# The Derwentside Story

**Derwentside District Council**
**1974 - 2009** 35 years Serving the People

by Chris Foote Wood

**NORTHERN WRITERS**

First published March 2009 by Northern Writers "Wor Hoos" 28 Cockton Hill Road Bishop Auckland County Durham DL14 6AH www.writersinc.biz

British Library Cataloguing in Publication Data
A catalogue for this book is available from the British Library.

ISBN 978-0-9553869-5-4

Typeset in 10/12pt Myriad Roman
Typesetting and origination, printed and bound by InPrint Unit 2C Hownsgill Park Consett County Durham DH8 7NU printing@derwentside.gov.uk

Produced for Derwentside District Council and for public sale.

Profits from the sale of this book go to the local Charity designated by the Council, the Willownburn Hospice Registered Charity Number 519659.

*To the People of Derwentside*

# Contents

## Foreword
### by Sir Bobby Robson

We live in a wonderful part of the world. Since Elsie and I returned to the area, we have been very happy here. We love the North East and its people. I was pleased and proud to be made an official "Ambassador of Derwentside" by the District Council in 2000, and it has been a great pleasure to represent the Council. Leaving aside myself, creating Ambassadors and Heroes to recognise the contribution made by so many people from all walks of life has been very much to the Council's credit.

When I was growing up in Langley Park, Derwentside was dominated by coal and steel. Railways linked our towns and villages. Now these great industries, which shaped Derwentside, have disappeared from the district. The closure of the pits, the steelworks and the railways caused the loss of tens of thousands of jobs and an exodus from the area. The fact that Derwentside has recovered from these massive setbacks is due in large measure to the efforts of the District Council, especially in bringing new jobs to replace the old. The population decline has been reversed. New housing has brought new life to our towns and villages.

When I was growing up in Langley Park, the local colliery was the heart of the village. I left school at fifteen and a half to follow my father Philip down the pit. In 51 years as a miner he lost only one shift – an incredible record – despite losing an eye in a pit accident. The principles I learned from my parents – unity, self-reliance and helping others – have provided the foundation for the close-knit communities typical of this part of the world. Although the pit closed many years ago, Langley Park has retained its sense of community. With new housing and other developments, Langley Park has mellowed.

For me, football has been a lifelong passion. When I first went to Fulham as an apprentice professional, my father insisted I continue to work as an electrician because he regarded football as a risky profession. Later he relented when he finally accepted that I needed full-time training to make the most of my sporting career. I have been fortunate to have played and managed at the highest level. After nine years in charge of a number of top European clubs, I got the chance to manage Newcastle United, the team my father regularly took me to see as a boy. This was my dream job – I was coming home. The five years I had at Newcastle were brilliant and I am proud of what I achieved.

Not for nothing I called my autobiography in 2005 "Farewell but not Goodbye." So in 2009 it is to be "farewell" to Derwentside District Council, but not "goodbye". All the good work the Council has done will continue to benefit this area and its wonderful people for years to come.

Sir Bobby Robson

## The Sir Bobby Robson Foundation

Over the last 15 years, Sir Bobby Robson has refused to give in to cancer no fewer than five times. To continue his fight to beat cancer, Sir Bobby has created a charitable foundation, the Sir Bobby Robson Foundation, to focus on the early detection and treatment of cancer and the clinical trials of new drugs that will eventually beat it. Through his Foundation, Sir Bobby's Big Goal is a campaign (hopefully the first of many) to support the new Early Cancer Trials Unit at the Northern Centre for Cancer Care, currently being built at the Freeman Hospital in Newcastle and to be named The Sir Bobby Robson Cancer Trials Research Centre. The money is urgently needed to fully equip the unit with treatment beds, treatment rooms, a state-of-the art laboratory, consulting rooms and offices. The building costs are being met by the NHS Trust and many of the staff in the unit will be funded by Cancer Research UK. To contribute to the Sir Bobby Robson Foundation, log onto www.sirbobbyrobsonfoundation.org.uk or send a cheque to: The Sir Bobby Robson Foundation PO Box 307 Heaton NE7 7QG.

*Sir Bobby Robson with wife Elsie starts a Charity Walk in his home village of Langley Park (EPC)*

**Derwentside District Council
Coat of Arms**

**ARMS:** *Barry wavy of eight Argent and Azure an Eagle displayed wings inverted Or gorged with a Mural Crown proper pendent therefrom by a Ring a Cross of St. Cuthbert and charged on each wing with a like Cross.*

**CREST:** *On a wreath of the Colours in front of Flames a Miner's Pick head upwards in pale and two Swords points upwards in saltire proper hilts and pomels Or pendent from the Pick by a Chain Argent a Roman Shield Sable charged with a Thunderbolt and on a Bordure Or ten Pellets.*

**BADGE** *A Fountain charged with an Eagle as in the Arms.* Motto 'DONEC DEFLUENT AMNIS' - Until the river ceases to flow. Granted 8th May 1975. *The Derwentside District was formed by the amalgamation of the Consett Urban District, the Stanley Urban District and the Lanchester Rural District.*

**The River Derwent**

The background of eight white and blue waves refers to the River Derwent, from which the District takes its name, the Derwent and other reservoirs, and the Rivers Deerness and Browney. The gold Roman Eagle is suggested by that in the insignia of the Lanchester RDC. This refers to the concentration of important Roman antiquities in the District - Dere Street, the Roman sites of *Longovicium* (Lanchester) and *Vindomora* (Ebchester) and the Roman cattle station at Stanley. Around its neck is a white ribbon from which hangs the distinctive cross of St. Cuthbert, seen in the arms of Stanley UDC and the device of Lanchester RDC. It is here coloured blue and refers to the numerous associations of the whole district with Durham's patron saint. The flames and crossed swords, from the arms of Consett UDC, represent the steel industry; and the pick, also from the Lanchester device, indicates coal-mining. Hanging by its steel chain is the Roman Shield from the crest of Stanley UDC, with its black background and circles for coal-mining, and gold thunderbolt for the Pontop Pike broadcasting station. The motto is appropriately in Latin to link with the Roman eagle, and is taken from Horace's Epistles. The two Ds indicate Derwentside District.

## The Derwentside Story

Midnight on Tuesday 31st March 2009 signals the end of Derwentside District Council after thirty-five years serving the people. As the clock strikes twelve, Derwentside and the six other district councils in County Durham will be abolished, to be replaced by a single, county-wide unitary authority. In its 35 years, Derwentside Council has faced many challenges, not least the almost total loss of its two main industries, coal and steel, and its railways. This is the story of how the Council met those challenges and built a better future for the District; how the Council tackled unemployment and decline, housing problems, industrial dereliction, poor health and lack of opportunities for its people.

In 1974, Derwentside seemed to be doing well. Consett Steelworks and its associated industries were still going strong, and although there had been pit closures, new firms had moved into the District. Yet only six years later, the closure of the steelworks and almost all the remaining pits left the area and its people in dire straights. There was a huge decline in population as around 20,000 people left the District to find jobs elsewhere. This and the steep rise in unemployment saw a massive drop in average earnings. Hundreds, indeed thousands, of private and council houses became empty and property values plummeted. The loss of younger and better-skilled adults left Derwentside's population with higher than average levels of the elderly, sick and disabled as well as the unemployed.

For all that the coal and steel industries had given the area much-needed jobs for a century and more, they also left the unwelcome legacies of injury, ill-health and skills based on industries now in serious decline. The closure of Consett steelworks and scores of pits throughout the District meant there was a great deal of industrial dereliction. There was also the problem of low aspirations and a relative lack of educational achievement. While in the past most of our local boys and girls could readily find employment as soon as they left school, better educational standards would be needed to meet the challenge of finding work in a rapidly-changing world.

And, whereas in the past the people of the area had put up with the pollution, dirt and noise of the District's old industries, this was no longer acceptable as a price worth paying. In any event, the District could not expect to attract new and more modern industries without removing the scars of the old industries and creating a more pleasant and healthier environment. Although many agencies had to be involved in the regeneration of Derwentside, it fell to the District Council to take the lead. These massive problems, the legacy of the past, had to be tackled, or the area would undoubtedly have fallen into terminal decline with an even greater loss of population. As it was, with fewer people resident in the District, there was a consequent loss of income to the Council in Council Tax.

Move forward nearly thirty years, and Derwentside has undoubtedly become a far better place in which to live, work and play. With the creation of thousands of new jobs, unemployment has been reduced to around the national average. The economy of the area, for so long dependent on just two industries, has been diversified beyond recognition. The environment has been vastly improved, new recreation and leisure facilities have been provided, new educational opportunities created, and the health and well-being of the people enhanced. New houses have sprung up all around the district, and the population decline has been reversed. Pulling the area back from the downward spiral of the 1970s and 1980s was a massive task, but one which Derwentside Council tackled with determination and ultimate success. The legacy which in 2009 the Council hands on to others is a District once more thriving and buoyant. Unlike in 1974, it is a legacy which is strong and well-founded. Derwentside can look to the future with confidence.

This book is dedicated to the hundreds of civic-minded men and women who have stood for election to Derwentside District Council and who have participated in its dealings in other ways, to all the dedicated staff who have worked for the Council over the years, to the Council's many partners, and above all to the people of the District who both councillors and council employees have been proud to serve.

**Chris Foote Wood**
*Author & Editor*

## Chapter One
# Land of the bright clear water

*From the time of the Romans; When Coal was King; West Stanley Pit Disaster; Consett Iron Co, Battle of the Blue Heaps, Railways; Communities & Services; Consett UDC, Stanley UDC, Lanchester RDC; Forced marriage.*

### From the time of the Romans

Derwentside takes its name from the River Derwent, which in turn gets its name from the Celtic word for "clear water". The District as we know it today can be traced back to Roman times. The village of Ebchester is where the Romans built the fort of Vindomora, thirteen miles south of Hadrian's Wall, at the point where Dere Street crosses the Derwent. Lanchester is also on Dere Street, and its fort of Longovicium was built about 160-180 AD. The origins of Stanley also date back to Roman times. It was the site of a cattle camp in the 2nd and 3rd centuries, and the Roman road known as Wreken Dyke ran from South Shields to the entrenchment on Stanley Hill. Following the discovery of the remains of a paved Roman road at New Kyo in 1897, there is every reason to believe that Wreken Dyke continued to Lanchester to connect with Dere Street. There was Roman iron-working at Ebchester. Mineral deposits of coal, iron, lead and lime have been exploited in the District ever since.

Industry in Derwentside began in earnest in the 17th Century when German sword-makers settled at Shotley Bridge on the banks of the Derwent. During the next 200 years a multitude of mills and forges sprang up, making use of the river as a powerful natural resource. Mills at Allensford, Shotley Bridge, Ebchester, Blackhall Mill, Derwentcote and Lintzford were used for the production of iron, wool, corn, flour and paper. By the 18th century the Derwent was home to an established paper-making industry. Shotley Grove Paper Mill, built in 1812, was the first in the North of England. Originally water-powered, it was converted to steam in 1860 and at one time employed 300 people. Although paper production on the Derwent ended in 1908, a large proportion of the nation's paper-making industry had rested here for almost a century. The Derwent Flour Mill at Shotley Bridge was also a significant industry of the 19th century. There was a flour mill at Shotley in the 14th century, and a corn mill had been established there since the 16th century. In 1872 a Federation of Co-operative Societies from Consett, Stanley,

*River Derwent (YG)*

*Ebchester Bridge (CFW)*

*Lanchester, entrance to village (CFW)*

*Shotley Grove (IP)*

*Shotley Paper Mills (MC)*

*Shotley Spa Well (FF)*

Shotley Bridge, Annfield Plain, Leadgate, Dipton, Tantobie, Blaydon, Tow Law and Burnopfield bought the Mill to provide supplies for the expanding Co-operative Wholesale Society. This remained in operation until after the second world war.

There were invigorating, iron-rich mineral waters at Shotley Bridge, and Jonathan Richardson, landowner, banker and industrialist, had the idea of making the town a second Harrogate. A saloon and bathrooms were built around the local well, called the Hally Well after the Saxon hal (whole in health). Ornamental grounds were laid out and an imposing hotel built. Although in the event Richardson's dream was never fully fulfilled – the growth of the industrial townships of Blackhill and Consett saw to that – the grounds became a resort for workers wanting to get away from Tyneside and Wearside. In one year alone the spa attracted 60,000 visitors. But industry eventually won the day and the spa faded.

"No scurvy in your skin can dwell
If you only drink the Hally Well"
*(ancient rhyme).*

## When Coal was King

By the mid-19th century the establishment of the major new industries of the area - iron and coal - the local economic importance of the mills was greatly reduced. Although there were coal mines in the Lanchester area as far back as 1500, significant mining in the district dates from the beginning of the 18th century. Coal is the most abundant mineral to be found beneath the soil of County Durham. The coalfields of Durham and Northumberland helped fuel the industrial revolution of the 18th and 19th centuries. Steam engines of every sort ran on coal, powering railway locomotives, ships and factories, as well as heating homes, offices and workplaces throughout the land. Derwentside had the good luck to stand on millions of tons of high-grade coking coal, the very best. As well as heat and power, coal produced scores of by-products for industries of every sort.

Coal mining and iron production began to dominate local economic and social life. Stanley and Consett were at the centre of these industries. The towns were ringed with collieries owned by the Lambtons and the Joiceys, John Bowes & Partners, and new joint stock companies like Holmside & South Moor and the South Medomsley Colliery Company, as well as the Derwent Iron Co. The iron and coal industries developed at the same time around Consett and Stanley. The first major coal mine in the area was sunk at West Stanley in 1833. The Derwent Iron Company was formed in 1841, with investment from the owners of three recently-sunk pits in the Consett area.

Coal is an extractive industry, so inevitably every colliery had a limited life, although many pits lasted over a century. Coal

*Five Medomsley pitmen (l-r): Jim Cant (horsekeeper), Isaac Brown (horsekeeper), Edmund Walton (onsetter), Bill Scarlett (deputy), Frank Pattison (bank hand & first aid man) (CB)*

*Double-decker pit cage (MC)*

*Thin seam (MC)*

*Salvation Army soup kitchen, 1926 General Strike (LHA)*

*Beamish Mary Pit (JH)*

*Oswald Pit (JH)*

*Derwent Colliery, Medomsley (MC)*

*Morrison Pit, Annfield Plain (JH)*

mining in the Dipton area goes back at least to 1731. There were early sinkings in the Hobson area in 1742. The Hobson Colliery, officially called the Burnopfield Colliery, closed in 1968. Tanfield Moor Colliery was sunk in 1768 for the Earl of Kerry. Reputed to be the oldest in the country, it was once owned by the first Lord Joicey, and closed in 1947. Oakey's Pit opened in 1783 and closed in 1934. West Stanley Colliery was sunk by Burns & Clarke in 1832 and was known locally as "The Burns Pit". William Hedley came to Craghead in 1839 and proceeded to sink the William Pit. The family went on to sink several other collieries in Craghead: the Edward, Busty, Oswald & Thomas Pits. Coal mining ceased in Craghead in 1969 with the loss of 1,600 jobs. A majority of the former pit employees found employment with the Ever Ready factory at Tanfield Lea. Other local pits included the Louisa, West Drum & Kettle Drum and Fanny collieries.

Hedley also sank the West Craghead Colliery at South Moor in 1839/40. It closed in 1863 but was re-opened in 1898 by South Moor Collieries Ltd and renamed William Pit after owner William Hedley junior. Always known as the Billy Pit, it closed in 1968. Other South Moor pits included the Charlie Pit and the Hedley Pit. Early local pits near Shield Row, Stanley, included the Hare Pit, Hound Pit and Knap Pit. Major coal owners in Stanley area included Burns & Clarke, Bowes & Partners, Morrisons, Bell, Hunter & Hedley, and Joicey. Marley Hill colliery opened in 1841 and closed on 3rd March 1983 when over 900 men were transferred or made redundant. Jackie's Pit between East Stanley and No Place opened in 1864 and closed in 1937.

The Louisa pit, Stanley, was named after the wife of William Bell, a partner of Hedley's. It was sunk by the South Moor Coal Co in 1863 and closed in 1962. The Louisa Sports centre, opened in 1980, stands opposite the site of the former colliery at the top of Stanley Front Street. Morrison North and South Pits were sunk in 1868. The South Pit closed in 1948. The Bute Pit at Tanfield Lea was sunk in 1839, the Wind Pit in 1896 and the Margaret Pit in 1903. This colliery closed in August 1962. Handen Hold Colliery was worked from 1860 to 1967. The Morrison Busty pit was sunk in 1923. It opened in 1927 and closed in 1973. Beamish Mary colliery opened in 1884, and closed in April 1966 when 400 men were

either transferred or made redundant. Marley Hill Colliery opened in 1841 and closed on 3rd March 1983. 733 miners found jobs at other pits, 33 were made redundant and 160 were kept on for salvage work. The Delight Pit, Dipton, opened in 1855 and closed in 1940. South Tanfield (Oxhill) pit opened in 1837 and closed in 1965. Burnhope Collieries (Fell, Annie, Fortune) opened in 1850, closed in 1949. East Tanfield pit was sunk by James Joicey in 1844 and closed in 1965. South Medomsley (High Stables, Dipton) pit opened in 1861, closed in 1980.

*Hobson Banner (JH)*

*Durham Miners Gala (JH)*

*West Stanley Pit Disaster – Thirty Survivors (JH)*

## The West Stanley Disaster

One of the worst mining disasters of the 20th century occurred at West Stanley Colliery on Tuesday 16th February 1909 when 168 men and boys lost their lives. At 3:45pm in the afternoon a muffled bang was heard from the direction of the colliery. This was followed 50 seconds later by a cataclysmic roar. A rising sheet of flames and dust was seen belching skywards from the mouth of the shaft. There was no doubt that something catastrophic had taken place. The whole community was stunned and bewildered. Word spread that the pit had "fired" (explosion). Soon hundreds assembled at the pit head. Womenfolk, fearing the worst, began wailing and screaming for their loved ones who were in the pit. Rescuers could not enter the pit until workmen had carried out the Herculean task of clearing the blocked shafts. The first rescue party went down shortly after 2am. What they found was death and destruction, as if they had entered Hell itself. The explosion had gone its full course, ripping through the seams and galleries. In the Towneley Seam, 64 men were dead. The Tilley Seam claimed 18. In the Busty, 38 were dead, and in the

Brockwell Seam, the deepest worked at the colliery, 48 men were found dead. Of the 168 victims, only 166 bodies were recovered at the time. Although it was known roughly where they were, it was thought too dangerous to try and retrieve the remaining two bodies. This was agreed by everyone and later the funeral service for the two men was held over the mouth of the pit. It was not until March 1933, some 24 years later, that the remains of the two men were discovered.

The King and Queen sent telegrams of sympathy. The funerals were started the following Sunday, with anything from 150,000 to 200,000 people in attendance. Most of the men were buried in big trenches at St Andrew's graveyard. Another trench was dug at St Joseph's for the Roman Catholics. A few were buried in private graves. A disaster fund raised £17,919 for the 238 dependents. 43 of the men who died were members of the New Kyo Constitutional club. There are four memorials of the Burns Pit disaster. The original, unveiled on 15th February 1913, was paid for by local workingmen's clubs. It stood at the front of Stanley Council Offices until 1936 when it was moved to the town cemetery. The second was unveiled on 16th February 1995 by Newcastle United manager Kevin Keegan. Kevin's grandfather Frank Keegan was one of the men rescued in 1909. He went home, changed his clothes and returned to help other trapped miners. £12,000 was raised with the help of South Moor Police and a charity game with Keegan and a Newcastle side. The third, placed at the site of the colliery shaft, was organised by the Stanley Hall Community Partnership and unveiled by pupils from East Stanley Primary School on 21st April 2004. The fourth, dedicated on Saturday 5th March 2005 by the Bishop of Jarrow, stands by the No.1 Trench Grave at the old council burial ground in Stanley. It was set up by a committee, inspired by Northern Echo reporter Chris Webb. A memorial service took place on the 100th anniversary of the disaster, Saturday 14th February, 2009 at St Andrews Church, Stanley. The Annfield Plain Gleemen and the Craghead Colliery Band took part.

*Waiting at the Pithead (JH)*

*Funeral of the Victims 21st February 1909 (JH)*

*Crowds watching funeral procession (JH)*

*Funeral Carriage (JH)*

*Burying in the Trenches (JH)*

*Burns Pit Memorial (JH)*

In the early 1900s, Thomas Baron was building the bridge leading from Consett to The Grove. When he left at night, it was several feet high, but on his return the next morning, the whole of his work had disappeared into some uncharted mineworkings.

Newcastle United manager Kevin Keegan among an appreciative crowd in Stanley

Kevin Keegan unveiling a memorial to the West Stanley
Pit Disaster, 16th February 1995 (JH)

ERECTED BY
STANLEY HALL
COMMUNITY PARTNERSHIP
ON THE SITE OF
THE BURNS PIT SHAFT
WHERE 168 MEN AND BOYS DIED
ON 16TH FEBRUARY 1909

West Stanley Memorial (MW)

Memorial Service (JH)

*Derwentcote Mill (CFW)*

## Consett Iron Co.

With seams of coal and ironstone being found close together, both could be won from the same mine. Ironstone deposits had been excavated in Derwentside by the German swordmakers in the late 17th century. Derwentcote Steel Furnace, built in the 1730s, used "cementation" to convert wrought iron into steel. Burning charcoal, the process took three weeks and produced ten tons of steel. The Furnace ceased production in 1891, became derelict and was restored by English Heritage in 1990. In the mid-19th century there were four pits at Consett, Nos.1-4, producing both coal and ironstone. The shaft of the No.1 pit was less than 100 yards from the roundabout on Medomsley Road. Consett became a centre for iron- and steel-making because of the ready availability and cheapness of three main ingredients: iron ore, high-quality coking coal, and limestone. In 1839 William Richardson – no relation to Jonathan - was taking the waters at Shotley Spa when he met John Nicholson, a local minerals expert. In 1840 these two and four other businessmen from Tyneside, including the managing director of the Northumberland & Durham District Bank, formed the Derwent Iron Co. It became the leading firm in the north, with 14 blast furnaces and rolling mills capable of producing 900 tons of bar-iron a week. There were twelve refineries, 22 steam engines and 35 coal and iron pits.

In 1851 the works were the second largest in the country, but by 1857 the company was in financial

*Consett Ironworks, Cogging Mill or Plate Mill (CHS)*

difficulties and became the Derwent & Consett Iron Co. This again ran into financial problems, and the company's creditors formed the Consett Iron Company (CIC) to take over the business. Consett Iron Co Ltd was floated in April 1864 with £400,000 capital in £10 shares. The Shotley Bridge Tinplate & Iron Co produced tinplate from 1840 and 1863 when it became the Shotley Bridge Iron Co. It made iron for three years before merging with the newly-formed Consett Iron Co. From 1882 the Company began to change over to steel production. By the 1890s CIC was employing 7,500 people, it owned ten collieries producing 1.3m tons of coal a year. By 1921

*Langley Park Colliery (MC)*

*Crookhall Colliery, Victory Pit (MC)*

this was 2.25m tons a year. As CIC became bigger and economically stronger it began to dominate the coal industry in the area. Major collieries owned by CIC included Consett, Delves Lane, Crookhall, Blackhill, Leadgate, Iveston, Medomsley, Westwood, Garesfield, Chopwell, Dipton, Marley Hill, Lanchester and Langley Park. In 1883 CIC owned 2,700 cottages at Consett, Blackhill, Leadgate and the outlying districts. In 1894 the Company owned nine collieries producing 1.3m tons of coal a year, two-thirds of which was converted into coke. The Company's weekly wage bill for their 6,000-strong workforce was £8,000, an average of 26s 8d a week per man. Besides having its own railways, CIC paid the North Eastern Railway £150,000 a year for the use of their tracks.

The original four German sword-makers who settled at Shotley Bridge were Oley, Vooz, Moll or Mole and Bertram. Other German families who followed on included Buske, Groate, Henkel, Shindlebrush, Vintner, Woper.

*The colliery manager's house in South Moor, built in 1906, was the first in the area to have a bathroom.*

The Quakers built a Meeting House at Benfieldside in 1790, and a new one at Snows Green in 1843. In 1814 a Methodist Church was built at Shotley Bridge on land given by swordmaker Christopher Oley. A small chapel was built in Derwent Street, Blackhill, in 1849 and a larger one in Durham Road in 1872. A Baptist Church was opened in Blackhill in the early 1850s. A Roman Catholic chapel was opened in Blackhill in the early 1840s and a new church built in 1857, helped by voluntary deductions from the wages of CIC workmen. The church of Our Blessed Lady Immaculate was opened on 24th July 1857.

*The 28-acre Consett & Blackhill Park was gifted by the Consett Iron Co in 1891.*

## Battle of the Blue Heaps

As both coal production and iron-making expanded, thousands of workers and their families moved into the area in search of work. There were tensions between these incomers and people already established here. There was also a religious divide. In November 1847 there were riots, known as the "Battle of the Blue Heaps". The Blue Heaps were the mounds of spoil between Consett and Blackfyne, which were occupied by the Irish and provided plenty of ammunition in the shape of small stones. The riots may have been caused by religious differences between Protestants and Catholics, but is more likely to have been due to problems involving differences between newly-arrived workers – mainly from Ireland - and those already established. The Durham Advertiser reported: *'a serious affray which occurred in the above neighbourhood* [Blackhill] *on the 14th inst., between the English and Irish workmen employed by the Derwent Iron Co'.* The Newcastle Journal said: *'Riot at Conside ironworks – some disturbance took place on Sunday at Conside ironworks near Shotley Bridge in County Durham. In consequence of serious disputes between the Irish and English labourers employed there, which have been aggravated by large numbers of the unemployed parties having come there from other places in the expectation of getting work in which they were disappointed'.* Around that time, riots were also taking place in Gateshead, Newcastle and Sunderland. Of 195 men sent for trial, only twelve, the supposed ringleaders, were actually charged. None was jailed, but each had to pay a £20 fine and was bound over *'to keep the peace for a twelvemonth'.*

*Memorial, Louisa Morrison Colliery Disaster 1947 (JH)*

*Causey Arch (YG)*

### The Railways

As Derwentside's great industries of coalmining and iron-making expanded, the railways grew with them, linking them together and speeding their production to their customers at home and – via the ports – abroad. Every town and village of any size – and some very small villages at that – had its own railway station, not only bringing in and despatching goods and materials, but also providing cheap, convenient and regular transport for passengers. Needless to say, as far as Derwentside is concerned, this once all-embracing rail network has now almost completely disappeared along with the coal mines and the steelworks.

### Tanfield Railway

One railway that has survived, thanks to the efforts of many volunteers, is in fact the oldest still in being – the Tanfield Railway, built to link Burnopfield, Tanfield Colliery, Marley Hill and Gateshead. Originally it was drawn by horses, later replaced by steam power. Construction of the Tanfield Waggonway from Sunniside to Causey was started in 1725, making the Tanfield railway the oldest railway in the world still working today. This involved building the Causey Arch, at 105ft the largest single-span bridge in Britain at the time (1726). During the 18th century the Tanfield Waggonway was the largest carrier of coal in Britain, and possibly the largest in the world. Originally built with wooden rails, in 1836 it was rebuilt as an iron railway. In 1841, three steam-powered stationary haulage engines were built, and in 1881 steam locomotives were introduced. The Tanfield railway was closed in 1970, but in 1971 a few local enthusiasts started on the long road to restoring it. The first section from Marley Hill to Bowes Bridge came into use in May 1977, and the Sunniside extension in July 1982. The first train from Marley Hill to Causey Arch ran on 27th July 1991, with the official ceremony on 15th August. The extension to East Tanfield saw its first passenger train on 18th October 1992. East Tanfield station was officially opened on 27th August 1997. The railway has been used as the setting for a number of episodes on the Catherine Cookson tv series.

*Hownsgill Viaduct (MC)*

*Hownsgill Viaduct (SW)*

*"The Wylam Dilly" engine, built by Wm Hedley in 1813 at Wylam at the same time as "The Puffing Billy", worked at Craghead Colliery 1862-1879 (JH)*

## Stanhope & Tyne Railway

Another significant railway was the Stanhope & Tyne from Stanhope in Weardale to South Shields via Waskerley and Consett. It was built to carry iron, lead and limestone from the Weardale mines and quarries to Shields for onward shipping. Limestone was an essential ingredient in making iron and steel, and the fact that the rail line passed though Consett was an added advantage. Waskerley, although now isolated and comprising a few houses, once had a goods station, sidings, engine sheds and a wagon repair shop. Unlike most railways, the Stanhope & Tyne was not set up by Act of Parliament, but by the old waggonway wayleave system. The land for the railway was leased from the Dean & Chapter of Durham Cathedral whose high rents eventually led to the railway's demise. With Robert Stephenson as engineer, the 15-mile upper section of the line between Stanhope and Annfield Plain was opened on 15th March 1834. The occasion was marred by the deaths of three people. These occured when a haulage rope snapped and four wagons ran out of control on the Weatherill incline above Stanhope.

The 12-mile lower section from Annfield Plain to South Shields was opened on 19th September 1834. A hundred wagons of coal from the Medomsley and Pontop pits were taken to Shields, pulled by a locomotive built at Annfield Plain. This engine burst its boiler in 1837, killing the driver and fireman. The line utilized every form of power available at the time: horse haulage, stationary steam engines, locomotive haulage, and self-acting inclines. With high rents and less traffic than anticipated, the Stanhope & Tyne railway went bust in December 1839. The Derwent Iron Co, which needed coal from Medomsley and limestone from Stanhope, bought the western section and ran it as the Derwent Railway until the line became part of the North Eastern Railway in 1863. In 1844 it was linked to the Stockton & Darlington Railway from Crook to Waskerley via Tow Law. The Hownsgill Ravine, 150ft deep and 800ft wide, at first had to be crossed by means of a stationary steam engine that hauled the wagons up the steep slope one at a time. This bottleneck was overcome by building the Hownsgill Viaduct, still known today as the Gill Bridge, in 1856. It is 700ft long, 175 ft high and has 12 arches each of 50ft span. 3.5m firebricks were used in its construction, which took 17 months to complete at a cost of £14,000. Thomas Bouch was the architect and John Anderson the building contractor. Seamen were used to put up the scaffolding. The viaduct bridge was opened on 1st July 1858 and remains a potent landmark to this day.

On 26th August 1911, a charabanc taking the Consett Co-op Choir to a Prudhoe Show lost control on Longclose Bank and hit a tree, killing ten members of the choir.

*NCB 'A' Class loco at Bank Top (AP)*

## North Eastern Railway

The North Eastern railway took over most of the local lines in 1854. In 1843 the Derwent Iron Co had constructed a rail line between Gateshead and Consett which branched off the Pontop railway at Tanfield Moor. By 1862 Consett had been connected to Durham and Cleveland, via Lanchester and Langley Park, for the transport of iron ore and coal. In 1867 the North Eastern Railway Company opened its eleven-mile Blaydon & Consett Railway serving the Derwent Valley. The growth of Blackhill station, the main station at the time in the Consett area, was due to the Derwent Flour Mill and the paper mills which used this station as their supply line. In 1894 stations at Leadgate, Annfield Plain and Shield Row were connected to Newcastle and Blackhill via Consett. Blackhill Station was originally called Blackfyne Station, and Shotley Bridge Station was originally called Benfieldside Station. These and most of Derwentside's other stations went with the "Beeching cuts" of the 1960s. For example, Lanchester station closed in 1965 after 101 years. The last passenger service had run in 1939, apart from annual excursions to the Miners Gala in Durham. The Annfield Plain branch line, opened in 1893, closed to passengers in 1955 and to goods in 1964. The line to Consett remained open until the Steelworks closed in 1980. It was then taken over by Sustrans as part of the C2C cross-country cycle route.

*West Stanley Station (JH)*

*Shotley Bridge Station (MC)*

*Shield Row Station (JH)*

*Annfield Plain station (JH)*

## Early days on the railway

Recalling his early days at work, railwayman John Grant wrote: "One of the first places they sent you to learn the road at Tyne yard was up to Consett steelworks. It was 14 miles up to Consett High Yard and when I say up, I mean up. The climb was hellish bad enough going up, but worse coming back down. It was one hell of an incline to bring the loaded steel wagons down en route to the Tyne. You needed every brake you had, be it vacuum, air or pinning the wagon brakes down with the brake stick. A few trains have, as they used to say, 'got away' down the bank. Having hauled them from the bottom yard, you went downhill from the top yard where the old Consett station and coal yard was, straight down to Stanley Level, then down from there past Beamish to South Pelaw, then onto the slow line into Tyne Yard where there was a couple of sand traps on the road down to the bottom. We used to take the iron ore from Tyne Dock bottom with two Class 31 engines on the front. The iron ore wagon doors were operated from inside the engine cab by a lever that operated the doors with the air brake pressure. When hauling the iron ore cars up to Consett, the doors on some cars sometimes opened themselves, spilling the iron ore pellets all over the ballast and down the embankments. Going up to Consett was a hell of a climb up, and one hell of a drop back down to Tyne Yard. You had to keep your wits about you and your brake stick handy".

Ransome & Marles of Newark opened their ball-bearing factory on Friday 1st October 1953, the first on the Greencroft Industrial Estate. Brigadier AR Lowe, Parliamentary Secretary to the Ministry of Supply, did the honours. The factory cost £400,000 and covered three and a half acres. The factory was expanded three times up to 1963 but was eventually closed and the production concentrated at Newark.

## Communities & Services

The Shotley Bridge and Consett District Gas Company was established in 1856. Two gas-holders were constructed at Shotley Bridge serving Ebchester, Medomsley, Leadgate and Consett. In 1947 there was a need to enhance the gas supply to the area but an extension to the Shotley Bridge facilities could not be justified on economic grounds. Because of the gas production capacity generated by Consett Iron Co, the Gas Company agreed to buy the additional capacity they needed from CIC. In 1869 the first water storage reservoir in the District was constructed at Smiddy Shaw near Waskerley to the west of Consett. Two additional reservoirs were built at Waskerley and Hisehope nearby to serve the demands from the expanding population of North West Durham

In 1831 Consett had a population of under 150. Lanchester was the largest village in the area and only Stanley Hall had any other significant population. Industrial development saw an influx of labour and by the 1850s Derwentside's population had grown to 20,000. Workers began to form distinct communities around the new collieries and steelworks. By the mid-19th century the Derwent Iron Co, as well as expanding its iron production, owned four pits in the area; it had interests in local and regional railways, and was developing houses, schools, an infirmary and recreational facilities in the Consett area. This paternalism was replicated by mine owners at Leadgate, Stanley and Langley Park. Derwentside's industrial culture was firmly established as one based on heavy industry providing both work and social facilities. Societies, clubs, sports leagues and branches of national organizations also proliferated under such names as "Consett & District", "Derwent", "Derwent Valley" and "North West Durham".

*Hisehope Reservoir (CFW)*

*Smiddy Shaw Reservoir (CFW)*

*Waskerley Reservoir (CFW)*

Derwentside prospered as local coal and steel production continued to develop well into the 20th century. Because of the inextricable link between the two industries, the whole of Derwentside also suffered hard times together. During the great depression of the 1930s unemployment in North West Durham rose to 45%, with over 60% in Stanley. After WW2 a North West Durham "Joint Committee for the Localisation of Industry" met to encourage industrial development in the districts of Chester-le-Street, Consett, Stanley, Lanchester. This was superseded by the North West Durham Joint Industrial Committee, in which Chester-le-Street UDC was replaced by Blaydon UDC. Under the Coal Industry Nationalisation Act of 1947 Consett Iron Co lost ownership of some 3,000 houses; nearly 12,500 acres of land; over 50 miles of railway; seven collieries at Consett, Chopwell, Garesfield, Langley Park, Leadgate and Medomsley; the Derwenthaugh and Langley Park cokeworks; the Crookhall washery, and power stations at Derwenthaugh, Chopwell, Langley Park and Templetown.

In 1951 there were still some 30 collieries operating in Derwentside, employing 17,000 people - 42% of all jobs in the District. With the run-down of the mining industry, employment in mining and quarrying in Derwentside fell to 2,500 in 1971. The last colliery in the district closed in 1980. Many men from the Stanley area had found jobs at British Steel's Consett works only for that too to close in 1980. Even in 1972 only 25% of workers in Derwentside had jobs which were not in some way dependent on coal and steel. Yet the historic skill base of mining, steel-making and their associated activities still bind Derwentside people together with a common heritage and community.

*Civic Centre, Consett (IP)*

**Consett UDC**

By 1936 the population of Consett was over 12,000. As elsewhere in Derwentside, local administrations were created to provide democratic representation and manage local services. Recalling Consett in 1880, RP Logan said: *'the Council were numbered twelve. The surveyor was Mr Shell and Mr Rippon was the foreman. It was a very poor town. The coal and ash carts came up the back streets. Netties were outside. There were no theatres in Consett'.* The population of Benfieldside rose from 534 in 1831 to 5,857 in 1882. Benfieldside Parish was created in 1847, the Local Board in 1866, and Benfieldside UDC in 1884. Blackhill Parish was created in 1894 when it had a population of 4,500. In 1903 Blackhill was the centre of the area, as Consett station had not yet opened. 68 trains passed in and out of Blackhill station every day. The Consett Local Board was formed in 1865 and in 1874 the district had a population of 9,500. The Consett Guardian newspaper was established in 1860. Consett Urban District Council was formed in 1937, amalgamating the small urban districts of Consett, Benfieldside and parts of Lanchester rural council (Ebchester, Knitsley and Medomsley). Consett had a population of 40,000, and in 1961 was of similar size, 38,720. The UDC had 29 members representing eight wards: Benfieldside, Blackhill, Consett North, Consett South, Delves Lane & Crookhall, Ebchester, Leadgate and Medomsley. In the early 1960s Consett UDC members between them could boast two Military Medals, three BEMs and an OBE. Five were JPs, but only four of the 29 councillors were women. Consett Civic Centre was officially opened by Cllr SA Breen, chairman of Consett UDC, on Monday 6th October 1969. A dinner-dance followed, with entertainment by the Consett Citizens' Choir and the Patchogue Plymouth (Crookhall) Band. The council chamber was built to accommodate 45 members (there being 27 councillors), so since 1974 some of Derwentside's 55 members have had to sit on the sidelines as it were.

Annfield Plain Co-op first opened in the 17th May 1870. The Society decided to buy a horse for £3 10s and a dog for 9 shillings. At one time it had seven branches, and in 1970 it became part of the North Eastern Co-op. The Central Buildings were opened in 1873. They closed in the early 1970s and were replaced by a residential home. Part of the store was rebuilt at Beamish Museum. There was an underground toilet in the centre of Annfield Plain. It was opened in 1907 but closed ten years later when a Mr Mumford fell down the steps and was killed.

*Engineer's Dept Staff 1974 (l-r): John Groves, Daniel Bennett, Colin Bell, Harry Anderson, Trevor Watson, Paul Nelson, Nigel Holmes, John Shepherd*

*Stanley UDC staff 1965 (l-r, back) Frank Vickers, Doug Robson, Colin Bell, David Riley; (front): Vera Daglish, Dorothy Armstrong, Margaret Hewitson, Malcolm Lynch*

*Stanley UDC team, 1972 winners Nalgo TP Easton Shields: (l-r back): John Walsh, John Mason, Fred Nevin jnr, Brian Shields, Adrian Evans; (front): Robert Cook, Jack McGurk, Fred Nevin snr, Norman Harrison, Terry Hodgson*

## Stanley UDC

Annfield Plain, Stanley and Tanfield Urban District Councils were formed on 1st October 1896. Stanley Council Offices – still in use today - opened in 1911. In 1937 these three urban councils merged with Craghead Parish to form Stanley UDC. In 1970, Labour took all 33 seats on Stanley Council. Cllr Norris Oyston, later to become leader of Derwentside DC, became chairman. Newly-elected members of the council included Cllrs Margaret Errington, Catriona Smith, Walter Armstrong, Rachel Montgomery, Bob Belton, John Evans, Ted Lightfoot & Ronald Dodd. A deferential press report said: *'They (the councillors) kindly gave the Stanley News permission to take photographs before getting back to business'.*

## Lanchester RDC

Lanchester had its own Rural District Council dating back to 1877. Much smaller in population than Consett and Stanley, inevitably Lanchester found itself the minor partner when the three authorities were amalgamated in 1974. Much of the Lanchester area looked to Durham City rather than Consett or Stanley as a major centre, adding to the unease which many felt about the merger. In the early 19th century Lanchester was the judicial centre for North West Durham. Petty Sessions were held there, and there was a lock-up. The Workhouse was opened in 1839. Its offices, built for the Board of Guardians, later became the Council offices, then the police station and courthouse, and now houses the library. In 1851 there were 140 houses in the parish with 752 residents. The opening in 1862 of the Durham-Consett railway line with a station at Lanchester prompted the next surge in development. Terraces of houses were built on land near to the railway station and along the roads linking the railway station to Front Street. By 1961 the population had reached 4,050 and the development of the village accelerated again. During the following eleven years four housing estates amounting to over 500 houses, two schools and an old people's home were built. These private estates were constructed by builders to their own designs, generally with garages. Part of Front Street was demolished and replaced by a row of shops that are typical of their period. In 1966 the railway was closed and has since been converted into the very popular Lanchester Valley Walk. In 1970 the by-pass was built, easing traffic congestion. In 1973 jobs were lost when the livestock mart closed, soon to be followed by the Siris factory. Since then there has been significant further housing at Valley Grove, St. Bede's Court, Oakwood, Greenwell Park, Fenhall Park and Lee Hill Court. However, fewer people now tend to live in each house, so the population of Lanchester ward, which was estimated at over 6,000 in 1973, dropped to 3,900 by 2001.

## Forced marriage

As was later to happen in 2007, in 1972 the government of the day decreed that there must be local government reorganisation, whether or not the people wanted it. The "two-tier" system of county and district councils was retained, but – in Durham and Northumberland at least - the districts got bigger and the counties got smaller. Consett and Stanley urban districts and Lanchester rural district were amalgamated in a single authority – Derwentside District Council. At the same time, County Durham lost huge swathes of land and population. No longer was County Durham the powerful and historic land between the rivers Tyne and Tees as Gateshead, South Shields, Sunderland, Stockton and Hartlepool all went their own way. Then, as in 2007, local councillors and Council staff alike faced a stark choice: accept the changes, albeit under protest, or leave local government altogether. Most chose to "stick with it" and do their best to make an unwanted, government-imposed system work. The fact that Derwentside District Council has had the success it has – and has overcome tremendous difficulties - is due far more to their efforts than to the wisdom (or otherwise) of government ministers and their advisors. Major changes in local government have taken place in 1896, 1937, 1974 and 2009 – at intervals of 41, 37 and 35 years. Presumably the next reorganisation is due around 2040.

The Annfield Plain council offices were located beyond the boundary of Catchgate at Harelaw.

Cllr Ronnie Dodd, Leader of Consett UDC

Cllr Ossie Johnson snr (OJ)

Cllr Larry Thomas (BT)

## Chapter Two
# Early days 1974 -1979

*Divided Loyalties; April Fools' Day; Norris Oyston, Selby Walker; mixed hereditaments; Joe Quinn, Terry Hodgson, Eric Davis; twin steel towns.*

### Divided Loyalties
Political and religious differences were brought sharply into focus in 1974 when the district's three local councils, based at Consett, Stanley and Lanchester, were brought together to form Derwentside District Council. The rivalry between Derwentside's two main centres of population, Consett and Stanley, still in evidence today, was even more marked then. With the steelworks still operating, Consett was relatively prosperous and unemployment low. Stanley on the other hand had particularly suffered from the steady closure of the pits, resulting in rising unemployment and lower average incomes. There was also a religious divide. Thanks to the immigration of Irish labour, mainly to the steelworks, Consett had a more Catholic and liberal tradition, while Stanley was rooted in Methodism. More than one new member of the local Council staff was asked "are you a Catholic or a Protestant?" and it was said that if you didn't have a cross hanging in your front window in Consett, you wouldn't get your Council house repairs done – with the reverse at Stanley. As the years have gone by, the religious divide has all but disappeared. While political and geographical differences remain, Derwentside councillors and Council staff have for the most part worked together effectively for the good of the District as a whole.

No civil marriages were possible in Derwentside in 1974 due to the closure of the register office at Hare Law. You could get married in church, but if you wanted a civil ceremony the nearest register office available was at Chester le Street. It was mid-1975 before a registrar's office was opened at Stanley.

*The Council was considering the appointment of a new Housing Manager. "We need someone to take us into the 21st century," suggested one councillor. "What we need is someone to get us out of the 18th century!" replied outspoken Labour Group Secretary Selby Walker.*

Long-serving councillor Jimmy Graham was a junior whip – at the age of ninety!

*Consett Steelworks – still going strong in 1974. Aerial view from West (IP)*

*New factory - Ransome & Marles (JH)*

Derwentside in 1974 was vastly different than in 2009. In 1974 the area was dominated by public service bodies: the District and County Councils, the health service, and the nationalized industries of steel, coal and rail. Derwentside District Council was one of the biggest employers in the area, and 2,000 of its 2,500 staff worked in the DLO (Direct Labour Organisation). Half the homes in the district were Council houses, so the Council had a massive influence as a landlord as well as an employer. While the pits were closing, new industry had come into the district, such as Ransome & Marles, Ever Ready, Patchogue Plymouth, Celluware, Corrugated Packing, Elddis Caravans, Feedex, Charnos, Eurochem, TMCO Products, Thorn Electric Industries and Armstrong Cork.

## April Fools' Day

For some reason, new councils always seem to come into being on the first of April – All Fools Day. Perhaps it's some senior civil servant having a little joke. Derwentside District Council, perhaps wisely, held its first formal meeting on Tuesday 2nd April 1974, at 7pm in the Council Chamber at Consett Civic Centre. The Council's 55 members, elected the previous May, had been holding "shadow" meetings in the interim, but this was the first formal meeting of DDC. First business was to elect the Chairman, Cllr Wilf Baker confirmed in office after being "shadow" Chairman for the previous year. Cllr Baker's first duty was to present a life-saving award to Robert Statt of 9 Victoria Terrace, Lanchester, for saving the life of a drowning child at Fleetwood on 15th August 1973. Cllr John Parkin was then elected Vice Chairman of the Council. A Council chairman has exactly the same position as a mayor. He/she is the civic head, representing the Council at public functions, and presiding at full council meetings. By convention, the Chairman is non-political during his/her term of office, usually a year.

*….but pits were closing (JH)*

Derwentside in 1974: area, 66,944 acres (105 square miles); inhabited houses, 35,464; population, 91,478; voters, 69,342; rate in the pound, 70p (total); district rate 19p; product of a 1p rate (nett) £69,000.

*Old Angle Mills (CHS)*

*Fell Coke Works & By-Products Plant 1960s (CHS)*

*Melting Shop: tipping open-hearth furnaces into 100-ton ladles, pre-1970 (CHS)*

*Red menace – Consett town centre 1970s (MC)*

*Oxy Steel Plant. CIC operated both LD & Caldo systems, the only works in Europe to do so (CHS)*

*CIC from the Grove Bridge (MC)*

## Norris Oyston, Selby Walker

Cllr Norris Oyston was elected as the Council's first Leader, the political head of the Council. "Where the buck stops" is on the desk of the Leader, not the Chairman or the Chief Executive. Oyston, previously Leader of Stanley UDC, had become Leader of the DDC Labour group after the elections to the shadow Council in 1973. Cllr Selby Walker was Labour Group Secretary, then the equivalent of Deputy Leader. While vastly different in character, they were an effective team. Oyston was a good public speaker and would articulate Council policy well. 'Norris Oyston was a good man, a hard worker,' said a later Leader, Joe Rhind, 'at that time the Council was trying to revive villages like Dipton that had suffered under Durham County Council's Category "D" policy. Their idea was to build council houses to replace the demolished terraces, but personally I would have preferred to see a mixture of public and private housing'. Walker exercised his power behind the scenes. Allegedly, he kept a dossier on every member and every senior officer. Walker even went so far as to keep copies of the Council's daily till receipts, and it was said that he knew at least as much about finance as the Council Treasurer. Recalling Oyston and Selby, former Council staff member Gilbert Green described them as a very effective double act. 'Selby shot from the hip. He would rant and shout. Then Norris would say much the same, but in a calm and reasoned manner, and get it through. Each was a foil for the other'.

*Norris Oyston – first Council Leader (NO)*

## Mixed hereditaments

The AGM set up the Council's various committees, the full Council was to meet on the first Tuesday of every month – no recess – and school governors were appointed. That was it, but the members stayed on for an "ordinary" meeting of the Council. One of their first decisions was to reduce the rates – by 13p in the pound for a "dwelling house", and 6.5p for "mixed hereditaments". This may have been to curry favour with the electorate, but the adoption of attendance allowances, £5 a day for meetings, £10 if for more than four hours, was to attract criticism from the public who expected their elected members to do the job for nothing. Word from the College of Heralds was awaited about the Council's Coat of Arms, meals-on-wheels were extended to Langley Park at the request of Cllr Vince Taylor, and attendance at conferences agreed.

The committee meetings that followed in the next few weeks determined the welter of matters large and small that have always been the lot of all local authorities. Group Secretary and strong man, Cllr Walker demanded to see the receipts and attendances at the district's two swimming baths; DDC planned to build 400 new Council houses a year for the first five years and modernize 600 existing houses; sale of Council houses (not yet compulsory) was refused on principle; Lanchester rent collectors were granted a new raincoat every year to bring them into line with their counterparts in Consett and Stanley; DDC continued the subsidy of the No. 763 and 764 bus services between Consett and Tow Law; standard home improvement grants were agreed up to £300 a time; a request by Esh Parish Council for DDC to introduce a waste paper collection service was deferred; there were to be 18,090 meals-on-wheels for the year with another 17,800 for luncheon clubs; Council mortgages of £700 to £5,000 over 10-20 years were granted; likewise 75% home improvement grants of £120-£1,500 were approved; Council workers in further education were reimbursed their travel, amounts ranging from £1.19 to £15; the Consett Corps of the Salvation Army was given a £200 interest-free loan, repayable over 12 months, to buy new uniforms: Securicor was paid £6 a week to transport Council cash. To create interest in the new district of Derwentside and to inform the public of its progress, the Council produced a bi-monthly magazine "Derwentside".

The No.1 edition came out in July 1974. As well as listing the 55 councillors and the ten most senior officers, the magazine gave some fascinating insights into seventies society, its conventions and fashions. The winner of the 1974 Council House Garden competition was Mr JG Routledge of 32 Parkside, Burnhope. DDC took over the competition from Lanchester and only covered the RDC area this first year. R Snowdon of 22 Eastern Avenue, Langley Park, was the 1975 winner.

As well as the councillors, staff inherited from three different local authorities had to learn to work together. Common procedures had to be agreed and implemented. It took several years before they became what future Chief Executive Neil Johnson called "a family". When DDC was set up in 1974, the senior officers of the Council were: Chief Executive & Clerk - Joe Quinn, Treasurer - Eric Davis, Chief Planning Officer - WF (Bill) Hetherington, Chief Technical Officer – Malcolm Davies, Housing Officer – Bill Middlemast, Chief Environmental Health Officer – Jack Richards, Parks Manager – George Tyreman, Civic Hall Manager – Tom Clifford, Baths Manager – Arthur Waller.

The second Chairman of the Council, for 1975-76, was Cllr John Parkin from Hamsterley. He was a face worker – a coal hewer – mainly in Hamsterley Colliery. 'It was all pick and shovel work in those days,' said John, 'I often worked in the Tilley seam, which was only 14-24 inches wide'. After 25 years in the pits, John was made redundant and subsequently worked as an EWO – Educational Welfare Officer. He was first elected to Consett UDC in 1970. 'The officers had more say in the days of the old urban council,' said John, 'whereas then meetings used to last only half an hour, with the new District Council in 1974 the councillors had to go into things in more depth'.

*Harperley Hotel (CFW)*

### Joe Quinn

"Joe Quinn was held in awe by staff who were very much aware of his 'presence', recalled Gilbert Green, "but he would say that his door was always open and he would see anybody at any time". Former clerk to Consett UDC, Quinn was a forthright character who didn't suffer fools gladly. Quinn was a hard-working Chief Executive & Clerk who "knew everything that was going on," according to another former colleague. Quinn died in August 1975 while on holiday in Los Angeles, aged only 57. Apart from service in the Army in WW2, Quinn had spent his life in local government. He had started as a junior clerk with Leadgate Council, and continued with Consett UDC when it was formed in 1937. He was appointed Deputy Clerk with Consett in 1948 and Clerk ten years later. He was Leadgate born and bred, and a passionate Sunderland supporter. "Joe Quinn was a far-sighted man," said former Consett MP David Watkins. Joe's successor was Terry Hodgson, the youngest Chief Executive in the country. He had been Deputy Clerk & Chief Executive with Stanley UDC. Personable and sociable, Hodgson had come through the ranks. At that time each department held its own Christmas party, and there was competition between them as to who had the best party. Hodgson made sure he attended every one. Neil Johnson was appointed Deputy Chief Executive in January 1976.

*May 1975: Cllr Wilf Baker hands over to new Council Chairman Cllr John Parkin (JP)*

### Terry Hodgson

When Terry Hodgson was appointed as chief executive of Derwentside District Council in 1975 he was the youngest in the country and possible the youngest ever to hold this office. Born near Settle in the West Riding of Yorkshire, Hodgson went to Clitheroe Royal Grammar School for Boys, leaving at 16 to start work as an "office youth" with Bowland RDC. Unable to take his professional exams until he was 21, Terry went to evening classes to learn shorthand, typing and English. "I can still touch type, and it has proved very useful," he said. Terry was the only boy in the class with 31 girls, one of whom became his first wife. At 20, Terry was married and had moved on to Gainsborough UDC in Lincolnshire as a committee clerk. There, in 1966, he ran his first general election as deputy returning officer. Then it was on to the Borough of Radcliffe in Lancashire as a senior committee clerk. His boss at Radcliffe, Town Clerk & Solicitor Arthur Fox, offered Terry free articles if he would stay, but Terry was on the move again. It was in fact fishing that brought him to Derwentside.

Terry was a keen fly fisherman, and in 1967 he organized a trip for his local fishing club to the newly-opened Derwent Reservoir. Terry caught nothing, but determined to go back and give it another try. So when he was short-listed for a job with Stanley UDC, he reckoned that it would be an evening meeting and he would have the whole day to fish. So it proved, but again

*Empire Theatre – saved by Derwentside Council who bought it in 1975 (LW)*

lost. After that, Hodgson operated a strict "need to know" policy, which sometimes excluded even the Leader of the Council. "I promised the members that they would be told at the appropriate time," said Hodgson.

One of the early problems that had to be tackled during Hodgson's tenure was to replace the huge amount of housing lost to slum clearance, particularly in the Stanley area. The Council had a programme of building 700 homes a year – a massive task. The Louisa Centre in Stanley and the Hobson Golf course clubhouse were built "in house". Hodgson also had to get the Council to adapt to their new role as a planning authority and to think more strategically. To this end he had two Council Leaders, Norris Oyston and Billy Bell, who were both pragmatic in their approach and put the local community ahead of their Party loyalties. In Hodgson's recollection, both were articulate and open to compromise. Joe Rhind, who became Leader in 1987, the year Hodgson left the Council, was more of a political animal. In 2008 Hodgson was still living near Consett and running his own consultancy company, advising on environmental and waste issues, and occupational health & safety. Motto: "finding the right path".

Terry did not catch anything – apart from landing the job as Assistant Clerk, with the promise of promotion to Deputy Clerk within the year. Stanley Council was as good as its word, and after first Jack Shipston and then Cecil Warren had taken their due retirement, Hodgson found himself deputy to Ronnie Callicott - at the age of 23. Meantime, Terry completed his DMA (Diploma in Municipal Administration), a four-year course involving night classes and day release.

When Joe Quinn got the job as Chief Executive of the new Derwentside Council in 1974, Terry was made one of two Assistant Clerks under Quinn and his deputy Bob Birtwhistle. Birtwhistle, a qualified engineer, soon left to take up an engineering job elsewhere, and Hodgson stepped up once again to take over as Deputy Chief Executive. On 20th August 1975 he got the news that Joe Quinn had died suddenly of a massive heart attack while on holiday in the USA. And so Hodgson became Chief Executive at the age of 28 years and one month. When Terry broke the news of Joe Quinn's death to tea lady Hilda Ashby, all she could say was 'He's not paid his tea money!' After his appointment as Quinn's successor, Hodgson had to promise Hilda he would keep his tea fund contributions up to date.

A confident young man, Hodgson never had any doubts about his ability to do the top job. He also had a different approach than many other senior people in local government at the time. Hodgson was very much the clubbable man. He would have drinks with the members after meetings, and played golf with both councillors and members of staff. "I found that if you could persuade people that a course of action was the right one, that generally worked," he said, "I was always at pains to assure the members that they were all part of the process". This skill came to the fore when the Council was seeking inward investment. Just once, a senior member of the Council "blabbed" too soon, and a potential investor was

### Eric Davis
Treasurer Eric Davis had a military background and was treasurer of Consett Golf Club. Davis had a dry sense of humour and could have been an after-dinner speaker. He suffered terribly from arthritis but never complained. Malcolm Davies from Stanley UDC, a more flamboyant character, became Chief Technical Officer. He had started as an engineer with British Rail. Robert Birtwhistle, who had been Engineer & Surveyor with Consett UDC and became Deputy Chief Executive and Clerk with Derwentside, left DDC later in 1974 to be Director of Technical Services at Northwich in Cheshire. Housing Officer Bill Middlemast administered the Council's huge stock of houses. With the letting of Council houses always an important item on the agenda, Housing Committee meetings sometimes lasted several hours, from 2pm in the afternoon to six or seven o'clock at night. The Council's catering manager Tommy Clifford, who sported a small moustache, was known as "Dapper Dan". The council-run Harperley Hotel – licensee Harry Munster - was reopened in time for Christmas 1974 after being extended. The Harperley was sometimes unkindly referred to as "The Ratepayers Arms".

*Consett Bus Station c1970 (WS)*

## Twin steel towns

The industrial town of Werdohl (pronounced "ver-dole") in Saurland, West Germany, became Derwentside's "twin town" in 1974 after initial contacts with Consett UDC. Cllr Baker led a delegation to Werdohl in July with a return visit by the Germans in October. The partnership agreement was signed on 6th April 1975. Both districts were prominent steel-producing areas, although there was a contrast. Consett's output was mainly mass-produced raw steel, while Werdohl made a variety of steel products. Since then, steel production in Derwentside has ceased altogether, and Werdohl's has markedly decreased. Nevertheless, the Town Twinning links helped to "forge" new relationships between the two communities.

*Planning Dept staff c1978 (PR)*

The Council advertised its services in its magazine "Derwentside". The library service, civic halls and swimming baths were featured. 'Bathing facilities second to none,' the magazine enthused, 'without doubt the wisdom and enterprise of the former Stanley and Consett Councils has endowed Derwentside with the finest sauna, remedial and bathing facilities in the region,' it claimed, modestly. Beamish Open Air Museum – admission 20p for adults, 5p for children and OAPs – had a two-page spread, as did Allensford Park and its lido, with

*Staff soccer team Jan 1988 (PR)*

'genial yet firm' Bill Hobson as the Resident Warden. Touring vans were charged 65p and tents 28p per night, and you could store your caravan for the winter for £8.25. 1974 was the era of the 75% home improvement grants. With a shortage of skilled workmen, many householders had been scrambling to meet the June 23rd deadline – extended to 30th September. In those days you could get a mortgage from the Council – up to 100% "Derwentside valuation". But the rate of interest was 8.75%, and the maximum advance was £8,000. In 1975 the Council declared eight Conservation Areas at Ebchester, Iveston, Lanchester, Satley, Shotley Bridge, Esh, Medomsley and Tanfield. And it was as far back as 1977 that Derwentside Council decided on its first "no smoking" policy, designating the auditorium and balcony at the Empire Theatre as no smoking areas. Approaching 2009, Cllr David Llewellyn reflected on 1974: "the district was put together by government regardless of local feelings. We had to make the best of it, and by and large I think we did a good job".

*Doing the Twist, early 1960s. (AP)*

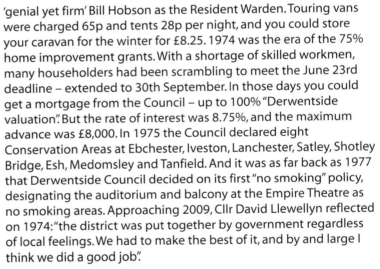

*Council Chairman Cllr John Parkin welcomes youth swim team from twin town Werdohl (JP)*

*Hot metal*

## Chapter Three
# Crisis, Protest & Fightback 1979-1991

*Marches & meetings; the "Mad Monk"; Maggie, Maggie, Maggie! Consett Crisis; "Town for Sale"; Billy Bell, Joe Rhind; Last train to Consett; Road to Recovery; Neil Johnson.*

**"Will the last one in Consett please turn out the lights"** *(graffito on a door at the derelict steelworks)*

### Marches & meetings

On 9th July 1980, a thousand Consett folk, steelworkers, their families and supporters from all walks of life, took a special train to London for a march, demonstration and mass lobby of Parliament. It was the high point of a widespread and passionate but ultimately doomed campaign to save the Steelworks from closure. The ISTC (Iron & Steel Trades Confederation) newspaper "Banner" reported: *'They came to march the streets of London, 1,000 Consett steelmen, townspeople and their families. They arrived tired and cold – the train was two hours late and without heating. But after being welcomed by local MP David Watkins and by ISTC national officer Ken Clarke the steelmen, led by the Consett band, set off in good heart. The rally at the Central Hall, Westminster, had to be cancelled due to late running, but the mass lobby of Parliament was impressive, even though not one Government minister would meet the marchers.'* Two teenagers, Bob Nixon (who had just left school and has no chance of a job) and Elaine Dixon (an ISTC member) handed in a 20,000 signature petition to 10 Downing Street. North West Durham MP Ernie Armstrong and Giles Radice, MP for Chester le Street, also took part in the march, along with many local councillors, trades union officials and members, and hundreds of local people.

The banners read: *'Consett Crusade'* and *'Consett in the black faced with sack'.* It was *'a march against madness, the march for commonsense'.* The ITSC argued that unemployment in the Consett area, already 13.8%, would be 40% if the steelworks closed, putting 3,500 people out of work. 65 people were chasing every vacancy. That month (July 1980) 1,400 youngsters would be leaving school, but there were only eight job vacancies available. In May, the ISTC argued, Consett had made £1m profit, in June £900,000. It was all in vain. The British Steel Corporation had decreed that the Consett works must close, and the Conservative government under Margaret Thatcher, just over a year after taking office, was determined to stick to its non-intervention policy.

*CIC Works at full blast (JE)*

*March on Westminster (CHS)*

## The "Mad Monk"

It was just Consett's – and Derwentside's – bad luck that the Secretary of State for Industry, the one person who might have been able to influence the decision at the highest level, was Sir Keith Joseph, the acknowledged architect of Thatcherism. Joseph's theories of monetarist economics were central to his policy doctrine, and they were applied without mercy. As Secretary of State, Joseph's approach was to alleviate the effects of closure rather than doing anything to prevent it. It was in December 1979 that the British Steel Corporation (BSC) announced its intention to close the Consett steelworks. The Hownsgill Plate Mill had been closed two months earlier on 12th October, putting 750 steelworkers – BSC said 430 - on the dole. The Council's Industry Committee met frequently. In a two-hour meeting on 11th September they protested the closure of Hownsgill, calling for urgent meetings with the Secretary of State for Industry (Joseph) and the chairman of BSC Sir Charles Villiers. Villiers did meet the Council on 30th October. On 22nd November DDC Chief Executive Terry Hodgson advised members to await the impending publication of the Derwentside Study. This report, by Coopers & Lybrands and the Building Design Partnership, was discussed by the Committee on 17th December, by which time BSC had announced that the Steelworks would definitely close. DDC set up an emergency Steering Committee which met with representatives of Durham County Council, British Steel Corporation

*March banner (CHS)*

*Consett Crusade (CHS)*

*Line of march through Consett (l-r): Cllr Willie Walton, Cllr Vince Kelly, Cllr Billy Bell, David Watkins MP, Cllr Jimmy Graham (Council Chairman), Cllr Bill Stockdale (behind), Bill Sirs (General Secretary ISTC), Bolsover MP Dennis Skinner, union official (LHA)*

(Industry) Ltd and regional government officials on Thursday, 13th December 1979. After the meeting, a joint press statement was issued, agreeing that an urgent programme of development was now necessary in Derwentside and that a joint approach would be made to the Government for additional assistance within the District.

A confidentiality promise had caused Hodgson some difficulties. Although the official decision to close Consett Steelworks was announced in December 1979, nine months in advance, Hodgson had been told about it by BSC Chairman Sir Charles Villiers a year earlier, but under strict confidentiality. When the rumours of impending closure reached a peak in the autumn of 1979, Hodgson had to play for time – he could not break his promise to Sir Charles. So he advised the Council Members to wait for the publication of the Derwentside Report which in the event came out days after BSC's closure announcement. Hodgson then had to tell the members that, as a result of the announcement, large parts of the Derwentside Study were now out of date - something he had known all along but had been unable to say. One benefit of knowing in advance was that Hodgson had been able to set in train plans for reclaiming the BSC site, which got under way within six months of closure with EEC money Hodgson had already prepared for ahead of the closure announcement.

Hodgson told the Industry Committee on 17th December: 'The problems now facing the District are considerably more severe than had been envisaged in the document (the Derwentside Study) when closure was forecast in 1985,' he said. The committee accepted that industrial development must be given priority over all other fields of activity. One of the recommendations of the Derwentside Study was the appointment of a Development Officer by the Council, with possible financial aid from the EEC (European Economic Community). £4m of EEC aid was also available for in-house training for industry moving into the steel closure areas, but an equal amount of "matched funding" would have to be provided from the UK. That meeting lasted four and a quarter hours.

Two days later, on Wednesday 19th December 1979, the DDC Industry Committee met senior members of the County Council at County Hall to formally ask for their support. The DDC representatives were: Cllrs Ken Robson (Chairman), Billy Bell (Leader), Joseph Redshaw, Bill Stockdale, Joe Walker and Selby Walker. The DCC members were: Cllrs Billy Nattrass (Chairman), Bill Firby, George Fishburn, Joe Graham, Ronnie Knowles, Jim McCallum and George Shields. Consett MP David Watkins and Durham & Blaydon MEP Roland Boyes had already pledged their support. Boyes had arranged for Henk Vredeling, EEC Commissioner for Employment and Social Affairs, to visit Consett at an early date. Arrangements were also being made for a delegation of non-UK Socialist members of the European Parliament with a particular interest in steel to visit the area in January. With other steelworks closures to come, the government had announced that £13m would be made available to the Welsh Development Agency for investment in Shotton and £3m to the Corby New Town Development Corporation for Corby, but no direct government assistance would be given to the local authorities concerned.

Chief Executive Terry Hodgson outlined the magnitude of the problems facing the District. Unemployment could rise to over 30%, and the situation was further complicated by the capital expenditure controls facing local authorities. It was estimated that the closure of Consett Works would result in increases in rates of 5p and 2p for the District and County

CIC "The big offices" (LHA)

Councils respectively, if there was no increase in the Rate Support Grant. The County Council was invited to accompany the delegation from the Council to visit the Secretaries of State for Industry and Environment. However, the County Planning Officer questioned the value of further increasing the industrial incentives offered by the Department of Industry, the County Council and the District Council and considered that it might be more appropriate for the finance which would be necessary to be used elsewhere. That evening a

special meeting of Derwentside Council confirmed all the decisions of the Industry Committee. In arguing for the retention of the Consett Works, the Trades Unions had pointed out that it had made a profit over the past three months. The Council agreed to support the Trades Unions 'in any positive and responsible action which they proposed to take to prevent or delay the closure', but recognised the need to 'prepare for the worst' as a matter of urgency.

Junction Bridge – what future for these two lads? (IP)

As the trades unions mounted a "Save Consett" campaign, a report entitled "Case for Action" was produced jointly by the District and County Councils and the British Steel Corporation and presented to government ministers on 13th February 1980. By 1986 over 7,000 new jobs would be needed. New roads and new industrial sites had to be built, as well as reclamation and town centre and village improvements. Over the next five years, something like £75m of new investment would be required. The situation at Consett was compared and contrasted with Scunthorpe, Llanwern and Port Talbot where steelworks closures were also pending. Sir Keith Joseph made a statement in the House of Commons on 19th June 1980. Consett was already a Special Development Area, and the English Industrial Estates Corporation would get about £12m to increase building over the next five years, he said. Consett would get £10m in derelict land grants. 80 acres of land would be developed for industry, he said. From a local point of view, it was at least a start, but far short of what was needed. Behind the scenes, senior government advisors were less than optimistic. 'They haven't got a cat in hell's chance,' said one. It was 8th December 1980 when Sir Keith finally met a delegation from the two Councils and the MP, but by then the deed was done. As a fraternal gesture, Derwentside's German twin town of Werdohl offered jobs to 100 redundant Consett steelworkers.

## Maggie, Maggie, Maggie!

As closure approached, Derwentside Council wrote to Prime Minister Margaret Thatcher, asking her to take responsibility for the action needed 'to alleviate the economic and social problems arising as a consequence of the closure of the steelworks'. But in response to a six-page letter from Terry Hodgson, Mrs Thatcher gave a short, sharp reply of just three paragraphs. 'We believe the measures we are implementing….are the right response to the problem,' she said, 'but there is always a limit to what is practically possible. It is no use building factories for which there are no tenants'. On another, more famous occasion, she said: 'there is no such thing as society'.

On 12th September 1980, steelmaking ceased at Consett after 135 years. In his book "Consett a town in the making" Tommy Moore described how it was his task to close Consett down. At 11.28am on the morning of 12th September, he "tapped" steel for the last time. And then he had a couple of pints 'to get rid of the bloody misery of it'. Years later, Tommy Moore wrote that he still missed the camaraderie of the steelworks, the rewarding hard work, and the beer and dominoes at the end of the shift. The decision to close the steelworks put 4,500 men out of work, with many more losing their jobs in associated industries. Overnight, Consett plunged from being a relatively prosperous town to an area of high unemployment, industrial dereliction and empty properties. Population decline accelerated as more and more people of working age left for jobs elsewhere, leaving behind the young, the old, the disabled and unemployed.

It wasn't just the steelworks. Most of Derwentside's coal mines had already closed, and the rest were soon to follow. In 1973, the year before DDC took over, the last big coal mine in the district – Morrison Busty – closed. Ball bearing manufacturers Ransome & Marles – later Ransome, Hoffman & Pollard – had opened a factory at Greencroft in 1953 with government assistance to reduce unemployment in the area. This closed down in 1981 with the loss of 1,250 to 1,500 jobs when RHM were given incentives to move production back to their Newark home base. In less than a decade, the Annfield Plain area had lost its two biggest employers. Another "new" employer, battery firm Ever Ready, was shedding staff at Tanfield Lea. By 1981 Derwentside had lost 15,000 jobs in two decades. Faced with such a serious situation, the Council had to act – but needed the help of government and the European Community to solve the District's grave problems. If Derwentside was not to go into terminal decline, two things were needed. One of these was not in any doubt – the determination of Derwentside people and their elected councillors and MPs to fight for the very survival of their close-knit communities. The other, the need for substantial financial aid from government and the EEC, was also, eventually, forthcoming as the powers-that-be finally had to accept that they could not ignore the pressing need of the District to rebuild its economy anew.

## Consett Crisis

The Council produced another report, "The Consett Crisis", outlining the economic and social problems of the district. This was presented to the Economic & Social Committee of the EEC when they visited Consett on 23rd October 1980. The closure of Consett Steelworks the previous month had reduced the economy of the area by over £100m, said the report. In 1975 the Works had employed 5,500, falling to 3,750 at the time of closure. In 1951, 16,900 of 39,700 people employed in the District (over 40%) were in coal mining. Since then, almost all the mines had closed, and by 1976 total employment in the District had fallen to 28,300. The unemployment rate rose from 10.1% in 1975 to 14.9% in 1980, with youth unemployment at 29.8%. Between 1951 and 1971 the population of the district had fallen from 102,400 to 92,000 and by 1980 it was about 89,000.

It was not possible for the Council itself to become actively involved in building large advance factories, which was the responsibility of EIEC (English Industrial Estates Corporation), but smaller developments could be done jointly by DDC and the County Council. Building the new roads needed was the responsibility of the Department of Environment and Durham County Council. In-house training required by incoming industrialists needed the support of the Manpower Services Commission and Durham County Council, with more facilities at Consett Technical College. There would be a bigger demand for executive housing in the area. One potential problem was that the capital expenditure reductions required by government could affect the ability of the Council to finance further development and environmental improvements. Failure to comply could lead to "retributory action" being taken against the Council by the Secretary of State. In other words, if Derwentside Council spent over its limits in trying to tackle the vast problems caused by the closure of the steelworks, the pits and large factories, the Council could be "fined" by government by substantial reductions in grant aid. Not so much "help yourselves" as "help yourselves, but not too much".

*CIC Entrance before closure (LHA)*

*CIC entrance after closure (IP)*

*Derelict Steelworks*

## "Town for Sale"

The closure of Consett Steelworks could have been the last nail in the coffin for Derwentside. Most of the pits in the district had already gone, the last one closing in 1980. From mid-1980 to mid-1981, Derwentside lost half its manufacturing jobs. Unemployment doubled to 27% by July 1981. By the end of that year, one third of men in the district were on the dole. Consett featured in a television documentary entitled "Town for Sale". What the district desperately needed was a business and job creation programme to combat the loss of its traditional employment base of coal mining and steel manufacturing. Almost overnight, Consett had plunged from being relatively well-off to an area of high deprivation. This was such a high profile and traumatic event that government could no longer ignore the area. Economic regeneration became the order of the day. To progress this on the ground, a Task Force was set up to promote the creation of new businesses and jobs. It had representatives from the District and County councils, government and public utilities. British Steel immediately set up an office of its job creation arm - British Steel Corporation Industry (BSCI) - and the District Council appointed its first Industrial Officer.

The Task Force was set up with four aims: new road links to the A1 motorway, building new factory premises, reclaiming the steelworks site, assistance to establish new industry. BSC (Industry) Ltd set up in Consett in 1979 to help new businesses get established. Money came from central and local government, BSCI Ltd, the European Community and venture capital companies. The Number One Industrial Estate at Consett was opened up. Eddie Hutchinson came to Consett in 1980 as part of the BSCI regeneration team based on the old steelworks site. In 1982 he transferred to the new public/private body DIDA (Derwentside Industrial Development Agency) which had its origins in the multi-agency Task Force established two years earlier. He was Chief Executive of DIDA 1988-2007.

The strategy was based around a drive to diversify Derwentside's industrial base by helping existing firms to expand, bringing in new employers from elsewhere and helping new businesses to start up. The Council also helped to set up the Derwentside Industrial Group (DIG), a forum for local businesses to join together and support the economic development of the district. In 1982 the District Council, DIG and BSCI established DIDA under the chairmanship of local businessman Brian Crangle. Laurie Haveron of BSCI was its first Chief Executive. DIDA took on BSCI's role in Derwentside, providing advice and support on business and financial planning and working closely with the District Council in creating new jobs. By March 1990 the numbers of unemployed in the district, 7,208 in September 1986, had fallen to 3,418. The end of the "red dust" from the Steelworks that used to blanket the town was a big environmental improvement, and also had a jobs spin-off. Speciality glass manufacturer Romag moved to Consett because of the clean air!

## Billy Bell, Joe Rhind

To meet the new situation, both councillors and officers had to find new ways of working. Cllr Billy Bell was the new Leader of the Council. He had taken over in 1979 when Norris Oyston lost his seat. As Leader, Billy Bell adopted a more democratic style. Selby Walker continued as Group Secretary. Members of the Council were becoming more demanding and less likely just to accept the decisions made by the leadership. But there were no councillors on the Task Force. This was something new for the Council members, and had to be handled diplomatically. Chief Executive Terry Hodgson provided the interface between the councillors and the Task Force, reassuring the members that their policies were being fed into its deliberations. In 1981 a "triumvirate" of senior officers was formed of Chief Executive Terry Hodgson, Chief Technical Services Officer Malcolm Davies and Chief Planning Officer Bill Hetherington. Davies was responsible for the reclamation of the former steelworks site and was awarded the MBE for his efforts. Deputy Chief Executive Neil Johnson later took over the top job from Terry and went on to devise what became the Genesis Project to bring economic activity back to the huge former Steelworks site close to the centre of Consett. In 1987 there was also a change of political leadership, Joe Rhind taking over as Council Leader when Billy Bell lost his seat. Rhind, born and brought up in Leeds, moved to Derwentside in 1968 to be near his wife's parents. Looking for a home for their growing family – they had five children – Joe and his wife Esme bought the former chief colliery electrician's house in Dipton and have lived there ever since.

*Billy Bell*

*Joe Rhind*

*Desolate scene after closure & clearance*

*The last molten iron from the blast furnaces tapped at Consett, 12th September 1980 (AP)*

## Last train to Consett

The last regular passenger service from Consett to Newcastle was in 1955. The last empty coal train left Consett in September 1983. The official "last train to Consett" ran from Newcastle Central Station to the High Yard at Consett on the 17th March 1984. The train guard was John Grant, a leading member of the Railways of Britain group. Organised by the Derwentside Rail Action Group, it was the first passenger train to Consett since the 1950s when passenger services were withdrawn and the line became freight-only. The freight was mainly iron ore from the terminal at Tyne Dock on the River Tyne, coal from the collieries up to Consett High Yard, and steel from the Low Yard back down to the Tyne. The line up to Consett was part of the old Stanhope and Tyne Railway, which opened in 1834, and ran from Stanhope to South Shields via Waskerley, Rowley and Consett down to Stanley, Vigo, Washington, Boldon and and into South Shields. After the closure of Consett steelworks in 1980 it was not viable to keep the branch line open just for a couple of coal trains a day.

John Grant wrote: 'for me, the journey started at Greensfield shed. It was a very cold and snowy morning. We picked up our engine and went down to Heaton carriage sidings. There we added eight coaches and went up to Newcastle ready for the journey to Consett. On arrival at Newcastle Central station with the set we found the platform awash with hundreds of train enthusiasts with their cameras, as well as both BBC and Tyne Tees television, radio and newspaper reporters. The train quickly filled up with those lucky enough to have tickets for the return journey to Consett. We picked up a further train crew at Newcastle from the Tyne Marshalling Yard depot as they were needed as conductors up

*Last train to Consett (CO)*

*Last freight train (CO)*

*Last coal train (CO)*

the Consett branch. People were lined up along the track all the way from Ouston junction where the line left the East Coast main line, up to West Pelton, then up the gradient to Stanley Level and then on again right into Consett. We passed Beamish, West Stanley, Annfield Plain, Leadgate and went on into the High Yard where we came to a stop next to where the old Consett station platform used to be. Huge crowds with banners and flags and a brass band greeted us. As there was no platform, the passengers had to alight from the train using special stepped ramps. It was the end of the line.' Not quite - Prince Charles came to Consett by train in December 1984.

## Road to Recovery

After Brian Crangle, DIDA chairmen included Mark I'Anson, who set up Integrated Micro Products in Derwentside in 1982, and its latest incumbent Owen McFarlane, who started AS&T Aerospace (now part of CAV Aerospace) in Derwentside in 1990. Laurie Haveron of BSCI was followed as Chief Executive by John Carney, formerly the Council's Industrial Officer, and then Eddie Hutchinson, previously a business adviser with both DIDA and BSCI. Many of Derwentside's business success stories began as venture capital-backed start-ups assisted by DIDA, including companies such as Derwent Valley Foods, CAV Aerospace and International Cuisine. CAV – which in 2008 employed 350 people in Consett

and around 500 worldwide – was close to Hutchinson's heart. Born in Crook in 1944, he joined British Aerospace in 1964 and trained as an aeronautical engineer. Hutchinson was sponsored by the company to take a degree and graduated in 1968, despite having earlier failed his 11-plus. He then went on to get an MA at Durham Business School. In 1971 he joined British Steel on Teesside where he worked on the financial side, before joining BSCI in 1980 and arriving in Consett in mid-1981. 'AS&T, as CAV were then known, were based in Haltwhistle but once we were aware of their interest I just picked it up and ran with it. This is the success story that has given me most satisfaction with my background in this subject,' said Hutchinson, who also told the Journal newspaper that things were not always so plush as in DIDA's modern £1m Steel House office accommodation. 'When I arrived we were based in some old huts which had been left over from the steelworks'. He recalled the inauspicious beginnings of another of Derwentside's success stories, Derwent Valley Foods. 'The four men behind the company were all senior managers in industry. Theirs was just the kind of product we were interested in, niche packaging, an adult savoury snack in aluminium packaging. Their business plan was a single sheet of A4 paper with nothing on it! We helped Derwent Valley Foods secure the venture capital finance, they got the thing off the ground and the rest, as they say, is history'.

*Chimney falls....(MC)*

*Going….*

*…going….*

*… gone*

One of the goals of DIDA was to focus on attracting the right type of company to Derwentside. One company Hutchinson singled out as being one of his high points is Bioprocessing which came to Consett in the early 1980s after it secured £600,000 of venture capital. The company, later known as Millipore and based on the town's No.1 Industrial Estate, became a world leader in cancer fighting drugs. In 1995 Hutchinson received an MBE for services to the business community. DIDA Director John Pearson, Director of Development and Asset Management for Derwentside District Council, said: 'I don't think anyone should underestimate the contribution Eddie has made – both in commitment and expertise'.

*CIC apprentices, the last intake 1979 (GS)*

*CIC apprentices, reunion 2008 (GS)*

**Neil Johnson**

When Terry Hodgson left the Council in 1987 to go into private industry, his deputy Neil Johnson took over as Chief Executive. Hodgson and Johnson were much the same age, around thirty, with Hodgson the older by less than a year. Their widely differing characters had made them a good team. Hodgson was very much the clubbable man, socializing with other officers and senior members of the Council. While friendly, Johnson tended to keep a professional distance with both officers and members, preferring not to join in the after-hours drinks and weekend golfing. As Chief Executive, Hodgson's main focus was on outside matters, while his deputy Johnson ran the office. To those who worked with him, Johnson could at times appear to be somewhat dogmatic but his motives were seen as sincere and he had a

*Neil Johnson (IP)*

genuine passion for the district and the welfare of Derwentside's residents. Neil Johnson spent the whole of his working life in local government. Born and brought up in Aycliffe, he left school at sixteen with five GCE "O" levels to start work as a "general division clerk" with Darlington Rural District Council. His first wage was £23 9s 11d a month. Nine years later he moved on the Spennymoor UDC as Deputy Clerk to Alan Roberts. When local government reorganization came in 1974, and Spennymoor was taken into Sedgefield District, both men moved to the new council. Roberts became Chief Executive, while Johnson was given a "third tier" post. Two years later he moved to Derwentside as deputy to Hodgson before being appointed to the top job in 1987.

With the closure of the East Coast deep mines, government attention had moved from the West to the East of the county. It was clear that Derwentside would have to stand on its own feet. At the same time, government was putting more and more pressure on local authorities, with the threat of capping – limiting or reducing Council Tax rises by government decree – a very real possibility. To meet this challenge, Council staff had to adjust to new ways of working and learn new skills. But there were other difficulties. The introduction of the Poll Tax by the Conservative government in 1989/90 created severe problems. While some individuals made a political protest by refusing to pay, many innocent people got into difficulties and were taken to court. The Council was in a dilemma – on the one hand, the Council was under a legal obligation to collect the Poll Tax and take enforcement action against non-payers, but on the other hand DDC had a social responsibility to all of its residents, particularly pensioners, unemployed and other vulnerable groups. Derwentside Council had yet to find its future role.

When Treasurer Eric Davis was chided by a colleague for driving on the wrong side of the road to take a short cut, he said: *"you can do what you like until you are stopped."* Davis once remarked, tongue in cheek: *"every year the Council should have a National Shooting Day, so let's start with the Council tenants."* Davis was generally quiet during Council meetings, but when he spoke on budget issues, his word was law. When Davis told the Council: ***"you can't do it, you don't have the money,"*** nothing more was said and the councillors moved on to next business.

*Pontop Pike television mast sent out its first pictures on 1st May 1953. In November 1955 it was extended from 300 to 500ft. At that time a Pye tv set sold for 67 guineas (£70 7s) and a tv/radio licence was £2.*

*Picture (right)*
*Glorious sweep of heather on Hedleyhope Fell (DS)*

## Chapter Four
# Building the Future 1991-2002

*Turbulent Times; Urgent Action; Watson, Earley, Malone; death of Harry Collinson; Broadband comes to Derwentside; CCTV; DurhamNet; Infonet; Alan Hodgson; Project Genesis; Shotley Bridge Hospital; Wind Turbines.*

### Turbulent Times

'One of Derwentside's most turbulent years' is how retiring Council Chairman, Cllr Keith Murray-Hetherington, described it at the Council's annual meeting in May 1992. But the District was already on the long road to recovery. Alongside the Council and government bodies, British Steel encouraged the setting-up of new businesses. Regional grants were co-ordinated by the Derwentside Development Agency. This combination of public and private investment got results. Of the 180 companies that invested in Derwentside between 1985 and 1996, 98 were new start-ups, 51 were expansions of existing businesses, and 31 were from inward investment. The formula: Business + Council + Workforce = Success.

Three companies who located in Derwentside in 1982 reflected on their success ten years later. 'I needed a lot of help at the beginning,' said Karl Sandoy, the Norwegian managing director of Grorud Industries, 'at first I had nowhere to work, and I used the Council Chairman's office as my office. The Chief Executive and all of his staff were there to help me. I haven't needed that now, but I know they are there. They do exactly the right thing, not to be blowing down your neck all the time, telling us what to do, but to be there when we need them'. Originally, Mr Sandoy employed six people. Ten years later, five were still working for the company – one having died in the meantime. 'They are loyal,' said Sandoy with great emphasis. The workforce had grown to 300+. It was a similar story at Derwent Valley Foods, who started in Consett in 1982 and became the country's leading producers of quality snacks. Their television adverts emphasised their location "Medomsley Road, Consett"'Staff turnover is almost zero. Our absentee rate is 1-2%, compared with an industry average of 5-6%, with some as much as eight, nine or ten per cent,' said Commercial Director Keith Gill, 'that's an indication of the quality of people we have'.

Mark I'Anson, Managing Director of Integrated Micro Products, was equally enthusiastic. 'The workforce are a major advantage for us, a committed and very skilled workforce,' he said, 'the lifestyle here (in the North East) is superior'. IMP was typical of many firms that have located in Derwentside. I'Anson and his business partner David Liddell were researchers with the Open University when they decided to form their own company. 'We knew how to build computers and we could see a gap in the market, but we lacked business experience,' said I'Anson, 'but help was at hand with Derwentside Council. They helped us form our business plan, and as well as grants, the most valuable help they gave us was introducing us to sources of finance'.

A new company, CAV Aerospace, set up in brand-new premises in Annfield Plain in July 1990. At that time just ten people were on the payroll. By 2008 CAV had a £6m annual turnover and employed a 700-strong workforce worldwide, 450 at the company headquarters on the No 1 Industrial Estate, Consett. With three divisions involved with aerostructures, ice protection and small component machinery, the company had other manufacturing sites in Leicester, Poland and the USA. 'Derwentside District Council had the foresight to make facilities available," said Managing Director and Chief Executive Owen McFarlane, "we were able to move straight into a 20,000 sq ft factory. Not only that, we were made to feel so welcome. The service and support we have had from the district council has been second to none'.

Mandy Scott built up AA Flags from scratch, with help from DDC all along the way. As sales manager for a Tyneside-based firm importing flagpoles, Mandy realised there was a market for flags made to order. When her employers went bust, she decided to set up on her own. She and her husband Laurie bought a large terraced house in Blackhill simply because it was cheap and had room for flag-making. Admitting she 'couldn't sew a button on', Mandy enrolled on an evening course at the local community centre but soon had enough business to take on her first employee. Helped initially by a £40 a week Enterprise Allowance, the business expanded. The Scotts moved into an even larger terraced house along the street, and then on to a factory unit on the Park Road South estate, both moves aided by DDC. 'The Council has backed us every step of the way and is still helping us,' she said. A £7,000 eyelet-making machine was bought with the aid of a 40% grant. By 2008 AA Flags employed 16 staff and had an annual turnover of £450,000. With demand for flags affected by the credit crunch and competition from Chinese printed flags, Mandy added garment alterations as "Quick Stitch." With clients all over the world, AA Flags has undoubtedly been a success story of backing local enterprise.

### Urgent action

Sometimes the Council had to take urgent action. In 2000 DDC economic head John Pearson discovered that stairlift manufacturers Bison Bede, who had originally started in an old school building in Leadgate, and had then moved to the nearby industrial estate and again to bigger premises in Castleside, were about to move once more but this time out of the District and into Northumberland. Within half an hour moves had been made to identify alternative premises within Derwentside. A funding package for the refurbishment of a building on Consett No.1 Industrial Estate was rapidly put in place, and Bison Bede moved there with the retention of over 100 jobs for the District. When Ever Ready drastically reduced its operations at Tanfield Lea there were already two empty buildings on the industrial estate that were in a danger if being pulled down. Pearson oversaw the drawing-up of an action plan for a major initiative to refurbish the empty industrial buildings and build new ones. With support from English Estates, Government Office North East, One NorthEast and EU funding, over £10m of capital investment was put in to refurbish buildings, improve the estate's infrastructure and build 60,000 sq ft of new factory space. Part of this initiative also saw the first Broadband installation in Derwentside. Over 500 new jobs were created on the Tanfield Lea site, significantly more than the 400 which were lost at Ever Ready. By 2008 a new £7m Business Centre was being developed to support further improvement to the site and additional job creation.

In 1999 the District Council established the Derwentside Engineering Forum (DEF) which brought together local businesses from key sectors of the local economy to develop joint initiatives to win new business, improve industry efficiency and create new jobs. The Forum also had great success working with local schools and Derwentside College to help develop engineering skills

and qualifications. By 2002, the number of unemployed in Derwentside had fallen to fewer than 1,500, the lowest since 1974. It was almost 9,000 in the early 1980s. The rate of fall was the greatest in County Durham. 2 million square feet of business space had been provided, and 6,700 new jobs created.

On one occasion, Derwentside's first Chief Executive Joe Quinn upset the civil service mandarins of Whitehall with his straightforward language. In those days it was customary for a local Council chief, writing to a government minister, to sign his letter *"I remain, Sir, your obedient servant, etc, etc."* Joe had written in with a request that government provide financial support to help the Council tackle areas of deprivation. The minister had given a typically bland and unhelpful reply. The minister's letter, no doubt penned by a London-based civil servant, included the phrase: *"from where I sit, looking out of my window, I cannot perceive your problems."* Joe replied: ***"from where I sit, looking out of my window, it is blindingly obvious. Yours faithfully…."***

*AA Flags – boss Mandy Scott at the back (CFW)*

### Watson, Earley, Malone

After two years as Deputy Leader of the controlling Labour group and the Council, Cllr Alex Watson was elected Group & Council Leader in 1991. He was to hold these twin positions for the next 18 years – an unusual record. Watson and the two men who were his deputies, first Kevin Earley and then Mike Malone, had a major influence on Council policy. In fact, when chief executive Neil Johnson left the Council in 1997, the Council operated a joint Member/Officer Management Team without a Chief Executive. The arrangement stood for five years before ending in June 2002 when Mike Clark was appointed as General Manager. 'When I took over as Leader, it was clear that much more needed to be done to reduce the high unemployment levels in the district and continue to clear the dereliction left by the closure of the Consett Steel Works,' said Alex.

To tackle these problems, in 1989 the Council had started Project Genesis with a high-profile board that included David Bellamy, North West Durham MP Hilary Armstrong, and David Weeks, Deputy Leader of the City of London, as Chairman. Little progress had been made. Under Watson's

*Alex Watson*

*Kevin Earley*

*Mike Malone*

leadership, the Council brought in private development company Dysart Developments to manage the project. Their appointment was and still is controversial, but Watson has always defended the decision. "Councils are good at providing public services," he said, "but there are some things that private enterprise can do better. Under Dysart's management, not only has the Genesis Project been an outstanding success, it has cost the Council very little in terms of direct cash payments". Watson pointed to the renewal of Consett bus station as an example. "Here was an ugly, badly-designed bus station that cost the taxpayer a million pounds to build in 1980. It was nick-named 'the Bull Ring.' Everybody hated it, there were muggings and vandalism. Thanks to Dysart, this monstrosity was demolished and we got a brand new bus station at no cost to the Council, saving us £200,000 a year in running and maintenance costs. Consett also got a new shopping centre and CCTV cameras were set up throughout the district. Other improvements included the by-pass from McDonalds to Blackhill. Dysart brought in companies like McDonalds and English Cuisine, taking on all the hidden costs of seeking out and making presentations to prospective clients like these, and again saving the Council money".

### Death of Harry Collinson

Beside the entrance to the Council Chamber is a simple black plaque with gold lettering which says: *"in memory of Harry Collinson 1945-91, Principal Planning Officer".* The death in 1991 of the Council's Chief Planning Officer Harry Collinson – shot by Albert Dryden in a planning dispute – was a profound shock to members and officers of the Council and to the general public. The events of that black day were recalled by retired Council officer Gilbert Green: 'the news filtered through in dribs and drabs. First, staff heard that there had been an incident involving Harry Collinson, then that he had been shot, and finally that he was dead. Even then, we could scarcely believe it, and we hoped that there had been a mistake and that Harry was still alive,' said Green; 'we were all numb with shock, and that feeling lasted for days. We were very much a family, and it was almost like losing a member of your own family. Collinson's natural instincts were with the downtrodden. He wrote letters in newspapers championing the cause of exploited plantation workers in South America. He was also a kind man, regularly picking up shopping for his elderly neighbours'.

The events of that day were widely reported – they were even recorded on television. Never before, it seemed, had a Council officer been deliberately murdered in the course of his duties. Peter Reynolds, DDC's last Director of Environmental Services, was there, and he confirmed that what happened was completely unexpected. This was how he remembers that traumatic day: 'Harry Collinson was a very consciencious officer. He was determined not only to do everything exactly correctly, but that everything should be done openly and honestly. All the necessary approvals were in place, and the Council could have sent a bulldozer in the night and knocked down Dryden's bungalow without anybody knowing. Instead, Harry arranged for the demolition to take place during the day, and he notified Dryden in advance. We had checked with the Planning Inspectorate that we were following correct procedures, and the police had been notified. Who told the press I do not know, but the media was there in force, including a television crew. I was the Senior Planning Officer at the time, and it was my job to record the proceedings. But it was our clear intention, and it had been agreed in advance, that if there was any form of obstruction – for example, if anyone had stood in the road to bar the path of the bulldozer – then we would all retire from the scene immediately and send the bulldozer away. Everything was to be as low key as possible, and in reality we did not expect to get the work done that day'.

As Harry Collinson approached the bungalow, Albert Dryden appeared with two others in the background. Without warning, Dryden produced a gun and shot Collinson dead. Dryden was subsequently convicted of murder and sentenced to life imprisonment. Gilbert Green believed the press was at least partly responsible for the shooting. 'They built up Albert Dryden to be some sort of folk hero,' he said, 'but Harry Collinson was a very fair man who went through all the legal procedures. Harry wanted things not only to be done correctly, but to be seen to be done correctly. In addition, it is inexplicable to many people as to why the police did not have an armed response unit at the scene'. 'Some people regarded Dryden as a harmless eccentric, but there were a few who stood outside the court and actually applauded him,' said the then Deputy Council Leader Cllr Kevin Earley. Ex-Leader Joe Rhind said: 'The murder of our Chief Planning Officer Harry Collinson was a huge shock to everybody. Never before had we thought that a Council officer, or a councillor for that matter, might be harmed in the course of doing his or her duty. Council staff were put under terrific pressure. For the first time, members of the public started to get aggressive. We had to bring in new procedures to try to avoid anything like this happening again'.

After Collinson's death, Ingrid Steele was appointed as Chief Planning Officer under the Chief Environmental Services Officer Peter Hunter. When Steele left in 1993, Peter Reynolds and Tim Wheeler jointly ran the Planning Department until 1995 when Reynolds was put in sole charge. Reynolds is a local lad through and through. He was born and brought up in South Stanley and went to Hustledown School and Lanchester St Bedes. Peter joined Derwentside District Council in September 1974 after completing his GCE 'A' levels, aged eighteen. He has worked for the Council ever since – almost the full 35 years of its existence. Peter started as a trainee planning technician earning £17 a week, far less than he had earned for eleven weeks that summer, labouring at Consett steelworks. Reynolds rose through the ranks to become Head of Planning Services in 1995 and Director of Environmental Services in 2003. In 2008 he was in charge of 200+ staff in planning, environmental health and general services (refuse collection, street cleaning, grounds maintenance). Peter's first boss was Chief Planning Officer Bill Hetherington. A tall, imposing man at 6ft 5in, Hetherington had spent a lot of time in South Africa where he'd had servants. One of Peter's first jobs was to go to the shops to buy his boss's favourite brand of cigarettes. Hetherington was a heavy smoker. Every lunchtime he would play poker with paper clips with his senior staff who included Jeff Singleton, Harry Collinson, Tom Stukins and David Keast. When Hetherington retired he was succeeded as Chief Planning Officer by Collinson whose death in 1991 sent shock waves that reverberated around the world. It had a devastating effect on everyone connected with Derwentside Council, but especially on Collinson's colleagues in the Planning Department. After Collinson's death, new rules were brought in to ensure proper registration and monitoring of planning applications. The Council thereafter reviewed its procedures, installing alarm buzzers in interview rooms. Staff were told always to ensure they had a safe means of escape, and to have a colleague with them if they had any doubts. Other staff were always on hand in case of trouble. Some people who had a grievance with the Council would threaten to "do a Dryden" if they didn't get their own way. Reynolds understands why some people get extremely upset when their planning applications are turned down. 'A planning refusal can mean that someone's hopes and dreams are shattered,' he says, 'we are the face of the Council and to some applicants it becomes very personal'.

*Laptop Learning (LW)*

## Broadband comes to Derwentside

Getting Internet and Broadband facilities into Derwentside was a bold initiative by the Council, the first in the North East to do so. 'At that time, Derwentside was still served by the old analogue telephone system and BT had no interest whatsoever in converting to digital,' said Deputy Leader Cllr Malone, 'so, with the help of an EU Grant the Council paid for 27 kilometres of fibre-optic cabling to be put into the ground. One firm in particular, Express Engineering at Tanfield, would not have located in Tanfield Lea with the loss of 250 jobs, without this new system being installed'. The network went "live" late in 1997 after the installation of the cable network. This was thanks to a genuinely ground-breaking deal with Telewest Communications who built the network as an extension from their base in Gateshead's Team Valley. This required a £1.2m investment. Derwentside Council was the first in the region to get a Broadband network and the accolade of being "far-sighted and innovative" was well deserved. 'Other providers like BT simply were not interested in a district like Derwentside with its relatively sparse population,' said Council Leader Alex Watson, 'we were not willing to wait to be last to be linked up with the world-wide net, but to be at the front of the queue we had to take action ourselves. Telecommunications are now as important as road and rail links to new industry looking to move into the area'.

*Donna Ryans of Delves Lane Junior School with the Robert Swan award for schools environmental projects (1996)*

The introduction of Closed Circuit Television (CCTV) has been one of the Council's most successful weapons against crime. It has been proved effective in both cutting and detecting crime and because of this people now feel safer. Derwentside installed CCTV in Consett town centre in 1997 and followed this a year later with another scheme in Stanley town centre. By 2008 there were 18 cameras installed in the two town centres alone. The cameras work on a private co-axial network in the Consett area and a fibre network provided by Telewest in the Stanley area. The traditional box cameras are installed on six-metre columns. Originally the Council planned to install 46 CCTV cameras, two for each ward, but this was ultimately increased to over 100. The network allowed DurhamNet, a partnership between DDC and Durham County Council, to be set up. By 2008 DurhamNet was providing IT services not only to the two councils, but also to other authorities and public bodies in Tyne & Wear and Northumberland. Its video conferencing facility has attracted interest from Germany, Italy and Spain as well as from the NHS, and DurhamNet has advised the British cabinet. 'Our initiative has had far-reaching, knock-on effects,' said Cllr Malone. In May 1998 DDC helped set up Britain's first online job centre. The Swift project, an on-line medical appointments system, was pioneered in Derwentside.

*Computer girls Cllr Evelyn Wilson (left) with Caroline Connolly (centre) and Jill Harris.*

*Computer lads*

In response to the increasing fear of crime within the Derwentside area, in 2003 the Council started to implement a pilot CCTV scheme with three cameras installed in three wards, Blackhill, Leadgate and South Stanley. These cameras utilised the existing Derwentside network connections and used wireless technology for connection to the cameras. The success of this scheme meant that a further 61 cameras were installed in other wards. The cameras are a Pelco Spectra III dome type, the wireless equipment is Proxim Tsumsami, and the monitoring software and encoders are provided by VCS. The three schemes are monitored by the Project Genesis management company from a central control room based at Ponds Court on the Genesis site.

### Alan Hodgson

Later to become Chief Executive of DurhamNet, Alan Hodgson was the lead officer in DDC's charge to embrace the Internet age. Hodgson, from North Shields, started work at sixteen as an apprentice mechanic with the NCB. While still in his teens, he learnt his basic IT (Information Technology) skills at South East Northumberland Technical College in Wallsend and became fascinated with computers. He moved on to work in the shipbuilding industry for several years. After a spell working in London, Alan returned to the North East as a data processor with Wansbeck Council. After five years there, in 1989 he joined Derwentside Council as Chief Information Officer. Up to that point, IT was mainly used in finance, but Alan was asked to include HR (human resources) in his remit. With an influx of new and younger councillors came the desire to try new ideas. The only computer power then available to the District Council was the shared use of Durham County Council's computer – a slow and tedious process. Then came the Poll Tax debacle. Introduced in Scotland in 1989 and in England in 1990, the new tax was hugely unpopular and was soon replaced by the Council Tax. All this meant huge changes to the Council's financial systems.

In 1995 new Deputy Leader of the Council, Cllr Mike Malone, and his predecessor, Cllr Kevin Earley, met with Alan Hodgson to discuss how the new and rapidly-expanding ICT (information & communications technology) could be used to better effect. The world-wide internet was just emerging, and it was clear that unless some radical action was taken, most Derwentside residents and businesses would remain "digitally excluded". These ideas crystalised at a two-day meeting in Preston. Alan went with DDC Policy Officer Lorraine O'Donnell and councillors Mike Malone and Jean Huntley. It was an eye-opener. Some councils had already started what were called FreeNets or TownNets – in other words, web sites. Community-based IT "platforms" were to be the building blocks of Derwentside's own internet revolution, and Stanley was to be the first centre of what eventually became Derwentside's District-wide network.

Alan, Lorraine and Economic Development Officer Con Crawford ("trust me to have two Northern Irish colleagues," said Alan) put together a bid for five years of SRB (Single Regeneration Budget) funding to provide access points in and around Stanley: schools, libraries, doctors' surgeries, and even a solicitor's office with free legal advice thrown in. The Stanley Infonet was launched in 1995 with one full-time technician and computer training provided by Derwentside College. By coincidence, British Telecom (BT) had just installed a new and up-to-date telephone network in the area. This was an initial advantage, but it quickly became clear that it would be far too expensive to expand the network using BT due to their charging policy at the time, so the Council looked for alternatives. Three companies responded, Telewest, Northern Electric and, belatedly, BT.

'At that time, it seemed inconceivable to many people that a small, semi-rural local authority like Derwentside could possibly be in the forefront of the new information technology,' said Alan, 'it was assumed that the large urban authorities would be the first in the field'. In the event, a joint financing scheme was agreed. DDC put in £650,000, enabling successful bidder Telewest to link Derwentside with their base at Team Valley in Gateshead. Without the Council's cash input, the scheme would not have gone ahead. And so little Derwentside Council became the first local authority in the country to have its own municipal IT network. As well as local communities, every industrial estate was linked up – a big asset for existing firms and a huge incentive to new companies to locate in the district. The Stanley Infonet was an instant success, and within two years DDC had successfully bid for a million pound grant from the Rural Development Commission to expand the Stanley Infonet into the Derwentside Infonet. This million "levered in" £3.5m of additional funding from UK government and European bodies. The crucial meeting with the RDC took place in London. This was a competitive bidding process, and the regional winner was to be either Derwentside or Tynedale. It was just before Remembrance Day. On their way to the meeting, Alan bought a tray of poppies and made sure every member of the team was wearing one – bound to impress RDC chairman Lord Shuttleworth. 'When we came out, we met Tynedale going in, and none of them had poppies,' Alan recalled with evident satisfaction. Derwentside won, and the rest, as they keep saying, is history.

The early implementation of new IT systems led directly to DDC gaining its first Beacon Status award. As other councils realized they had to catch up, Wear Valley and Teesdale paid Derwentside to manage their IT systems for them, bringing DDC vital revenue. Gateshead Council likewise asked DDC for their help, and the system grew and grew. In 2008, DurhamNet, a partnership between Derwentside and Durham County Council, employed 40 people and serviced around 1,600 clients. As well as headquarters offices in Durham, there was a brand new £5m state-of-the-art data processing centre at Tanfield, opened in 2008. In 2007 DurhamNet made a profit of threequarters of a million pounds, shared between the two councils, from a turnover of £12m. The "business benefit" to DDC was around £3.5m a year.

**Project Genesis**

After 1980, Derwentside was faced with two major problems: the huge area of industrial dereliction close to Consett town centre, and how to replace the jobs lost due to the steelworks closure. And so in 1994, the Council sought to tackle these twin evils with Project Genesis, created by the Council and private developers Dysart Developments Ltd. Dysart took on the regeneration and development of the former Consett Steelworks site, 750 acres close to the centre of Consett, following its clearance and decontamination after the Steelworks closure in 1980. Project Genesis is unique in that development profit is shared between the developer and the Genesis Trustees who administer a fund for the benefit of the area and its people. One beneficial scheme has been the CCTV system, which provides greater security for Consett and Stanley as well as rural areas. Dysart was run by husband-and-wife team Jack and Caroline Fawcett, well known for their development work across the country and particularly the North East. They retired in 2004 and sold Dysart to Morris Muter, who put new impetus into Project Genesis, building on the solid foundations established by the Fawcetts. Food manufacturer International Cuisine, which employs over 500 people, had set up in Hownsgill Industrial Estate; Derwentside College had a new building; the Victoria Centre, bus station, Wetherspoons and McDonalds had brought more shopping and leisure choice to the town; Derwentside Industrial Development Agency and the Innovation Centre had new purpose-built offices in Ponds Court; and new homes had been built on Project Genesis land, including the ongoing Fell View development by Barratts and The Chequers, a development by Dysart Residential Ltd. Soprano's Italian restaurant was the most recently completed project. The new Consett Bus Station was opened in January 1995 by Cllr Eric Turner, Council chairman, and local resident Ray Sheldon who was at the opening of the old bus station in 1930, replaced by the much-disliked "Bull Ring" around 1970.

*Old Bus Station, Consett (AP)*

*The "Bull Ring" – Consett Bus Station 1972 (AP)*

*Consett bus station 2000*

Victoria Centre clock

Dysart boss Morris Muter at The Chequers

Cllr Bill Stockdale contemplates a helicopter ride (WS)

Jack Fawcett (Dysart) talks to Tony Blair

Tony Blair with developer Jack Fawcett (centre), opening of Victoria Centre, Consett on 21st July 1995

Under the Town Clock (l-r): Neil Johnson, Harry Guildford, Alex Watson, Caroline Fawcett (Dysart), Alan Atkinson.

Blackfyne School flag

Victoria Centre

Derwentside College (CFW)

Hot metal carrier, Park Road Consett (CFW)

The old Technical College, Consett (AP)

New houses, Hallgarth, Consett (CFW)

No.1 Industrial Estate (CFW)

Greencroft Industrial Estate with wind turbine (YG)

Phileas Fogg tv advert (UB)

Plans for the future, Trevor Watson 1980

*Stanley town centre*

For the future, a 100,000 sq ft retail park on Berry Edge was planned, and more shops on Front Street in Consett town centre. There were also plans for a sports and leisure complex, and more housing of mixed tenure. Morris Muter, Managing Director of Dysart Developments and the driving force behind Project Genesis, said: 'Consett has been completely transformed and the infrastructure of the town is now very strong. Project Genesis has brought in jobs, retail choice and residential opportunities. The partnership between Derwentside District Council and Dysart Developments has been a strong one, and has given rise to industry, commerce and leisure, which seemed simply unrealistic when the steelworks closed down. Some £50m has been invested in the town to date, and our current plans allow for the same amount to be spent over the next five years, as we further develop retail, leisure and housing projects, as well as providing more industry and office space'.

The Northern Echo of 12th March 2005 reported: 'a milestone in the development of the former Consett Steelworks site. The plans will see the demolition of the last remaining steelworks building on the site - the former generator now known as Generation House. The new George Wimpey buildings form part of a wider patchwork of development which has breathed new life into the steelworks site'. Council leader Alex Watson told the Echo: 'We had earmarked land for just over 500 houses on the site and really we have now reached that target, with the latest development bringing the total up to 457 homes. During that incubation period, we looked for partners to get things moving with the private sector. We found that to access grants, we would have to set up a charitable trust'. The Council teamed up with Dysart, the company behind the Newcastle Business Park - which had attracted £150m-worth of investment and 4,500 jobs. It led to the launch in 1993 of Project Genesis, with a design brief for an area of around 700 acres. Coun Watson said: "What we were looking for was a plan which was sustainable, and which took the environment into account. After the pollution of the steel works, with its red clouds of dust, we wanted something different, and it has become the first truly green development - and the biggest in Europe at that.

'The steelworks left its legacy of contaminants and the Genesis Project had been given £9.6m to reclaim the site. Removing the slagheaps was not possible, so housing has been kept to the periphery of the site - enjoying views over the Derwent Valley. Among the housing developments which have already been built have been 50 homes at Phoenix Court, Blackhill, 77 homes by Miller Homes at Hall Cottages, and 20 homes by Northern Housing Association in Victoria Street, Berry Edge, Consett.

In August 2003, Barratt started building 125 executive homes in Berry Edge, Consett. The company, working with civil engineering contractor and consultants Hellens Contracts and White Young Green, spent £1.8m decontaminating the site. Project Genesis has now secured permission for 79 high-quality properties on land south-west of Knitsley Gardens, Templetown. This development had come under fire from residents, whose recreation area was to be replaced by one half the size. The Wimpey development, while on the former site, is not part of Genesis. Apart from the housing, there has been a range of other developments, including the new Derwentside College, Steel House, McDonald's Restaurant and International Cuisine - bringing 500 jobs. Several factories have also sprung up on the periphery. An Innovation Centre, built for the Derwentside Industrial Development Agency, at Pond's Court. There are also plans on the drawing board for a £14m wet and dry sports centre and a hotel complex to complement the newly built Italian restaurant. Project Genesis Managing Director Morris Muter said: 'While progress may seem to have been slow, much has been achieved to date. And we now have renewed interest from various quarters which would allow new initiatives which we are working on to come to fruition'.

*Villa Real roundabout (CFW)*

Reflecting on the development, former Deputy Leader Kevin Earley said: 'Project Genesis was bold and innovative, but it involved officers and members in a lot of work'. Former Leader Joe Rhind said: 'Genesis has not fulfilled its original intentions. One reason is that it did not become the green energy-producing scheme we had in mind. For some inexplicable reason, the civil servants in London decreed that Consett was "not windy enough" to justify a wind farm'.

*Clock presentation: Chief Executive Neil Johnson gets his retirement present from Cllr Alex Watson*

The Lanchester Joint Hospital Board built an isolation hospital at Tanfield in 1901/02 for £7,000. It closed in 1946 but the building still stands. The Tanfield National School opened in 1844 was later known as the Board School. It was demolished in the 1960s.

*One memorable occasion during Cllr David Llewellyn's term of office as Council Chairman came when the Commonwealth Games torch passed through the District.*

## Shotley Bridge Hospital

While there has been a reduction in services at Shotley Bridge Hospital, Cllr Malone was certain the situation would have been worse but for the Council. "Derwentside Council has been effective in maintaining some services at Shotley Bridge Hospital when there was a danger of it being closed down altogether. Some services were lost, but Shotley Bridge has been maintained as a community hospital with maternity, minor surgery and cancer treatment services," said Cllr Malone, "Now that the NHS Trust has brought land from the original owners English Estates, the hospital's future is much more secure". When the hospital was again under threat of closure in 2007, the Council and Derwentside Partnership funded a recovery package and major investigation into the role and future of the facility. The report was produced in 2008 and in January 2009, weeks before DDC was due to come to an end, Durham PCT advised the Council that the Hospital would be retained as a community hospital, accepting the recommendations made by the Council in the report, thus protecting and sustaining the hospital for the future. In 1997 DDC took up a call from fellow ward Cllr Dot Atherton for an investigation into the apparent "cluster" of throat cancers among former Consett Steelworks employees. The research, costing £50,000, was funded by the Council, County Durham Health Authority and British Steel. Fitkids, started by the Council in October 1995, provided activities for boys and girls aged five to seven at Belle Vue Leisure Centre, Consett.

When the hospital was again under threat of closure in 2007, the Council and Derwentside Partnership funded

*Shotley Bridge Hospital (YG)*

a recovery package and a major investigation into its role and future. The report "Protecting and Sustaining the Hospital for the Future" was produced in 2008. In January 2009, weeks before the Council was due to come to an end, the Durham PCT advised the Council that the Hospital would be retained as a community hospital, accepting the recommendations made in the report.

## Wind Turbines

Building wind turbines in Derwentside has achieved the targets for the whole of County Durham. Much of the district lies in windy upland areas, and it is no surprise that Derwentside has been at the forefront of harnessing this natural asset. In the main, people have accepted this addition to the landscape, which some see as striking and others as intrusive. There were seven wind farms in the district in 2008, six in operation and one soon to start, not including domestic wind turbines or small-scale micro wind turbines. The operational wind farms at Tow Law, High Hedley, Holmside, Greencroft and Langley, plus another to be built at Tow Law, had a total capacity of 24MW from 29 turbines.

*Wind turbines, Burnhope (CFW)*

*Wind turbine, Craghead (CFW)*

*Hownsgill Viaduct (CFW)*

*Lanchester (CFW)*

*Wharnley Burn (YG)*

*Causey Arch (YG)*

## Chapter Five
# Missed Opportunities

*The "two-tier" system; Unitary bid rejected; Referendums; Stanley Town Council; the axe must fall; Last Chairman; Last Councillor, Last Building*

### The "two-tier" system

Long before Derwentside Council was set up in 1974, there had been much debate about how local government should be organized, or rather, re-organised. Many people thought the traditional "two-tier" system of county and district councils, with services split between the two, was inefficient, outdated and confusing to the public. The idea was to have single "unitary" councils responsible for all local services, as was already the case with the large urban authorities. The only question was, how large or how small should these new unitary councils be? The debate came to a head in the early 1990s when Sir John Banham was given the job of looking into each area and coming up with recommendations. He started with County Durham and Cleveland. Durham County Council promoted the idea of a single, county unitary council, which ultimately did come about in 2009. In 1992 the eight Durham district councils banded together with the aim of each one becoming a unitary authority in its own right. This would have meant the end of Durham County Council, although the eight district councils would no doubt have run some services like education, police and the fire & rescue service on a joint basis. In the event, only Darlington gained unitary status and broke away from Durham to join the other new unitary councils in the Tees Valley.

'The Derwentside community we believe to be close knit, cohesive and with a point of view decidedly different to that of its neighbours,' said the Council's submission to the Local Government Commission, 'our history dates back to Roman times, but the effects of the industrial revolution have given our towns and villages strong economic and social ties. The rise and fall of coal-mining and iron and steel production has dominated the local economy and social life of Derwentside. Workers formed distinct communities around the collieries and steelworks. Strong cultural links were established between the workers in these industries. The social infrastructure, welfare facilities and housing owed their very existence to the Iron Company and the mine owners. Later these were largely to pass to the District Council, reinforcing the community's reliance on the local authority. Societies, clubs and sports league proliferated within the district.

'In 1951 there were still 28 collieries operating in Derwentside, providing employment for 17,000 people (42% of jobs in the district). By 1980 the last deep mine had closed and manufacturing industry was contracting. By the end of 1982, more than 8,000 manufacturing jobs had been lost. The once mighty Consett steelworks, which in its heyday had employed more than 6,500 people, ceased production on Friday 12th September 1980 – a devastating blow to the whole of Derwentside's community to whom coal mining and steel making had become a way of life. The residents of Derwentside looked to the District Council to take a lead – firstly in fighting to stave off closure, and then to drive forward the policies for regeneration'.

### Unitary bid rejected

The report described how the Council had set up an Industrial Development Programme in 1979, and the Derwentside Task Force and the Derwentside Development Agency three years later. Project Genesis, said the report, was the largest development in the country at that time, as well as being innovative and self-sustaining. The district council pointed out that the ratio of electors to councillors was 5,700:1 for a county councillor and 1,250:1 for a district councillor. Turnout in district elections was 48%, compared with 39% in county elections.

*"Closer to the People" Derwentside Council makes the case for unitary status for the District (MW)*

*"The Big NO" Referendum result 19th June 2007. County Durham's district councils make their voices heard, but was anyone in government listening? (MW)*

In 1989, only five of the eleven county divisions in Derwentside were contested. The report had all-party support and was signed by Council Leader Alex Watson, Leader of the majority Labour Group, Cllr Bill Stockdale, Independent Group Leader, and Cllr Denise Bullivant on the behalf of the Conservative councillors. The joint submission by the eight districts was titled "Closer to the People". In the event, it was rejected in favour of the two-tier system, ie the status quo, for Derwentside and six of the other districts, with Darlington alone gaining unitary status.

### Referendums

The possibility of a change from the "two-tier" system of district and county councils to a "single tier" system of all-purpose, unitary councils was again raised in 2003/04. After overseeing the introduction of the Scottish Parliament and the Welsh Assembly, following successful referendums there, the Labour government chose the North East as its test bed for democratically-elected Regional Assemblies in England. For the people of Durham and Northumberland, there was to be a second question in the Referendum of November 2004. As well as saying "yes" or "no" to a democratic regional assembly, residents of the two county areas were asked a second question on new local unitary councils. If there was an overall "yes" vote for a regional assembly, both county councils and all the district councils would be replaced by unitary authorities. Voters were asked what size these new unitary councils should be – single counties, or smaller? Along with all the other district councils, DDC supported the smaller option of three unitary councils within County Durham.

In a letter to all Derwentside residents in 2004, Executive Director Mike Clark said: 'Derwentside District Council supports the government in its desire to create a Regional Assembly for the North East. As a Council we believe that this would give greater power to the region. There is general agreement that the current two-tier structure should be replaced by all-purpose Councils, which will provide the best solution for the people of the County. However, Derwentside District Council agrees with research carried out by Birmingham University, that the County would be too big and the Districts too small to create the kind of local government which is small enough to be responsive to local needs whilst having the capacity and resources to deliver quality services. Derwentside District Council believes that a single Unitary Council based on the County boundary, with a population twice the size of Newcastle City Council, would be too large and remote to respond to local needs. Derwentside is happy therefore to recommend that the government dispense with both the District and County Councils, which is in line with the findings of the University of Birmingham, in favour of creating three unitary Councils covering the whole of the County'.

All three party Leaders on Derwentside Council were in favour of the "three district" solution for County Durham: Alex Watson (Labour), Watts Stelling (Independent) and Keith English (LibDem). In the event, the North East voted overwhelmingly – almost 78% - against an elected regional assembly, so the question of unitary councils did not arise. The "status quo" was to remain, including the "two tier" system and – ironically – the indirectly-elected Regional Assembly set up in 1999, of

*DDC hosts a meeting of district councils to agree a co-ordinated response to government on the thorny issue of unitary authorities, Council Leader Alex Watson in the chair. (MW)*

which Cllr Watson was now Chair. He retained that position until the English Assemblies were abolished in 2009. Referendum result (47.7% turnout): 22% yes 78% no. On the second question, options for new unitary councils in County Durham (Derwentside voters): for a single county authority, 13,734 (43.8%); for three district councils, 17,648 (56.2%). Derwentside recorded the second fastest result, beaten by Redcar by just four seconds! Derwentside was fastest with the "local" result, beating Wansbeck by 1min 11 sec, thanks to DDC electoral officer Jim Thompson and his team.

### Stanley Town Council

There was another, more local referendum in 2005. In response to a petition to form a Town Council for Stanley, Derwentside Council instituted a local referendum in June 2005. In a 34% turnout, around 40% voted in favour and 60% against. North Durham MP Kevan Jones was very much in favour of a Stanley Town Council, and in the event the Office of the Deputy Prime Minister granted permission. This followed a campaign by local people and a petition of over 2,000 names. Although the petition represented only 10% of the population that would be covered by the Town Council, that was all that was required by law. The campaigners promised that the Town Council would increase the pace of the regeneration of the town, and it was established in 2008. The introduction of a unitary system of local government in 2009, with one local Council covering the whole of County Durham, raised the prospect of Town and Parish Councils – they have exactly the same status – taking more responsibility for administering local services. Right across the county, in those areas without these grass-roots bodies, there were moves to set up new Town and Parish Councils.

### The axe must fall

After this latest review of local government was announced in July 2007, battle was again joined. As in 1992 and 2004, the district councils banded together to put their case. As in 2004, all parties on Derwentside Council were in favour of having three councils in County Durham instead of one, as again proposed by Durham County Council. They organized another referendum, asking the people of the county which solution they preferred. The answer came back loud and clear: 76% of those who voted were against a single council for County Durham. DDC Deputy Leader Cllr Mike Malone wrote to Works & Pensions Minister Peter Hain, as well as all 362 Labour MPs (most of whom failed to reply), who supported the referendum decision. 'This is a matter for local people to decide. If a proposal is rejected by the local people in a referendum, then their views should be respected,' he said. Cllr Malone said: 'MPs and Durham County Councillors should take note of Peter Hain's comments as they support the foundations of local democracy'. Nevertheless, the government decided in its wisdom to ignore the results of the referendum and impose single county unitary councils for Durham and Northumberland. The legislation was passed on 2nd October 2007, paving the way for the new Durham County unitary authority to be elected in 2008 and to take over the existing County Council and the seven District Councils in 2009. Derwentside District Council would cease to exist on 31st March 2009.

*Stanley from West (CFW)*

## Last Chairman

The last ever Chairman of Derwentside District Council 2008/09 was Cllr Eric Turner. "It's something to remember – I've been very conscious of the fact that I'm the last ever chairman – and many times I've carried out my duties with a heavy heart, knowing that this would be the last time. I've found it a bit emotional," said Eric, a district councillor for twenty years, "people will have to realize that from April 2009 they will have only two councillors to represent them, instead of seven – six on the district council and one on the county council".

## Last Councillor

Marion Wotherspoon from Castleside was the last Councillor to be elected to Derwentside Council. Marion won a by-election on 17th July 2008 to fill the vacancy left by the death of Independent Cllr Gordon Glass, a well-regarded local figure. Marion is a Parish Councillor and was persuaded to stand by other members of the Parish Council. Castleside is a single member ward and Marion stood to ensure that Castleside had representation on the Council for its remaining months. Although she was aware that she would be a District Councillor for a short period of time, she has nevertheless found herself with plenty to do. Originally from Consett, Marion moved to Castleside 25 years ago, she has two sons who were both brought up in Castleside and attended the local school. She worked at various post offices in the northeast before deciding on a career change and becoming in her own words 'a very mature student' at Teesside University, where she studied and gained a degree in occupational therapy. For the past ten years she has worked in mental health services, as an occupational therapist and in 2009 was on secondment doing developmental work in primary care mental health services in Gateshead. Marion first became involved in community activities as a Friend of Castleside School when her sons were pupils there. She wanted to become more involved with the community and decided to stand for the Parish Council, and was elected as a Parish Councillor in 2007 She subsequently became involved in Castleside & Muggleswick Community Partnership, where she is now the treasurer. She describes herself as 'completely independent'.

One dissatisfied customer was a man who had been refused a home improvement grant. He marched into Chief Executive Joe Quinn's office and demanded to know why. When Joe learned that the man's house already had all the standard amenities, he reiterated that he simply was not eligible for a grant. "Who do you think you are, God?" the man demanded. "As far as you and your grant application are concerned, I might as well be," replied Joe and bade the man good morning.

*Last Chairman, Cllr Eric Turner (MW)*

*Well regarded: Cllr Gordon Glass*

*Cllr Marion Wotherspoon – last to be elected*

## Last Building

One of Derwentside District Council's most ambitious development projects, the £6.8million Tanfield Lea Business Centre near Stanley in County Durham was due for completion in March 2009 and was to be the last building to be completed by the Council before it went out of existence on 31st March. Described as "revolutionary" and "iconic", the three-storey building provides 40,000 sq ft of modern office and workshop accommodation. The Business Centre was set up with a new approach to lettings to encourage young entrepreneurs to pursue self-employment.

*Villa Real Business Centre*

Facilities in the Business Centre include a communal atrium with kitchen facilities; 45 office units ranging in size from 100+ to 1,000+ sq ft; fully-equipped conference and meeting rooms for hire; fully-manned reception with a wide range of office services; Telephony and Broadband connectivity; car parking; 24-hour access to individual office units. Derwentside District Council's Principal Development Officer, Ross Bullerwell, said:'This major development will have a significant impact on the economy of Derwentside, and will ensure that public sector developments continue to lead the way in encouraging economic growth and sustainability in semi-rural locations'. Neil Jukes, Area Leader for builders ROK said:'This is a flagship scheme for us'. DDC Economic portfolio holder, Cllr David Llewellyn, said:

'Tanfield Lea Business Centre will be a huge boost to the economy of Derwentside'. Ed Rowley, Acting Dircetor of Regeneration at One NorthEast said the centre had the potential to create over 30 new businesses, with around 200 jobs.

Tanfield Lea Business Centre is aiming to achieve a high BREEAM (Building Research Establishment Environmental Assessment Method) rating. The Business Centre, located close to the A6706 road to Gateshead and Newcastle, was built thanks to funding from the District Council (£2m), One North East (£3m), County Durham Economic Partnership (CDEP) and the European Regional Development Fund (ERDF) with £1.8m.

*Under construction: Tanfield Lea Business Centre (CFW)*

Referring to the enforced amalgamation of county & district councils: *"Trying to get Districts and Counties together is like mating Pandas, they are only interested in chewing their own bit of bamboo!"* (anonymous email).

*Local historian JW Armond wrote: "if one pictures the bustling Front Street outside the Empire Theatre on a Saturday night, people issuing forth from the Freemasons Arms Public House and Bridgewater's Fish and Chip Shop converging on the Empire until the street was packed with people, the traffic held up and Police being called in to deal with the crowds. Why – because they all wanted to see 'Way Down East'(\*) showing at the Empire – the premier cinema in the region." The Empire had a strong claim to be the most prestigious class 'A' cinema in North West Durham. (\*) classic 1920 silent film by DW Griffith.*

When Gilbert Green first came to work for Consett UDC, Thomas Watson Bell was Clerk, in effect the Chief Executive. *"In his black homberg hat, black coat and pinstripe suit, he looked every inch like the traditional bank manager – just like Mr Swindley in Coronation Street or Capt Mainwaring in Dad's Army,"* recalled Gilbert, *"he was plain spoken, but always thought he was right. He was followed by Joe Quinn who had a much younger outlook. He would cultivate the members. Generally speaking, he always knew how to achieve his desired result".*

Consett was the first town in the world to have a Salvation Army Corps Band. The brass band was formed in December 1879 and went out on the streets playing at Christmas. The original band consisted of just four players. The Army's motto: "conquer the world with blood and fire".

Consett official guide 1960s: *"to assert that the Consett Iron Company Ltd IS Consett is not an overstatement."*

The famous court case, Miller v Jackson, arose from cricket played by Lintz Cricket Club in the village. Cricket had been played there since 1905, but in 1972 new houses were built next to the ground, one owned by Mr & Mrs Miller who sued the cricket club for damages caused by balls hit into their property, and they sought an injunction to stop cricket being played there. The Millers were awarded £150 damages, later raised to £400, but the injunction was refused on appeal. Appeal Court judge Lord Denning said: "after these 70 years a judge of the High Court has ordered that they must not play there any more. He has issued an injunction to stop them. He has done it at the instance of a newcomer who is no lover of cricket. The whole village will be much the poorer. And all this because of a newcomer who has just bought a house there next to the cricket ground. I am of opinion that the public interest should prevail over the private interest. The cricket club should not be driven out".

*Stanley UDC Chief Surveyor Harry Snowball had an artificial leg. As he could be heard clumping down the corridor, staff were alerted to his approach and would always be "hard at work" whenever he came into the office.*

South Moor Park was created in 1920 as a memorial to the employees of the South Moor Colliery Co. who died in WWI. Alongside the gates are the names of local people who had been killed in the war. Two names had to be deleted when it was discovered that the "victims" had not actually died.

*The most famous "other Stanley" is the capital of the Falkland Islands. There are Stanley towns in Australia, Canada, Hong Kong, the Republic of Congo, Egypt and several in the USA. There are Stanley villages in Yorkshire and Scotland, plus Stanley near Crook. Mount Stanley is a mountain in the Ruwenzori Range in Uganda, and there is an Owen Stanley mountain range in Papua New Guinea.*

A parliamentary report of 1777 recorded local workhouses for up to 30 inmates in operation at Tanfield, and for up to 20 at Kyo. In his 1797 survey of the poor in England, *"The State of the Poor: A History of the Labouring Classes in England",* Sir Frederic Morton Eden reported: *"Tanfield contains about 2,000 inhabitants, mostly coal miners. Wages of labourers in husbandry are from 1s 4d to 1s 6d a day, and of coal miners, 2s to 3s. Farms are small. Potatoes are much grown, which now form the chief diet of labourers' families. The cheapness of fuel seems the cause why this very useful vegetable is more used in the North than in the South of England. Here, as in other coal countries, the surface of the earth is neglected for the inside. It may be doubted, however, if the mines about Tanfield have of late been profitable. The rents of collieries have decreased and many have been shut up. Two paper factories employ about 10 men each. Number of ale-houses, 16. 130 houses pay tax, 270 exempt. There are about 20 Poor in the Workhouse. Other distressed families, which are very numerous, are relieved at home. Table of diet: Breakfast, every day: hasty pudding, with milk or beer; Dinner, Sunday, Wednesday: butcher's meat with pease pudding or other vegetables; Monday, Thursday: pease soup and bread; Tuesday, Saturday: boiled barley and milk; Friday: suet pudding and dumplins [sic]. Supper, Sunday, Wednesday, Saturday: broth and bread; Monday, Thursday: milk, boiled with oatmeal; Tuesday, Friday: milk and bread."*

## Chapter Six
# Consolidating the Legacy 2002-2009

*Partnership, progress & achievements; New management team; SPICE for kids; LEAF youngsters to it; Sounds like ABBA; Older people get SWIFT; Mike Clark, John Pearson; Derwentside Business Centre; Bank deposits frozen, Iceland Blog, Consett Sports Village*

### Partnership, progress & achievements

'Partnership is the only way forward,' said Council Leader Alex Watson in his 2002 review, 'although the Council has had to accept substantial budget cuts, it has used substantial amounts of its own core budget, along with government money and other funding it has successfully attracted to the area, to carry out a number of major improvements in Derwentside. As well as working with other agencies the Council is clear that consultation with the public is essential. The Council was one of the first

compared with 2.3% in 1999/00, target for 2004/05 was 18.0%; new community facilities at Craghead, Stanley and Consett; CCTV established for Consett and Stanley – to be rolled out throughout the district; Stanley Civic Hall becomes the Lamplight Arts Centre; Empire Theatre, Consett, to reopen after refurbishment; over 100 community groups given Top Sport and Top Play bags, full of sports equipment; Derwentside Football Development Scheme initiated and developed; Golf

*Alex Watson and Mike Malone (AW)*

authorities in the area to establish a Citizen's Panel. If the regeneration, revitalization and renewal of our District is to be completed, all our energy needs to be directed into working together in partnership'.

Watson listed some of the Councils' achievements: reduction in unemployment to 5.1% from a high of 28% in 1982, ie from 9,000 to less than 1,500; crime levels in the district falling by 15% since 1999; over £32m of extra funding secured for the District since 1992; saving 1,050 tonnes of carbon emitted to the atmosphere in 2001; in six years, 18% improvement in the average efficiency rating of private house, 22% for Council houses; 11,000 concessionary bus passes issued, a 48% increase over the previous year; 9.0% of waste recycled in 2001/02,

Merit Award Scheme introduced; Community Tennis Partnership developed; development of Derwentside Doorstep Walks; proposed redevelopment of View Lane Park, Stanley; replacement Fire Scheme – grants to replace existing coal or solid fuel fires with more fuel-efficient heating systems for families on benefits.

The Council's Corporate Plan 2006-2010, updated each year, continued to produce results. In 1982 unemployment in Derwentside had peaked at 28%. 8,900 people were on the dole, well over twice the national average. 25 years later, the District's unemployment rate was down to the national average of 2.1%, almost zero in practical terms, with fewer than 1,200 people unemployed, thanks to new job creation.

The partnership between the Council, DIDA and other organisations had secured over 200 businesses and 7,000 new jobs for the District. Well over half of these new jobs were in businesses that were new start-ups, a large number involved in high technology products and processes and serving international markets. Many of these had grown to employ several hundred people. Derwentside had become increasingly focused on developing business start-ups, and its success in this field gained the District Council national recognition in 2005 when DDC became one of only four councils in the country to be awarded Beacon Status for supporting new businesses. In 2003 Owen McFarlane of CAV Aerospace became chairman of DIDA – Derwentside Industrial Development Agency – and oversaw its change to DEA – Derwentside Enterprise Agency – in September 2008. This was the merger of three organizations, DIDA, the Derwentside Business Network and the Derwentside Engineering Forum. 'DIDA always was a broad church,' said McFarlane, 'Its focus has been on creating jobs, particularly high value, high technology jobs. DEA now includes the council, business, banks, lawyers and education. With changes in local government, it is essential that the loyalty and goodwill built up over the years is not fragmented'.

Strategic Pernership) and a partnership in every ward; Housing developments including the District's first build-your-own estate at The Grove; Estate Action in four areas; One-stop shop and call centre developed; Citizens' Panel created; Derwentside College relocated to a custom-built facility on the Genesis site;. In 2007 it was announced that co-developers Barratt Homes and Project Genesis were to build 277 houses and 64 apartments on the Genesis site. The project was to take six years at a cost of around £6m. Derwentside's success has attracted the attention of other local councils. In July 1999, officers and members from Carlisle City Council visited Derwentside to learn how DDC set up its Customer Team and the problems it had to overcome. Mike Clark and Jerry Miller gave presentations, and two leading councillors, Deputy Leader Mike Malone and Lyn Boyd also gave their perspective.

*Chief Executive Mike Clark (CFW)*

### New Management Team

The Council's Management Team was still changing and adapting. In 2002 Mike Clark was appointed "General Manager", Alan Hodgson and Keith Robinson moved on, and five new directors were put in place: Gordon Elliott (Corporate Admin & Policy), Steve Melvin (Housing & Capital Works), John Pearson (Development & Asset Management), Peter Reynolds (Environmental Services), Alan Smith (Finance). Steve Melvin originated from Chester le Street. Previously ten years with Sunderland City Council, he had worked for DDC for 12 years;. Gordon Elliott, born and brought up in Winlaton Mill, studied town & regional planning at Dundee and Glasgow Universities. After ten years with Newcastle City Council he became Gateshead Council's Head of Policy before joining DDC as Head of Corporate Strategy in May 2002. Elliott was responsible for Best Value, the new Corporate Plan and the establishment of the Local Strategic Partnership. Peter Reynolds was: born and grew up in Stanley. He joined DDC straight from school in 1974 as a Trainee Technician in the Planning Department, rising through the ranks to become Head of Planning Services in 1995. Alan Smith went to Spennymoor Comprehensive School, and worked for Sedgefield District Council, before joining DDC in 1991 as Project Accountant. John Pearson, born and raised in Derwentside, gained an honours degree in Public Administration at Sheffield; became a Director of Derwentside Industrial Development Agency, and was Chairman of Derwentside Economic Development Forum. Alan Hodgson moved to Durham County Council but still did work for Derwentside as head of DurhamNet. Keith Robinson, who joined DDC from Durham CC in 1974, retired in June 2003, handing over to Alan Smith. In 2003 Clark became Executive Director with Human Resources and the Leisure Department directly under him.

Another success was bringing Council Tax rises under control. 'When I first came on the Council, we were in danger of being capped or even surcharged,' recalled Cllr David Llewellyn, 'the public wanted value for money and an end to huge increases. We have now pegged the Council Tax at zero increase for the last four years. The days of budget meetings lasting until 2am while the members argued about small amounts of money have long gone'. The Council's first Corporate Plan was drawn up in 1999, and reviewed in 2001 to cover the period 2001-2005. 'For the first time, the Council adopted a Corporate Plan and a constitution,' said Cllr Mike Malone, 'our decision to institute Investors in People for officers and members alike in 2003 was unique at the time. It led to Derwentside gaining four Beacon Council awards. Procurement and efficiency targets were set and met. To save on staff costs, we agreed work sharing with Chester le Street on procurement and Sedgefield on finance. Legal services were brought "in house"'.

There had been improvements throughout the District: Consett bus station, opened in 1974, was demolished in 2005 and a new one built; a 25-metre pool and leisure pool were added to the Louisa Sports Centre, replacing the Burns Leisure Pool (Stanley Baths) which was demolished in 1997; wheelie bins introduced, with the "twin bin" system; industrial estates developed; Stanley Town centre pedestrianised; the Derwentside LSP (Local

## SPICE for kids

SPICE – Special Project to Implement Children's Elections - was launched in 2001 with the aim of involving young people in democracy and community issues. The first Young People's Forum election count took place in Consett Civic Hall on Monday 25th November 2002. 66 candidates contested 23 seats on the Children's Panel (5-11 year olds, 15 seats) and the Youth Panel (12-19yrs, 8 seats) with a highly commendable 40.5% turnout. SPICE Project Officer Sharon Robinson: 'all of the young people and their teachers have worked very hard to make the elections a success'. Cllr Lyn Boyd, Executive Member for Community & Culture: 'it is by involving young people in the decision-making process in this way that we hope to demonstrate that the Council is interested in their views and that they can influence the decisions that are made'. But SPICE was much more than just holding elections. SPICE worked with children and young people in Derwentside to: involve them in making important decisions; make sure that they are involved in their community; help them to have their right to be involved in any decision that affects their lives and be taken seriously; support them to understand how the Council works; encourage them to get involved in positive activities.

Many of SPICE's achievements have been through the Young People's Forum, a group of youngsters aged between eight and 19 elected by other young people. Through the hard work of the Forum members, SPICE got a mobile youth bus, known as "Ellie", and a rewards scheme running in schools known as SPICETACULAR, for school pupils achieving improvements in healthy eating, school attendance, homework and so on. Any child or young person in the district can get involved in SPICE in some way. In its first seven years Spice involved more than 9,000 young people and 40 schools in its pioneering programme which won the Government's prestigious Beacon Award for its work with "positive youth engagement". In 2004 alone, over 1,000 young people in the district benefited from the 17 grants awarded by the Young People's Forum through the Spice project. The Council's SPICE programme achieved a number of awards and accolades for work with children and young people including Public Management Leadership Award (2004); Beacon Award for Positive Youth Engagement (2006); Durham Constabulary Streetsafe Award for the Youth Bus (2006); Investing in Children (2007); Overall winner, Engaging with Young People, North East ShiNE Awards (2008).

A glittering awards ceremony was held at the Derwent Manor Hotel near Consett in 2008 to honour some of the district's young people for their outstanding citizenship, both at school and in their local communities. Emma Andrews was there to meet "the pride of Derwentside". This was her report: "At 6.30am on the dot, every single morning, teenager Jack Hocking walks through the gates of Consett Community Sports College ready to start his working day. Fifteen-year-old Jack is a valued member of the caretaking team at the school where he juggles his duties with his studies in English, Maths and Science. It is a remarkable turnaround for the teenager who just a few months ago was playing truant for weeks at a time. Unsettled by a move away from his beloved grandfather, Jack was stuck in a vicious circle of missed lessons and low self esteem. 'I couldn't see the point of going to school,' said Jack, 'and I had missed so much I thought I would never catch up. I was out of control and I couldn't see a way forward. I didn't think I was good at anything'.

"It would have been easy for his teachers to give up on him but that's not the way things are done at Consett Community Sports College says teacher Trevor Davis who was determined to find a way to bring Jack back to school. 'I could see that Jack had so much potential,' said Trevor, 'and I didn't want him to waste it. I have always had faith in him. We finally hit up on the idea of Jack coming in to work with the caretakers John, Chris and Andy – and we've never looked back. I have never seen a boy of his age change so much in such a short space of time. Jack is a happy, personable, polite and hard-working young man whose confidence has soared. And he always has a smile on his face. He is a true inspiration'. Jack's turnaround earned him the special Making a Difference In School award. Jack was one of 71 young people to be honoured for their outstanding citizenship. Award winners aged from seven to 18 were presented with certificates celebrating their achievements.

"Parents Peter and Barbara and caretaker Chris Rusling led the cheers and whoops as Jack walked up on stage to accept his award. 'We are so proud of him for who he is and what he has become," said Chris. "Jack has transformed from a boy who hated school to a star pupil with a 100 per cent attendance rate. His commitment is outstanding'. Other winners included Sam Richardson, a pupil at Grove Primary School in Consett, whose dedication and tireless energy in a physically demanding daily exercise class earned him an outstanding Commitment to a Healthy Lifestyle award.

*Jack Hockling (centre) with his "Making a Difference" SPICE Award, with Angela Harrington and Dave Fordy, DDC Head of Achievement.*

*Big Brother winner Anthony Hutton (DK)*

*Host Richard Salkeld (ITV Tyne Tees) interviewing seven-year old Morgan Coult, the Improving the Environment (Junior) Award winner. In the background are Kath Ivens, District Programme Co-ordinator, Groundwork, and Cllr Eric Turner, Chairman of Derwentside District Council, who presented the award.*

*SPICE winners with Council Chairman Cllr Eric Turner*

Sam, eight, has dyspraxia – a condition that affects his balance and co-ordination. But since he has been attending the school's movement group four mornings a week he has come on in leaps and bounds. His proud parents Lisa and Lee, brother Ben, 10, and head teacher Liz Hulme were at the ceremony to see him pick up his award.

"A determination to overcome the odds also characterised award winner Craig Beard, 16, an apprentice mechanic at Skill Training, Tanfield, Stanley, who has Cerebral Palsy. 'This affects Craig physically but because he is so determined and strong willed he has not allowed this to stop him from achieving his life-long goal of being a mechanic," said Michelle Laws from Skill Training, 'he not only gives it his all while training, he is a fantastic support to other learners. I think Craig is amazing and his commitment to help others always takes priority to his own needs. Craig is a star.' Craig's parents Debbie and Leigh were self-confessed emotional wrecks by the end of the night. 'We are bursting with pride,' said Leigh, 'Craig really is a true inspiration to everyone.' Operations Manager Alan Barkas, who works alongside Craig on the apprenticeship scheme, said: 'he is an absolute joy to work with. He's hard working, talented, committed and always willing to help others in any way he can. If there were more people like Craig the world would be a better place'.

"That was a feeling echoed by Consett police Inspector Andrew McConnell who was blown away by the insight and quick thinking of one very special little boy. Connor Wilkinson, 11, was out playing in woods near his home with friends when he spotted a young boy out on his own. 'I asked him where his Mam was but he couldn't tell me anything,' said Connor, 'I knew that it wasn't right that he out on his own so I ran home to tell my Mam and she rang the police.' The police, it turned out, were already searching the area looking for a five-year-old autistic boy who had been reported missing by his foster-carers. The boy was found, and returned home safe and well – but it could have been a very different story if it wasn't for Connor, said Inspector McConnell. 'Connor acted in a very mature manner in firstly identifying a problem but then having the sense to do something about it,' he said.

"For Chairman of the District Council, Councillor Eric Turner, who was on hand to present some of the prizes, the commitment and enthusiasm of the young award-winners was quite simply breathtaking. 'Each and every young person here tonight has done something extraordinary, whether it's caring for fellow pupils at school or making a real difference to other people's lives'. North East Tonight presenters Philippa Thomson and Jonathan Morrell, Tyne Tees weather man Bob Johnson and talk show host Jeremy Kyle were also keen to recognise the young people's achievements, sending their congratulations to the winners via a satellite link. While VIP guest, England goalkeeper Carly Telford, declared herself overwhelmed at the end of a fantastic night. Carly, 21, from Stanley, is herself an inspiration to young people across the North East. She had a dream – and she went for it – achieving her true potential and believing in herself. Carly represented her country in the Women's World Cup in China and is a first team regular at Leeds United. She debuted for the national team in March 2007 against Scotland where she impressed commentators and scouts alike with a skilled and concentrated performance, helping England to a 1-0 victory.' You have got to be focused and you have got to really, truly believe that you can do it,' said Carly, 'these young people all show an incredible determination to make a real difference at home, in school and in their local communities. I think they are all fantastic'".

Television journalist Richard Salkeld is another SPICE success story. He joined the Derwentside Young People's Forum in 2000 and was a member for five years, representing the Castleside ward, helped produce the SPICE newsletter and host talent shows. Richard helped encourage better working between councillors and young people. In 2004 he became the region's first Youth Advocate. In this high-profile role he helped raise the profile of the region as well as promote learning, training and other opportunities open to young people in the North East. In 2004 Richard went to Leeds University to study Broadcast Journalism, while still an active member of the SPICE project and Young People's Forum. He was part of the team who helped secure Derwentside winning the Beacon Status award for "Positive Youth Engagement" in 2006. Richard also worked on the Ellie Youth Bus for several months as well as hosting the homecoming celebrations of Big Brother winner Anthony Hutton. In 2008 Richard presented a feature for North East Tonight about why he loves his home town, Consett - a place he is proud to call home.

# AB@H

## Sounds like ABBA

Aspirations Begin at Home (AB@H) was set up by DDC to raise educational standards and help young people achieve their goals. To help a youngster raise his/her aspirations, the whole family needed to be involved. So AB@H also helped adults develop IT skills through training sessions and with a 24-hour helpline. The high-speed connectivity of the Broadband Internet, coupled with local educational support brought increased access to learning - a key enabler for the development of a more self-reliant, robust local economy. This in turn improved the quality of life and prosperity local residents. Although the initiative was primarily targeted towards young people, the Council added sessions for adults to help raise aspirations. Training courses included: Internet, e-mail, Microsoft Office and the opportunity to access accredited courses eg European

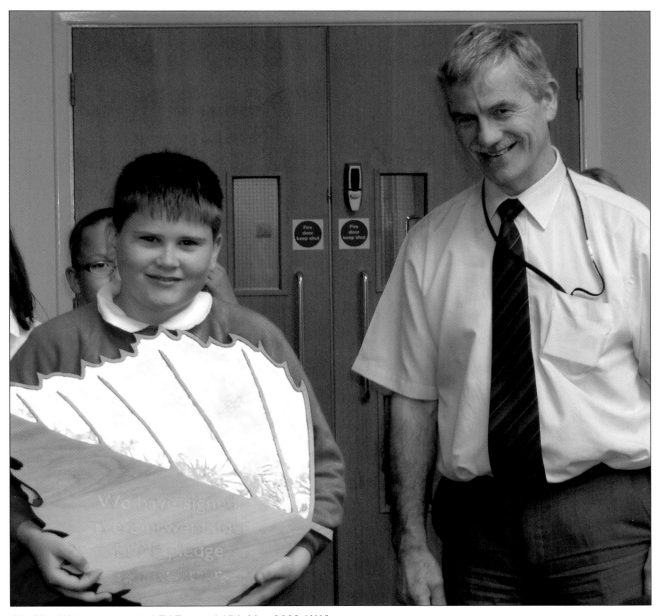

*Cllr Alex Watson presents LEAF award 15th May 2008 (AW)*

Driving Licence. The adult training sessions were flexible and easily adapted to fit different lifestyles. DDC supported AB@H with a range of initiatives from a team of IT Technicians on hand to help the local community and a 24 hour telephone helpline. Five new IT apprentices were taken on by DDC to work on the AB@H project, based at the Council Offices in Front Street, Stanley. The scheme provided laptops for Key Stage 3 pupils at Stanley Comprehensive School. Funding for this project included £440,000 from the Government's Neighbourhood Renewal Fund, £280,000 from the Department of Trade and Industry, £150,000 from the Stanley Green Corridor Neighbourhood Management Fund and European Funding The plans for this ambitious scheme triggered BT to make Broadband available for everyone in the Stanley area.

### LEAF youngsters to it

The Derwentside LEAF (Litter Education & Awareness Focus) campaign 2008 – "Don't LEAVE your Litter" - was a high profile promotional campaign, aimed at young people from pre-school to school-leavers, and at community centres and local businesses. The scheme involved working with local artists and dramatists to make the litter message fun and accessible to local people, especially the young. LEAF's £76,000 funding came from the Neighbourhood Renewal Fund and the Working Neighbourhood Fund. The project was run in partnership with environmental charity, Groundwork West Durham & Darlington. In February and March 2008, ten primary schools, ten community groups, four secondary schools and several nurseries were involved in drama and art projects based on the LEAF message. At a celebration event, some of the project's young participants from Catchgate Community Primary School received a carved wooden plaque and other prizes for their participation in the scheme. LEAF 2, the second phase of the project, saw a further 25 primary schools, ten community groups and four secondary schools undertake the LEAF challenge between May and July 2008.

## Older people get SWIFT

SWIFT, short for "uSer orientated and Workflow Integrated FederaTion of service providers for the elderly" (surely the most tortuous acronym ever invented), was an EU-funded project that used the Internet to boost the independence and improve the quality of life for elderly and disabled people. For example, SWIFT pioneered an appointments system that significantly reduced missed appointments and improved contact between the elderly and the various agencies and organizations involved in their care. Cambridge Professor Nigel Harding of Health Systems Co-ordination, one of the main partners in the SWIFT consortium, said the system 'could literally make the difference between life and death'. Derwentside was chosen for a pilot scheme in 2002 because the district has a significant proportion of over-65s and 'an incredibly robust and advanced information and communications technology infrastructure'.

Individual councillors can and do make a difference. When Cllr Michael Brough was first elected in 1979, he was aware of the lack of facilities in his ward for older people. On his request, the Council converted an empty shop in Betjeman Close into a communal room, and also provided eight tables and 32 chairs. East Stanley Workingmens Club donated a dartboard, playing cards and dominoes as well as tickets and bingo cards. A committee was formed, and over the years activities grew and an adjoining shop was taken over. It was converted thanks to an interest-free loan from the Council, paid back in just 15 months. At one time the committee was making and serving 80-90 meals at a time. This ended in the year 2000 when the six remaining members of the original committee of eleven – five having sadly died in the meantime – felt they were too old to carry on. "I am privileged to have worked with these wonderful people, and I am immensely proud of their wonderful achievements," said Cllr Brough. "Encouraging older people to learn how to use computers and get on the world-wide web, is well worth doing. It enhances their quality of life," said Cllr Mike Malone, "yet the District Auditor challenged us as to whether this was a 'proper use of public money".

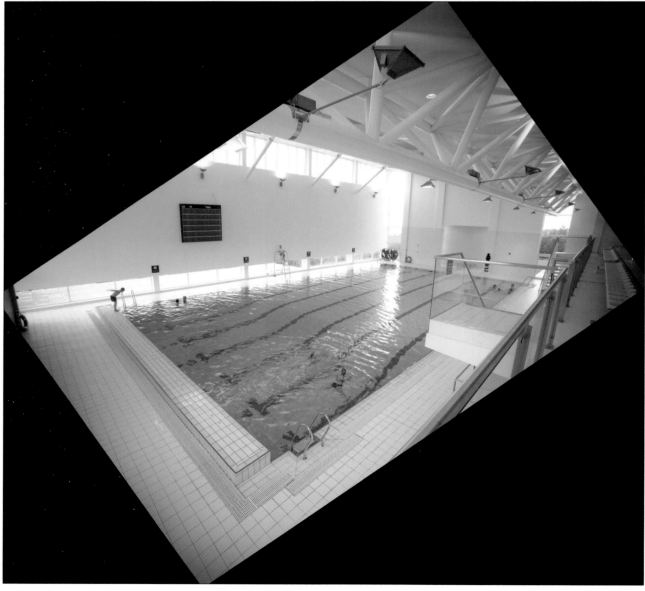

*An unusual view of the new swimming pool in Stanley (MW)*

**Mike Clark**

DDC chief executive Mike Clark was born in 1960 at Queen Elizabeth Hospital, Gateshead. The third of four children, Mike and his two elder brothers and younger sister were brought up by their parents John and Marjorie in their Burnopfield Council house. John was an NCB engine fireman, travelling the rail lines linking all the local pits from his base at Hobson Colliery. Marjorie later worked as a school crossing warden and school meals assistant. Although Mike's parents were not overtly political, national political issues were often discussed at home. Mike joined the Labour Party when a student and was an activist, leafleting and door-knocking. After attending Burnopfield Junior and Tanfield Grammar schools, Mike took a BA degree in government at Newcastle Polytechnic, 1978-81. His choice was influenced by the fact that his then girlfriend Lynda – now his wife – was already doing a BA in librarianship at the Poly, a year ahead of Mike. They married in 1981 and have three children, Gabrielle, Alexander and Oliver.

On leaving Newcastle Poly, Mike looked for work, but in 1981 finding a job was not easy. Wanting to stay in the area and work locally, Mike was taken on as a Trainee Housing Officer with Chester le Street District Council. Already very much inclined to public service, Mike had seen severe housing problems in Newcastle and had done a dissertation on housing as part of his degree course. 'I had a great desire to do something good in the North East. I was committed to the region and still am, very much so,' he said. After five years as a Local Government Officer, Mike had worked his way up to Area Housing Manager with Middlesbrough Borough Council. He could have had further promotion with Middlesbrough, but in October 1989 he took the chance to join his home district of Derwentside as Tenancy Services Manager. One factor that played a large part in his decision was a change in the political direction of the Council. 'Many new members had come onto the Council the previous year,' said Mike, 'I knew that a lot needed doing in the district, and hearing the then Deputy Leader of the Council speak at a housing seminar, persuaded me that the political leadership was up to the challenge'.

A little more than two years later, Mike Clark took over from Gordon Johnson as Chief Housing Officer, despite the offer of a better-paid position with his old employers Middlesbrough BC. Later Mike was told that Cllr Kevin Early, who had taken over as Deputy Leader, had told his fellow councillors: 'Newcastle United made a mistake letting Andy Cole go. Let's us not make the same mistake'. Like most other councils in the North East, Derwentside faced severe housing problems: hard-to-let properties, falling waiting lists, rising rent arrears, problems of repairs and maintenance. 'At first we tried a policy of repairing and improving our Council houses, in the hope that more people would be attracted to apply

*Mike Clark*

for tenancies,' said Mike, 'but when that failed, we had to look to more radical policies of part demolition and redevelopment through housing associations and the private sector, while improving our remaining properties.' Through Estate Action, the Council got government grants to improve four of the five housing estates most in need of redevelopment. In all, eight priority estates were improved.

In January 1996 the Council reorganised its management structure and Mike became Director of Community Services under Neil Johnson. Prior to this the management team consisted of Neil Johnson; Brian Shields, Director of Central Services; and John Hall, Director of Customer Services. The management team then became: Neil Johnson; Dennis Harris, Director of Works (who subsequently left in March 1997 and was replaced by Barry Edge); Alan Hodgson, Director of Human Resources & Technology; Keith Robinson, Director of Corporate Finance; Mike Clark, Director of Community Services; and Malcolm Davies, Director of Environmental Services.

On taking the top job, Mike had a long list of priorities. The Council needed to prepare for a difficult CPA (Comprehensive Performance Assessment) inspection by the Audit Commission, and complete an options appraisal of its housing stock. The recently set up Leisure Trust needed reorganizing, and there was the problem of replacing Stanley Baths. 'Most of all, the Council needed to get control of its budget,' said Mike, 'there was still the threat of capping, and it was an absolute priority that Council Tax increases had to be reduced to prevent the Council being 'fined' by government taking grant funding away from us'. This full agenda also involved totally reorganising the Council's management structure and responding to the government's proposals for local government reform.

After seven years as Chief Executive, Mike was proud of what the Council had achieved under his tutelage. 'Council Tax increases have been brought down to zero for the last four years; we have an economy we can be proud of, thanks to our very successful Strategic Partnership; the Council has won many awards, including three Beacon Status awards [later four] for our work with young people, with ICT and for getting people into work; we have helped create a green and attractive environment; the health of the people has improved  - life expectancy has increased significantly – and we are one of the few councils in the North East that has stabilized and indeed increased its population. As a Council we have certainly given value for money. I'm proud of everything we have done – proud of our achievements on behalf of the community and proud of the people who have worked for and with the Council over the years, their dedication and commitment being the basis of our success'.

## Derwentside Business Centre

Derwentside Business Centre, on Consett Business Park, is made up of the main Business Centre, the E-Business Centre, the New Business Centre, three Terraced Units and a 10,000 sq ft factory. The 10,000 sq ft Derwentside Business Centre was opened in 1992, and the 8,000 sq ft E-Business centre in 2000. The 10,000 sq ft New Business Centre, split into 18 Units, was opened by One NorthEast Chairman Margaret Faye in January 2004, the event enlivened by a splendid cake baked by Sandra Clennell of "Sugarfun", Consett. North West Durham MP Hilary Armstrong opened the Terraced Units and Factory (a total of around 20,000 sq ft) in March 2006.

## John Pearson

Deputy Chief Executive John Pearson was born in the Richard Murray Hospital, Blackhill, the son of John and Audrey. His dad was an electrician at Consett Steelworks and was one of those who lost their job there in 1980. John attended Greencroft Secondary School before gaining a degree in Public Administration at Sheffield Polytechnic and taking a temporary job with Derwentside Council in 1981, having completed a year's placement there in 1980. Part of the attraction in coming home was that he had met his future wife Julie, a Bonus Clerk at the Council, during his placement. They married in 1984 and have two children, Jenny and Stuart. In June 1982 John took up a permanent position as Industrial Assistant in the Council's newly created Industrial Development Department under its first boss

*Opening new business centre, January 2004, Margaret and Alex cut the cake (MW)*

*Peter McDowell, Margaret Faye and Alex Watson admire the cake. David Lllewllyn isn't so sure (MW)*

John Carney. John became the Council's next Industrial Officer in 1988. During this time the Council supported John's further studies and he balanced work and family life with studying in his own time for post-graduate Diplomas in Finance and Marketing and then an MBA, gained with Distinction, in 2000. This helped him to rise to the position of Head of Economic and Community Development then Director of Development and Asset Management in January 2003 and Deputy Chief Executive in June 2007.

*Villa Real Business Centre (MW)*

## Bank deposits frozen

Derwentside Council had a total of £7m deposited with three of the Icelandic banks (Glitnir, Landsbanki and Kaupthing, Singer & Friedlander) that went into into administration or receivership in Autumn 2008. £5m of this was due to mature on or before the 28th October, but along with many other local councils and other public bodies in the UK, the Council was clearly going to have to wait for its money. All of the DDC investments were made during 2006 and 2007. With Landsbanki in receivership in Iceland, the Government was trying to establish what this means for UK wholesale creditors, including local authorities. The Government had also taken action by freezing the UK assets of Landsbanki, to help ensure that UK wholesale creditors of Landsbanki are treated fairly. Heritable, the UK subsidiary of Landsbanki was in administration in the UK. The same situation applied to Kaupthing Singer & Friedlander, the UK subsidiary of Kaupthing also in administration in the UK. For Glitnir Bank, the parent company was in "receivership" in Iceland.

The Council's deposits were not lost at that stage, although at the time of writing it was not clear whether all or part would be returned. The Council had always followed government guidelines and the banks the Council invested in had all been independently assessed for financial standing and viability by the major ratings agencies, Moody's, Standard and Poors & Fitch's. These banks were further examined by the Council's Treasury Management consultants to determine what were the reasonable levels of investment with each individual institution. All the Icelandic banks the Council dealt with were judged suitable for investment purposes, and over 100 authorities across the country also took decisions to invest with them.

## Iceland Blog

***Tuesday 7th October 2008, 5.07pm:*** DDC Chief Executive Mike Clark, at home in Durham, gets an email from Dave Watson, head of financial services. "We could be in trouble. One of the Icelandic banks we deposited £2m with has gone bust. This loan is due to be repaid to us on Monday". Clark replies: "don't jump off the bridge just yet. What do our financial advisers say? Are any other Durham authorities involved? We need a brief for the members". Clark has a meeting at Durham County Hall at 8.30am next morning – one of a regular series to make arrangements for the new unitary county council to take over all local government services in County Durham on 1st April 2009. ***Wednesday 8th October 2008, 7.12am:*** Council Leader Alex Watson catches the National Express InterCity train to London Kings Cross for a meeting of the English Regions Network (ERN). Alex is chair of the North East Assembly and also chair of the ERN. ***8.25am:*** As the train approaches Doncaster, Alex gets a call on his mobile from Mike Clark. Alex learns the Council has £2m invested with an Icelandic bank, the loan due to mature on Monday – five days away. The position is unclear. Will the Council get its money back? ***8.30am:*** Clark goes into his meeting at County Hall. No-one mentions Iceland. ***12noon:*** Back at the Civic Centre, Clark gets another email from Watson. Only three other councils in the North East have investments with Iceland banks. The financial advisers and the Local Government Association are compiling a national list. ***4.30pm:*** Council cabinet members are briefed. ***Thursday 9th October 2008: 7.45am:*** Watson gets the first of many press calls, from Kelly Woods of the Newcastle Evening Chronicle. He promises to get back to her. Watson rings Clark – already at his desk. "It's worse than we thought," says Clark, "we have £7m in the Icelandic banks. Only £1m is due on Monday, but a further £5m is due at the end of this month". While many other local authorities and other public bodies in the same position refuse to speak to the media, Watson decides to tell all he knows. ***11am:*** Watson and Clark meet in the Leader's office. The line is "we can deal with this. We may stand to lose £350,000 worth of interest, but we are confident the Council will recover the whole of the capital invested. Any loss of interest on this scale will not affect the Council's activities or have any impact on Council Tax". Watson's view is that a Labour prime minister, having bailed out the private sector, is compelled to offer similar support to the public sector. Watson fields almost constant press calls all day. He speaks to several newspapers, three radio stations and is interviewed at the Civic Centre by BBC television. This footage is featured in the teatime regional and national news bulletins. ***3.30pm:*** Watson briefs Deputy Leader Mike Malone who arrives at the Civic Centre from his teaching job. ***4.30pm:*** Clark briefs Executive members and opposition leader Watts Stelling. **Friday 10th October 2008, 10am:** Watson and Clark confer by phone. There will be no early resolution to the problem.

## Consett Sports Village - the dream lives on

Ambitious plans for a major new sports complex on the Berry Edge site – the Consett Sports Village – were on hold in 2009, but in the last months of its existence Derwentside District Council had secured £15m of funding to ensure that replacement sports facilities – a new swimming pool and leisure centre - would be built, leaving open the possibility that the full scheme could still come to fruition in the future.

The Consett Sports Village project was first considered by the Council in June 2003. Replacement facilities were urgently needed because of the deteriorating "fabric and functionality" of the Belle Vue Swim Centre and Belle Vue Leisure Centre. In October 2004 Members agreed to seek development of a new, comprehensive sports complex at Berry Edge. As well as providing much-improved sports facilities, the Sports Village would also have had the potential to work with other organisations, and so reduce the revenue costs of operating sports facilities in Consett, and support regeneration of the District.

The Sports Village was planned to include a six-lane Pool, four-court Sports Hall, Fitness and Gym Suite, four-court indoor Tennis Pavilion, a three-court academy-status Squash Centre, three five-a-side outdoor Football Pitches, a floodlit artificial Senior Football Pitch, a Turf

Plateau accommodating up to 13 junior or nine adult football pitches, a six-lane outdoor Athletics Track and a new District Stadium capable of hosting non-league football teams and cup finals. A national-standard Cross-Country running track would run around the perimeter of the site. The proposals also included the incorporation of teaching and training facilities in partnership with Derwentside College and Durham County Council.

To deliver the Sports Village, the Council set out to secure funding totalling £28 million, including £6 million from the District Council, £1 million from the Football Foundation, £2 million from Sport England, £1 million from One NorthEast, £5 million of Olympic Legacy funding, £1m from the Lawn Tennis Association, £2 million from the Project Genesis Trust and £10 million from Durham County Council. The proposal would also have involved an array of agreements and tenancies with local organisations and clubs to create a fully-integrated facility serving a wide range of local people and groups.

During 2007 it became clear that not all of the original £28m funding that had been potentially available would in fact materialise. Delays in decisions and changing priorities meant that funding organisations could not

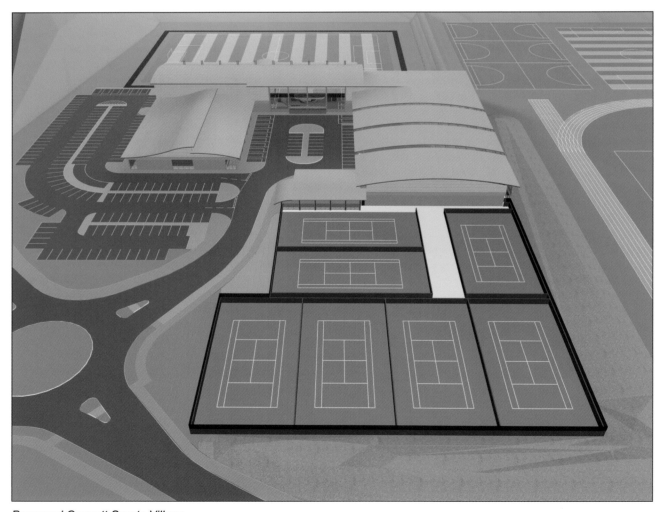

*Proposed Consett Sports Village*

commit to the Sports Village project, at least to the level they had previously indicated. Other issues remained to be resolved, including grant conditions that would have increased the operating costs of the Village. As a result, in 2008 the District Council agreed to progress a project that would initially involve delivery of a new facility to replace the aging Belle Vue Swim and Leisure Centres, but would also retain the potential to add significant further facilities and services, in line with the original Sports Village concept, as funding became available. The District Council secured the £15m funding needed to provide replacement facilities, but, under Local Government Reorganisation protocols, required the permission of Durham County Council in order to proceed. This permission was sought in July 2008 but, at the time of writing, Durham County Council had yet to make a decision.

Cllr Owen Temple, LibDem Leader on Derwentside Council and an elected member of the new Durham County Council unitary authority, put this question at the DCC meeting on 4th February 2009: 'I have been given assurances by Derwentside's Section 151 officer that that the £13.15 million contribution from Derwentside District Council included in the "Business as Usual" submission to build a new Sports Centre in Consett is fully funded. I therefore accept that that contribution is fully funded. Does the Cabinet Portfolio Member for Corporate Resources [Cllr Michelle Hodgson] accept the assurances of Derwentside's Section 151 officer, that the £13.15 million contribution from Derwentside District Council included in the "Business as Usual" submission to build a new Sports Centre in Consett is fully funded?' The answer was: "I wouldn't want to challenge the professional opinion of an Officer of another Council".

Whellan's 1894 Directory of County Durham refers to three "extensive collieries" at work in the parish of Dipton. The Delight Pit, sunk in 1854, employed 260 men and boys and produced 400 tons of coal daily. The main seams were the Hutton, 6 feet 6 inches; the Main Coal, 3 feet; and the Busty, 4 feet 11 inches, at a depth of 684, 420, and 384 feet respectively.

*Denise Bennett always enjoyed going to events with fellow-councillor Harry Guildford.* "He made conferences fun," *she said,* "Harry could always enliven the dullest proceedings with his witty quips and asides".

Cllr Kenny Robson was having difficulty hearing everything at council meetings, and so he went and got a new hearing aid. On being asked if it helped, he replied: *"Yes, it's a Godsend, especially being able to switch it off when certain speakers decide to air their views!"*

*On a visit to Vaux Breweries, each of the councillors was given a baseball cap with the company logo on the front. Cllr Jimmy Graham asked for an extra one, saying he had two young grandbairns and they must have a cap each. After some trouble, Jimmy got a second cap – only to give them both to another councillor who had two young children.*

For several years Cllr Eric Turner patrolled the streets of Consett as the local traffic warden. *"When I left that job, I stayed away from Consett for six months, fearing a backlash,"* he said, *"but when I did finally go back, the first person who spoke to me said 'Eric, when are you coming back?' So I must have done a good job."*

*When the old Stanley Baths was officially opened, the councillor who was doing the honours was told to step back by the photographer and stepped back into the water.*

One of the scenes in the 2000 film "Billy Elliot" was filmed in the changing rooms of Langley Park school. The village has also been used as a location for other film and television productions, including " (1974), "The Stars Look Down" (1975), "A Captain's Tale" (1982), "Ripping Yarns" (1977) and the BBC television comedy "The Fast Show". The main attraction for film and TV companies is Railway Street which remains essentially unchanged from the time it was built in the late nineteenth century. In 1988 the group Prefab Sprout released an album called "From Langley Park to Memphis."

*Railway Street, Langley Park (CFW)*

## Chapter Seven
# Personalities past & present

*Norris Oyston, Billy Bell, Joe Rhind, Alex Watson, Selby Walker, Bob Gardner, Dave Hodgson, Kevin Earley, Michael Malone, Bill Stockdale, Watts Stelling, Larry Thomas, Jimmy Graham, Owen Temple, Harry Guildford, Liz Coulson, Eric Turner, Janice Docherty, David Llewellyn, Ossie Johnson, Anne Taylor, Carl Marshall, Dennis Lavin, Carl Christer.*

### Norris Oyston (Leader 1973-79)

Derwentside Council's first Leader, Cllr Norris William Oyston was an articulate and accomplished political performer. He was born at Catchgate near Annfield Plain in 1923 and educated at New Kyo Secondary Modern and Stanley Grammar Schools. Norris left school at sixteen to start work with the NCB as an apprentice joiner. He worked at South Medomsley colliery and Eden colliery, Leadgate, finishing work at Stony Heap. He retired when the pit closed. A quiet man at home and work, Norris came to the fore as a councillor and was an effective first Leader of Derwentside Council, after taking charge for the Council's "shadow year" of 1973/74. Norris was first elected to Stanley UDC in 1958, representing the Collierley [correct spelling!] ward, Dipton. He was Chairman of Stanley Council 1970/71 when it was an all-Labour Council. Norris would undoubtedly have been Leader more than the six years he served in this position, but he lost his seat in 1979 – by just 20 votes - and subsequently failed to win it back. Norris Oyston had a wide knowledge of heraldry, and he supported the name "Derwentside" for the new District in 1974, pointing out that the River Derwent "washed" all three constituent parts of the District, Consett, Stanley and Lanchester which at one time extended as far as Castleside. Oyston played the piano, as did Group Secretary Selby Walker who also had a fine singing voice. Norris died in 1999, aged 75. His widow Margaret Elizabeth (Peggy) recalled that Norris took everything in his stride and seemed to enjoy the challenge of setting up the new authority. His sons Malcolm and Norris also worked for Derwentside Council.

*First Leader – Cllr Norris Oyston (NO)*

### Billy Bell (Leader 1979-87)

William Bell, who represented Catchgate, was a head teacher. According to some of his contemporaries, he was somewhat aloof and preferred to operate behind the scenes. LibDem Leader Owen Temple recalled the Labour leader as "ruling with a rod of iron", but former Independent Cllr Pat Holmes remembered Bell as "a gentleman". A rare triumph for the opposition in Bell's time as Leader was to gain school governor places, previously all reserved for Labour members only. Of his predecessor, Joe Rhind said: "Billy Bell was not a dogmatic Leader. He would listen to peoples' opinions".

*Billy Bell*

*Joe Rhind*

### Joe Rhind (Leader 1987-91)

Joe Rhind came from Leeds to the North East to teach in Gateshead. In 1968 he and his wife Esme were looking for somewhere to live when they landed on the house at Dipton that has been their home ever since. It had to have character and to be big enough for them and their five children. The former chief colliery electrician's house satisfied both criteria. Joe was soon involved in local politics and became District Secretary of the Labour Party. He had been politically active since 1950 when as a student he heard a speech by Keith Joseph, later to become a close advisor to Margaret Thatcher. On local issues, as a "Category D" village, Dipton needed new homes to replace those demolished under the county structure plan. As District Party secretary Joe Rhind was in a good position to resolve conflicts within the Labour Group on the Council, and when Billy Bell lost his seat in 1987, Joe was elected as Group Leader. Joe says he was fortunate when he became Council Leader to have a good set of Council officers to work with. His verdict: "Housing Manager John Hall had a good team around him, as did the Leisure Director Dennis Mitchinson. Brian Shields was a fine Financial Officer. We had an excellent works department, headed by Malcolm Davies with his deputy Dennis Harris looking after the practical side. We built houses that were far better than any the Council had built before. One good thing the officers did was to ensure that we developed our trading estates. Alan Hodgson led the Council's drive to install IT, something I was already aware of and fully supported".

There was a change of culture on the Council as Joe Rhind introduced more open government: "One change I instituted was in planning. Previously decisions had been made by a small sub-committee meeting on site. Instead of making decisions on the spot, the sub-committee would bring back recommendations for the Council to consider. I also allowed the opposition to see all Council papers, something that had never been done before. There had been a lot of secrecy and I was determined to bring things more into the open. I also tried to get the whole Council to work together and to put aside the traditional enmity between Stanley and Consett. One reason I think I got the job as Leader was because I did not belong to either faction. In my role as Secretary of the District Labour Party, I would speak to everybody and treat all members equally. I would always listen. As Leader you often have to make the final decision, but I would always consult with officers, councillors and others before making up my mind. I would like to be remembered for bringing the Council together and opening up our procedures to the opposition and to the public".

Joe gave strong support to environmental group Sustrans and their plans to build the C2C cycle path through the district. "Some people thought a rail line would be preferable, but that was just not on. I told the members and the public that this would not only provide recreation for the local population, it would also bring visitors to the district and that could have a spin-off with new industrial development for the area." For the same reasons, Joe also supported planting daffodils and putting up works of art. "When we first planted daffodils, a lot of people said it was a waste of money and many of the flowers were pulled up or destroyed. Now the daffodils are left untouched and people wouldn't do without them. Likewise with works of art: like the Millenium Bridge at Gateshead, they attract attention to the district and give a fillip to the area".

As Council Leader, Joe Rhind oversaw the introduction of wheelie bins in Derwentside, the first district in the North East to do so. There was widespread opposition, not least from the workforce who at one point went on strike. 'We had months and months of negotiations with the unions," said Joe, "they were brought in at the start of the process and eventually everything was agreed. I regarded bringing in wheelie bins as making life easier for the workforce, but it is a fact that there was a reduction of jobs, with of course a reduction of cost to the council taxpayers. I first saw wheelie bins when I visited our German twin town, and I could immediately see the advantages'. Joe Rhind exuded an aura of reasonableness, but he could be tough. He had been a rugby player and referee – "a game for hooligans played by gentlemen" (as opposed to soccer, "a game for gentlemen played by hooligans"). Joe played wing-threequarter for West Leeds Old Boys RFC in 1975 when they won the Yorkshire Cup. "I was captain on either side of our winning season, but missed out that one year," he said, still rueful over 30 years later. As to his legacy as Council Leader, Joe said: "bringing the Council together as a more uniform authority, and opening things out both to the opposition and the public". Cllr Eric Turner rated the former Council Leader Joe Rhind as "a level-headed man who listened to all points of view".

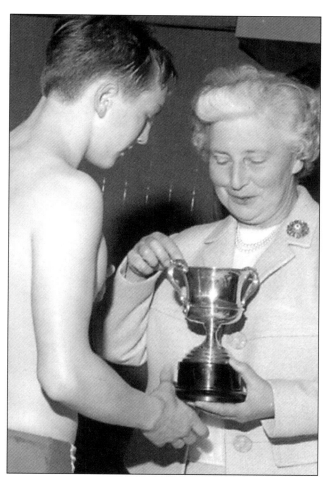

The redoubtable Cllr Rena Mohon presents a swim trophy (SW).

### Alex Watson OBE (Leader 1991-2009)

Alex Watson was born in 1942, the sixth and youngest son of Alexander and Edith. There were twelve years between the oldest and youngest boy, but no daughters! At first the family lived in a flat above the "Tea Shop" – a large big food store – in Newmarket Street, Consett. Soon after Alex was born they moved to a terraced Council house in Stratford Gardens, where Alex and his brothers were brought up. Now Alex and his own family live on Medomsley Road, Consett, famous for the "Phileas Fogg" snack adverts. Alex Watson senior, who originally came from Alston in Cumbria, was traffic under-manager with the Consett Iron Co. Edith, Consett born and bred, married young and became a full-time housewife and mother. Alex junior went to Consett Church of England School and left at fifteen to follow his father into the Steelworks, as did hundreds of young men at that time. It was the same for the sons of miners, sons following dad to work down the pit. Young Alex started in the boilershop, heating rivets. He moved on to "The Mills", loading and stocktaking. In his early twenties, Alex moved on to work as an auto-setter operator for mining engineers RB Bolton on the Castleside Trading Estate, staying with them for over thirty years until the company went out of business in 1995. Alex was works convener for the AEU engineering union at Boltons for 29 years, and this led to his

*Alex Watson*

involvement in the Labour Party. Watson was first elected to Derwentside District Council for the Consett North Ward in 1979. He became Leader in 1991, and his 18 years in the post is a rarity. Council Leaders are invariably subject to plots to unseat them, and Cllr Watson's long tenure alone is proof positive of his political skills. Council Chairman Eric Turner's verdict on Watson: "a real personality who tries to do his best for all". Watson was awarded the OBE in 2007.

### Selby Walker (Group Secretary 1973-84)

In 1975 DDC saved the Empire Theatre from demolition by buying the empty building. The driving force for the purchase was Group Secretary – effectively Deputy Leader - Cllr Selby Walker. He was an old-style "hell fire" councillor who called a spade a spade and stood on many people's toes, but his heart was in the right place. Selby Walker had a prodigious memory, and carried a briefcase stuffed with papers and reports of all kinds. Selby had another side to him. He was a good piano-player, sang and enjoyed amateur dramatics. With his background of mining and the Miners' Welfares, which provided recreation facilities such as playgrounds, parks and welfare halls for local communities, Walker was strongly supportive of a similar policy for the Council. Whenever the NCB put up property for sale, Walker was

all for the Council buying it. A Stanley councillor, he supported the purchase of the Empire Theatre in Consett, without which the building would undoubtedly have been lost. As the pits closed, the Council also took over assets from the miners' welfare charity CISWO. As a result of this policy, Derwentside built up the biggest land bank of any equivalent council in the country. This huge land bank proved vital when it came to economic redevelopment, both as an asset to sell and to control development of the land. Selby stood down as Group Secretary in 1984 to become Council Vice Chairman. He got his wish to be Chairman of the Council, 1985-86, before retiring in 1987. Bob Gardner took over as Group Secretary, 1984-85.

### Born in the USA

Bob Gardner has the unique record of being the only Derwentside district councillor born in the USA. At the time of the 1926 General Strike, along with many others from Derwentside and the North East, Bob's parents John and Eva went to America in search of work. But things over there were no better than here, so the couple returned. Meantime, young Bob was born in 1927 near Scranton in Pennsylvania. Bob could have claimed joint American citizenship, but that went by the board. Bob, who was appointed as a Magistrate in 1966, was first elected to Consett UDC in 1970. In 1974 he became Chairman of the Health Committee and was alter Chairman of the Housing Committee. Bob taught at various schools in the District including Benfieldside Secondary Modern. He was headmaster of Marley Hill junior school and Consett junior school. It was at the latter school that he formed Consett Junior Brass in 1973 with fellow teacher David Jackson, bandmaster with the town's Salvation Army Band. Consett Junior Brass went on from strength to strength, still being conducted by Jackson in 2009. When Selby Walker stood down as Group Secretary in 1984, Bob Gardner took over that role: he had recently retired from teaching. Unfortunately Bob suffered a heart attack in 1985 and retired from the Council. He was followed as Group Secretary by Ken Robson (1985-87). After that, the position became Deputy Leader.

## Kevin Earley (Deputy Leader 1991-95)

After a few years in London working as a radiographer, Kevin Earley returned to his parents' home in Blackhill before getting married and settling nearby. When he was first elected to the Council in 1987, Kevin was a student teacher, studying for his degree at Northumbria University in Newcastle. While working in London, Kevin was shocked by the blinkered views of people in the South who regarded the North as "the frozen end of nowhere." Realising that there was some truth in this view, Kevin decided to do something about it, joined the Labour party and stood for election to the Derwentside District Council in 1987. At 29, he was the youngest member. 'I was lucky in that two of the previous councillors for the area, Vince Kelly and Kenny Robson, were very experienced and gave me good guidance. Vince was Chairman of the Labour Group, and Kenny was Deputy Leader under Billy Bell,' he recalled. As a mark of respect for Cllr Kelly, Kevin named the second of his three children after his mentor.

*Kevin Earley*

Earley joined the Council at a tumultuous time. Many of the old faces had gone, and there was a substantial faction of younger Labour councillors, led by Cllr David Hodgson, who wanted the Council to take a more radical stance on social issues. After a year, Hodgson replaced Alex Watson as Deputy Leader. His reign lasted only two years, and in 1990 Watson was back as Deputy Leader under Joe Rhind. When Rhind lost his seat in 1991, Watson became Leader with Earley as his deputy. They ran in tandem for four years. While Watson retained his day job as a fitter, Earley, who was also a county councillor, gave up work to become a full-time politician despite the meagre allowances. 'It was an exciting but challenging time,' he recalled. The Council's budget had to be reduced to avoid capping, and the massive task of replacing lost jobs meant the Council had to forge much closer relationships with private industry. 'On a percentage basis, we were the third highest spending authority in the country,' said Kevin, 'I well remember 'Derwentside' being read out in the House of Commons, third on the list of high-spending councils'. The introduction of the Poll Tax by the Conservative government in 1989/90 drove a wedge between councils and their electors. When people were prosecuted, fined and even jailed for refusing to pay the Poll Tax, it was the Council who got the blame.

But there were plenty of pluses. 'We went for every grant we possibly could; we got Estate Action money every year, the Rural Housing Initiative resulted in bungalows being built in Ebchester; we brought flats over shops into use; gas to Burnhope; and got substantial European grants,' said Earley. By vesting some of its land holdings in "arms-length" trusts, the Council ensured that the eventual profits from development were reinvested in the area and not siphoned off by a government which insisted that 100 per cent of capital receipts had to be used to reduce debt – a short-sighted policy. The hated "Bull Ring" bus station at Consett was replaced at no cost to the Council, and the wheelie bins were finally paid for, saving £750,000 from the Council's revenue budget. Earley instigated the cavity wall insulation of every Council house in the district in 1993/94, making Derwentside one of the first authorities in the country to achieve this. In 1995, Earley decided he could no longer afford to be a full-time councillor earning just £3,000 a year, so he stepped down as Deputy Leader to be replaced by Mike Malone. Earley remained active on the Council as a committee chairman and chairman of the Labour Group. He stood down as a councillor in 2003.

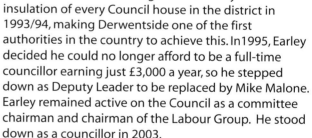

DurhamNet Chief Executive Alan Hodgson might have had his career cut short early on. When he sent a memo to neighbouring district councils, complaining about the "total lack of co-operation" from Durham County Council, DCC Leader Cllr Don Robson demanded the person responsible should be given the sack. DDC Leader Alex Watson refused, but the row quickly blew over. 'Later Don and I met at a Cliff Richard concert – we had both been dragged there by our wives – and he was fine,' recalled Alan. Alan also had early difficulties with his DDC colleagues. 'At first the Treasurer and Chief Executive were not convinced of the need for our own IT service, and it was the members of the Council who really pushed for it,' said Alan.

*At a one-day sale in July 2002, DDC offered cut-price compost bins at £12 for 220-litre compost bin (rrp £39.95) and £15 for the "giant" 330-litre compost bin (rrp £49.95). A previous home composter sale was held at Morrison Busty and Chester le Street Riverside in 1999. Composters costing £34.95 and £39.95 were on sale for £10 and £12.50.*

## Michael Malone (Deputy Leader 1995-2009)

Mike Malone was born at Pity Me near Durham. He went into the Merchant Navy, and then took a job as a steelworker before deciding to become a teacher. He took the Catholic teacher's certificate, and went on to gain a BEd degree in English and geography, followed by an MEd in psychology and education. In tandem with Leader Alex Watson for DDC's last 14 years, Malone could always be relied on to study every report in great detail, giving a deep analysis and asking penetrating questions that required answers. No officer could expect an easy ride when Malone was at a meeting. His thinking covered every field of Council endeavour. 'We took on board the modernisation agenda well before it became a government requirement. Likewise, the Council adopted best practice in advance of legislation. In the late 1990s, we stopped being paternalistic and inward-looking and became more entrepreneurial and risk-taking. The Council reduced its workforce through efficiencies, out-sourcing and partnerships'. The one thing that is most likely to raise Malone's hackles is someone saying "that's not a Council responsibility". During his term of office Malone served the Council as Government member champion, led on Best Value, CPA, Procurement and Member Training, and supported the introduction of the EFQM management model working with the lead officer Tom Gorman.

In 2005, Cllr Malone climbed Mount Kilimanjaro in north-eastern Tanzania with Esh Group quantity surveyor Jason Dixon. They took the 50-mile Rongai route up the mountain and raised more than £5,000 for charity. They took six days to reach the 19,265 ft. summit and camped overnight with Tanzanian locals. Blackhill councillor Malone, 61 at the time, lost 11lb during the trip. The temperature was more than 30C at the bottom but -27C at the top. The money raised went to St. Mary's

*The start of the Blackhill & Consett Park restoration. Chief Executive Mike Clark and Deputy Leader Cllr Mike Malone plant a tree, 7th January 2002.*

RC Church in Blackhill, which was to celebrate its 150th anniversary in 2007. 'We were extremely well looked after, but it was very tiring. It did not really hit us until the last 5,000 ft. It was incredibly difficult in terms of effort to keep going,' he said, 'it was very energy-sapping and I remember feeling a profound weakness'. Cllr Malone gave Newcastle United shirts to porters and their children for helping to carry their kit. Reflecting on his time as a Councillor: 'it has been a privilege to serve you, the people'.

*Mike Malone climbs Mount Kilimanjaro (MJM)*

### Bill Stockdale (Independent)

A steelworker's son, Bill Stockdale was born in Leadgate and represented the village on DDC for 24 years, 1979-2003. Bill, a local head teacher who played cricket for the village side, had no thoughts of getting involved in politics until he was asked to stand by the newly-formed Derwentside Independents in 1979.'The Labour Vice Chairman of the Council was all set to become Chairman, but I surprisingly defeated him,' said Bill. The new Councillor for Leadgate made an immediate impact. He demanded opposition representation on an important and influential new committee, the Industry Committee, and to his delight he was made a member. Stockdale, in 2008 the sole remaining member of the original Industry Committee, recalled meetings with Sir Charles Villiers and Sir Keith Joseph MP. Villiers was Chairman of the British Steel Corporation 1976-80, and Chairman BSC (Industry), 1977-89. Joseph was Secretary of State for Industry 1979-81. At first there were only seven members on the Industry Committee. Its meetings were held in private to maintain commercial confidentiality, resulting in some criticism, but the new committee was effective in bringing new industry to the area after the fiercely-fought campaign to

*Bill Stockdale*

stop the closure of Consett Steelworks in 1980 finally failed.'The Council spent a good deal of time and money in attracting new industry, but it had to be done,' said Bill. When he became captain of the council cricket team, which included both councillors and officers, Bill found the social and sporting contact made it easier to negotiate with the Labour leadership on council matters. This resulted in the Independents being given their own office in the Civic Centre for the first time.

Meanwhile, Cllr Stockdale turned his attention to the organisation of the Independent Group.'Up to that point, individual candidates had financed themselves and had written their own separate manifestos,' he said, 'I wanted to put the opposition on a level playing field with Labour. I re-organised the Independents into two sections. The social side had a monthly meeting for councillors and supporters which raised money to fund elections, and the district councillors agreed a common manifesto that we could all support'. When the registration of political parties was brought in by the Labour government, the Derwentside Independents adopted their own logo to go on the ballot paper.'We changed the ethos of the Independents from being mainly professional people, putting the emphasis on people who were well known and active in their own

area,' said Bill,'I wanted us to be as far as possible on equal terms with Labour, but we never had a whip and any member who felt strongly about a particular issue was free to vote the way they wanted'. For three years, Stockdale stood down as Group Leader while he studied at Durham University. Blackhill councillor Bob Atkinson, ex-manager of Consett Steel Plant, became Leader during this period, with Stockdale as his deputy.

The Independents reached their lowest ebb in 1995, reduced to five members on the Council due to what Bill calls "the Tony Blair factor". Gradually they recovered lost ground and established themselves as active community councillors. By 1999 there were 15 Independent members on the Council, one of whom was Watts Stelling. At this time, thanks to the more enlightened approach of the majority party leadership of Alex Watson, the Independents were able to take a full part in the "scrutiny" function of the Council, and were given scrutiny committee chairmanships. Under the leadership of Cllr Stelling, a Stockdale protégée and also a Leadgate councillor, by 2007 the Derwentside Independents gained the largest representation they had ever had on DDC, 23 out of 55 members.

Recalling Labour members of the Council, Stockdale had some trenchant things to say.'Selby Walker from Stanley was a powerful force. He had a dossier on every member and every senior officer. Dave Hodgson from Crookhall was left wing, but a good politician and a clever debater. He often made things difficult for us. Blackhill councillor Kevin Earley, deputy leader for a while, was always something of a grey eminence, a power behind the scenes'. Stockdale retired as a head teacher in 1989 and as a Councillor in 2003. Five years later, aged 80, he was still running the Leadgate History Society and the Men's Forum. In 2008 Bill finally got round to building himself a new house on the plot next door. 'I've had planning permission for thirty years, so I thought I'd better get on with it,' he said. As a former long-serving local councillor, Bill is particularly proud of his role in leading the campaign to bring a doctor's surgery to Leadgate when the previous branch surgery was closed. Ewen House now stands as a testament to his efforts.'The Derwentside Independents have produced some of the highest turnouts in local elections in the region, and we certainly made Derwentside Council more democratic.'

## Watts Stelling (Independent)

Stockdale's successor Watts Stelling was born in Leadgate and went to Leadgate County School and Moorside Secondary. A talented footballer, Watts was taken on by Derby County as an apprentice professional and was all set for a pro career in soccer when he suffered an injury that ended his hopes of fame on the field. For the next twelve years Watts worked for CIC as an analytical chemist in the Technical Research Department on the main site at Consett. After the closure of the steelworks in 1980, Watts went to work for Newcastle University as a lab manager and was there for 23 years. Although a "dyed in the wool" Labour supporter, Watts was disillusioned with his local DDC councillors and was elected as an Independent in 1999. He had already made his mark as a local resident, regularly taking advantage of the opportunity to speak at Development Control Committee meetings so much so that he was dubbed "the five-minute man". Watts spoke on local planning issues and complained about a sickly stench coming from a local factory.

Watts' mentor was Cllr Bill Stockdale, who had been his head teacher at school. Both men fully supported the decision to set up the Derwentside Independent Association – which includes other members as well as councillors – as a political party. 'We are a regular political party but we are not involved in national politics,' said Watts, 'most importantly, we do not operate a party whip and members are free to vote as they think fit'. Choosing candidates for local elections has rarely been a problem for the Association. If more than the requisite number want to stand in a particular ward, a panel of senior members makes a decision after interviewing all the would-be candidates. This has led to at least one member leaving the association and standing as an "Independent" Independent. "It just doesn't make sense for four independents to stand in a three-seat ward, especially if there are places available in another ward," said Watts.

With Labour's majority since 2007 down to just three overall, the 23-strong Derwentside Independent group – later down to 21 - could not be ignored. With the support of the three LibDems and the two other Independents, plus a few Labour rebels, proposals by the ruling group could be defeated. In September 2008,

*Watts Stelling*

the proposed sale of Council land to Derwentside Homes was vetoed by this method, although later reversed. On a more positive note, the support given by the Independents to the proposed replacement sports facilities in Consett has been, in Watts' opinion, crucial in keeping the scheme alive after the Council's initial plans for a major Sports Village complex had been halted due to its cost. 'We persuaded the Council to go for a less ambitious replacement scheme, otherwise it would have been sunk without trace,' said Watts. Although partly responsible for the rejection of the original scheme, having voted not to support it, the Independent Group is fully supportive of the Council in ensuring that the £15 million funding now available is secured to provide new sports facilities in Consett. Watts' late father was also called Watts but got "Danny" at the pit. "Make a difference where you live" was his advice to his son.

The population of Derwentside on Census Night 21-22 April 1991 was 86,046. Stanley had a population of 17,100 and Consett 29,700. The 2001 census showed that the population of Derwentside was 85,065, a drop of just 1.1% compared with ten years previously. The number of households however increased from 34,904 to 36,482, mainly due to a 49% increase in single person households. The average household size was 2.3. Owner-occupation in the district had risen to 69%, an increase of 3,006. The latest survey was done in 2006, estimating Derwentside's population at 86,500.

*Consett UDC adopted warship HMS Hydrangea in February 1942. Built in Glasgow, she was a 925-ton Flower Class Corvette with a complement of 85-109 men. She saw action in the Atlantic and the Mediterranean, and sank a U-boat off the south-west coast of Ireland. After WW2, she was sold to Hong Kong and converted to carry cargo. Renamed Hydralock, she ran aground and sank in the Formosa Straits in February 1957. In 1998, her ship's badge was handed over to Derwentside Council.*

### Larry Thomas MBE (Conservative)

Derwentside's first Conservative councillor and Group Leader was Lawrence Arthur Thomas, known as Larry. He was a Welshman who met his wife Bessie (nee Shackley) at the end of the war. They settled in Bessie's home town of Consett. Larry was elected to Consett UDC in 1950, the first Conservative on the Council. When the steelworks closed in 1980 and it was all "gloom and doom", Larry was optimistic. 'Consett will survive,' he said, and he was right. He was awarded the MBE in 1981 and two years later retired from DDC after 33 years as a councillor. Larry Thomas went to school in Wales with George Thomas, later to become Speaker of the House of Commons. The two men met up again on 25th April 1982 when Speaker Thomas was preaching at the 25th annual miners' service in Hetton Methodist Church. It was a happy occasion. Castleside councillor Dorothy Graham took over as Conservative Group Leader. She was followed by Denise Bullivant from Lanchester.

*Cllr Eric Edwards receives his 25-year long service award from DDC Chairman Olga Milburn in 2007, a year late (MW)*

*A 30-year award for Cllr Larry Thomas, from Council Chairman Cllr Jimmy Graham 1980 (BT).*

### Jimmy Graham (Labour)

Long-serving councillor Jimmy Graham, who died in 2008 at the age of 95, was a "Junior Whip" – at the age of ninety! He stood down in 2007 after 50 years as a Councillor, but died the following year. In 1997 Cllr Graham, the "Father of the Council" was presented with an inscribed watch to mark his forty years' service as a district councillor, first with Stanley UDC and then with Derwentside DC. He had been Chairman of both authorities. Jim and his wife Bet had recently celebrated their diamond wedding. Jimmy, a mechanic by trade, worked for the Northern Bus Co. for many years. He was later taken on as a School Board man (or, more colloquially, the "kiddie catcher"). Jimmy "never missed" a council meeting, and his particular interest was as Chairman of the Crematorium Committee. Jimmy was known as "the man with the carrier bag." In his later years Jimmy was a widower who fended for himself but didn't like to spend any money. Whenever there was a Council "do", when all had eaten Jimmy would be there, collecting left-over chicken legs. Perhaps his experiences growing up hungry in the 1920s and 1930s was responsible. On a visit to Vaux Breweries, each of the councillors was given a cap with the company logo on the front. Cllr Jimmy Graham asked for an extra one, saying he had two young grandbairns and must have two caps. After some trouble, Jimmy got a second cap – only to give them both to another councillor who had two young children.

### Owen Temple (Liberal Democrat)

LibDem Leader Owen Leighton Temple first served on DDC 1983/86 as an SDP/Alliance councillor, and returned to the Council in 2007 as a LibDem. Despite his Consett North ward being represented by three councillors from three different parties, there was no problem agreeing to spend the ward's £60,000 capital initiative fund on a state-of-the-art recording studio in Consett YMCA. Ex-teacher Owen gave the Council a "plus" for strengthening the economic base of the district by building business premises and other measures, but a "minus" for – in his opinion - making too many decisions behind closed doors with press and public excluded, despite the more open style of leadership compared with twenty years earlier.

Beamish village was bombed by German planes early in the morning of Friday 1st May 1942, shortly after an air raid warning that gave people time to get into their shelters. Some houses and shops were damaged, but no-one was hurt. As a bomb disposal squad was approaching, a second bomb exploded, damaging the railway and a footbridge, and fracturing a water main. At 9.05pm that night, a third bomb – not previously spotted – exploded. Eight children and adults were killed, seven seriously injured and 28 others injured.

### Harry Guildford MBE (Labour)

Harry Guildford has been involved in so many local organisations there isn't space to list them all. Suffice to say that not only was he asked to open the new headquarters of Esh Parish Council, they named the building after him! Born into a mining family, Harry has lived in Langley Park all his life. He spent most of his working life as an electrician at the local colliery. One of his apprentices was none other than another son of Langley Park, Sir Bobby Robson. Harry recommended Bobby to Newcastle United, but they said he was too small and Bobby went to Fulham instead. Harry was the last Chairman of Lanchester RDC. He recently found an expenses claim from that time – just over £13 for four months (ie a pound a week). Harry was a parish councillor for more than 30 years, twice Chairman, and was District Council Chairman 1996/97. His Chairman's charity was the Heart Foundation, taken up after his son-in-law had a heart transplant. "I always treated the Council officers with respect, and I listened to everybody's point of view," Harry reflected.

*Harry Guildford opens the new Esh Parish Council offices, named after him, in 2008 (EPC)*

*Liz Coulson*

### Liz Coulson (Labour)

Elizabeth (Liz) Coulson represented Quaking Houses where she ran the village shop. For many years she lived in the pub, the Smelters Arms at Castleside, run by her son. Liz stood no nonsense and was a stickler for procedure, qualities that stood her in good stead during her time as Senior Whip of the Labour Group. Liz helped raise funds for a brand new village hall. She not only started a pensioners' lunch club, she also cooked the meals. Cllr Coulson, twice Council Chairman 1993/94 and 2005/06, was a founder-member of the Quaking Houses Community Association. She supported the South Moor Hospital and the Save Shotley Bridge Hospital campaigns, and the Macmillan Nurses. As Chairman, she met children from Chernobyl who were hosted by the Consett Detached Youth Churches Project. Liz died in January 2007.

*Janice Docherty*

### Janice Docherty (Labour)

Through the Council, Cllr Janice Docherty has been at the forefront of setting up Aspirations Begin at Home (AB@H), its first priority to help local children who were falling behind in their first two years at senior school. "Learning to use computers can be of immense help to children at this stage, but to be effective, the whole family has to be involved," said Janice. The first tranche of AB@H saw 300 families with school-age children helped with computers and training. With other family members included, this involved a total of 900 people. Janice reckons that in her time as a councillor, her ward has benefited from £10m of investment, including £750,000 towards Craghead village hall and £250,000 for childcare facilities, including pre-school children. "The District Council has regenerated Craghead & South Stanley," she said.

## Eric Turner (Labour)

Cllr Eric Turner was the last ever Chairman of Derwentside District Council 2008/09. This was his second year of office, as he was also chairman in 1994/95. Eric was Chairman of the Planning Committee for ten years, he believes a record stint. A joiner by trade, he was particularly proud of his role in getting a brand-new community centre built for Hamsterley and Low Westwood. Eric acted as Clerk of Works to ensure that the job was done right. The £36,000 cost was raised mainly by local efforts, together with a grant from Durham County Council. Even then, they were two or three thousand pounds short. Local County Councillor Don Robson came up with the answer. Another project at Burnopfield could not go ahead, so Robson arranged for the money to be "vired" to Hamsterley.

In his long career, Eric has done two other jobs. For 26 years, he helped his wife Enid as postmistress at Hamsterley Post Office, which fortunately escaped the 2008 cuts thanks to the issue of motor vehicle licenses. A previous job saw Eric patrol the streets of Consett for several years as the local traffic warden. 'When I left that job, I stayed away from Consett for six months, fearing a backlash,' said Eric, 'but when I did finally go back, the first person who spoke to me said 'Eric, when are you coming back?' So I must have done a good job'. The one project that Eric is most proud of, the one he calls "my baby", is the provision of a new primary health centre at Hamsterley Colliery. Dr Drought, who had a surgery in Low Westwood for many years, was looking for new purpose-built premises but could not find a suitable piece of land. Eric applied his local knowledge and came up with a council-owned site at Axford Terrace. After protracted negotiations and problems with a main sewer running through the site, the scheme was just about ready when Dr Drought announced his intention of retiring. The torch passed to Dr Levick who said the site at Axford Terrace was not big enough for what was needed. Once again Eric went on the search around his patch, and located a big enough piece of land at Hamsterley Colliery, also Council-owned. The process started all over again, and eventually the new premises were opened in 2008 – a full five years after the initial scheme had been mooted. 'You have to be persistent to see things through,' said Eric, 'but I am proud of the fact that Hamsterley Colliery now has a doctor's surgery which it has never had before'.

*Cllr Derek Hume receives his 25-year long service award from DDC Chairman Eric Turner in 2008 (MW)*

HMS Anchusa was adopted by Stanley UDC in 1942. She was a 1,000-ton Flower Class corvette, built by Harland and Wolf. She carried a 2lb, 4-inch gun and had a complement of 85-109 men. She did duty in the North and South Atlantic, the Mediterranean and the Channel, mainly as convoy escort, and won battle honours. She was sold by the Admiralty in 1946.

*Albert "Jinks" Harrison of Towneley Street, Stanley, was walking his dog Billie around the Council ash tip on 13th November 1948 when he came upon the dead body of Sarah Ellen Watson. A local man was convicted of the killing and sentenced to 12 years imprisonment. Jinksy was fined for not having a dog licence.*

Hillary Rodham Clinton's grandfather Hugh Rodham was born at Oxhill near Stanley in 1879. Hugh, an overman at the local colliery, emigrated to the USA in 1883. He died in America in 1965. His son Hugh Ellsworth Rodham, born 1912, married Dorothy Howell in 1942. Hillary Clinton is the eldest of their three children.

*Some years ago, the then Chairman of the Council was horrified to find that the caterers for the annual Civic Ball would be charging "corkage" for the wine they supplied, a standard practice in the trade. At £5 a bottle for 100 bottles, it would amount to £500, in the Chairman's mind, just for removing 100 corks. Days later, the Chairman came into the Civic Centre, his face beaming. "I've solved the problem," he said proudly, "I've told the caterers to use screw-top bottles – so no corkage charges". His face fell when he was told that corkage would still apply.*

*David Llewellyn*

## David Llewellyn (Labour)

It was his wife Carol that brought David Gwyn Llewellyn to Derwentside. Born in Southampton and with a Welsh family background, David met Carol while a student studying economics and politics at Newcastle University. She got a job at Moorside School, and the couple settled in Consett with David teaching history & economics, first at a school in Blaydon and then at South Stanley Comprehensive. He now works part-time as a supply teacher. A long-time Labour Party activist, David was first elected for the Blackhill ward in 1987. He was Chairman of the Council 2002/03 and was particularly pleased to officiate at the reopening of Blackhill & Consett Park. Llewellyn's mentor was Cllr Vince Kelly who with fellow-councillor Ken Robson had run a "Back to Blackhill" campaign. Slum clearance in the area, while necessary, meant that many people had to move out of Blackhill. What was needed was new housing to replace the old. The Council built an unusual split-level development in Church Road, and the Pemberton Road estate. Church Road has been a success and the houses are still in high demand, while Pemberton Road was the last major development of its kind before the 1990s when Council house building was virtually ended. After spells as Vice Chair of the Housing Management Committee and Chair of Finance and Resources, Cllr Llewellyn took over the economic development portfolio in 2003. He saw the provision of business unit space as being particularly important. 'Without a thriving economy, there is no real future for any area'. David pointed out that the majority of the income of the Economic Development Department comes from its own resources of rental income, rather than from the Council taxpayers direct. He was very pleased to be part of the team that secured a Beacon Status award from the government for business start-ups, due to the hard work of the Economic Development Section.

## Ossie Johnson (Labour)

Cllr Ossie Johnson's father – also named Oswald and also called Ossie – was a founder-member of Derwentside District Council in 1974 after previously being a member of Stanley UDC. In 2008/09 Ossie junior, elected to the new Durham County unitary council, found himself repeating the experience of his father who likewise bridged old and new councils in 1973/74. Ossie snr, a primary head teacher at Craghead and South Stanley, was a committee Chairman on both councils. After attending St John's College, York, and Newcastle University and gaining BEd and MEd degrees in design technology, Johnson followed his father into the teaching profession, becoming Deputy Head of a special school in Bishop Auckland. Cllr Johnson is proud of the fact that he was the "Centenary Chairman" of the Council. One of many highlights of his year of office came when Ossie inaugurated the annual district inter-golf tournament involving the area's four clubs – South Moor, Consett, Beamish and Hobson. Another was attending a reception on the aircraft carrier Illustrious, berthed on the River Tyne, given by the Mayor of Durham whose authority had adopted the ship. As a councillor for Lanchester since 1996, Johnson has always worked closely with local residents. Many of his constituents still hark back to the days of Lanchester RDC, and with the abolition of DDC Johnson can see a bigger role for Lanchester Parish Council. Ossie was elected to the Parish Council in 1991, was Chairman 1994-97 and again from 2008.

*Ossie Johnson*

## Anne Taylor

Reflecting on her time on the Council, Cllr Anne Taylor said: 'I hope in years to come the residents of Havannah Ward will enjoy the fruits of my labours, in particular Oakey Park, View Lane Park, Shield Row Park, East Stanley bowls facility, Louisa swim centre, Tangle Wood Mews Residential Care facility, creating employment and training opportunities for approximately 120 local people. I have worked passionately and enthusiastically for the democratic opportunity of a directly-elected Youth Forum, achieving Beacon Status and the

*Cllr Anne Taylor with SHINE Award winners (AT)*

regional SHINE award which recognised the pro-active work within Derwentside in creating open dialogue between youth and their elders; and helped bring to reality a mobile youth unit aptly named "Ellie" the Youth Bus. I would like to thank the residents of Havannah who trusted and supported me during my 18 years as their representative; they were my enthusiasm for change and creation of opportunity. It has never been plain sailing. At times I have had a rocky journey, but I have always come back fighting. I can hold my head high and say I worked very hard and always fairly for the people'.

At the Council AGM on 11th May 2004, retiring chairman Denise Bennett announced that Cllr Tracy Davinson had give birth to a baby boy, Jacob, weighing 8lb 12oz. This may have been the only occasion when a sitting member of the Council had given birth.

*The highlight of the annual Derwentside Show was the Show Queen final at Consett Civic Hall. "Show your old lady she isn't like the back of a bus" and "is your girl friend a beauty queen?" said the adverts, urging the men of the district – in somewhat non-PC fashion - to enter their wives and girlfriends for the competition.*

The introduction of the Twin Bin system was controversial. The then Deputy Leader Kevin Earley remembers a placard saying "Hang Kevin Earley".

## Carl Marshall

Learning Portfolio holder, Cllr Carl Marshall from Stanley was first elected to Derwentside District Council in 2005 at the age of 24. He is the youngest Councillor ever to serve on the Council, and is one of the youngest Council Cabinet members in the UK. 'It was a great privilege for

*Carl Marshall*

me to be elected to the Council's Cabinet,' said Carl, 'it gave me a broader outlook on how the Council operates, and provided opportunities for me to further influence the work of the Council. The Portfolio for Learning covers many key areas of work. I have particularly enjoyed working with our excellent staff, who have always been supportive to me in my role'. One of Carl's proudest moments as a Councillor was representing Derwentside at the National IRRV (Institute of Revenues Rating & Valuation) Conference, where the Council's Revenues & Benefits Team was highly commended for their work. Carl is optimistic for the future. He has been elected as a member of the new unitary Durham County Council, and is excited by the prospect of helping establish this new Council for the people of Derwentside.

## Dennis Lavin (Labour)

Dennis Lavin was born in East Stanley and lived in New Kyo since the age of four. He worked as a civil servant, including four years in Kent. His great-uncle on his mother's side, Jack Burridge, was a member of Stanley UDC. Dennis's grandfather Jack Lavin was steward of the Irish Club in Station Road, Stanley, now called the Hibernian Club. Dennis first stood for Council in 1979 as an Independent, and was beaten by just six votes. Later he joined the Labour Party and was elected for the South Moor Ward in 1999, then for Annfield Plain Ward in 2003 after a boundary change.

*Cllr Dennis Lavin (right) presenting a cheque for £1,500 from the Members Initiative Fund to Ernest Wilson, Chairman of Oxhill Youth Club management committee in 2008 for security lighting at the club. This is typical for all Council Members who each have an allocation from the Fund to use in their ward (DL)*

*Carl Christer*

## Carl Christer (Labour)

Many councillors take on roles far beyond their basic responsibilities as a ward member, not just within the Council, but in the wider community. One such example is Labour's Carl Christer. His current (2008) and recent positions include: Executive Member & Community Safety Portfolio holder; Branch Chair, Public & Commercial Services (PCS) Union; previously national Chair of the PCS Regional Development Agencies Co-ordinating committee & a TUC Northern Regional Council Member. As Housing portfolio holder 2004/05, chaired the Council's Housing Stock Large Scale Voluntary Transfer Steering Group. Board Chairman, Derwentside Homes Ltd; School Governor, Annfield Plain Primary School, 2001/03; Annfield Plain community appraisal steering group 2001/03: Executive member, Annfield Plain Community Partnership 2003/08 (Secretary 2003/05); Chairman, Annfield Plain Branch Labour Party 2002/date; North Durham Constituency Labour Party: Executive 2002/08, Youth Officer 2002/04, Membership Officer 2006/07; Derwentside Domestic Violence Forum Management Committee 2006/07.

*Pictures (right)*
*1 River Derwent (YG)*
*2 Shotley Bridge (YG)*
*3 Lanchester Church (CFW)*
*4 Sheep may safely graze (CFW)*
*5 Gibside*
*6 Gill Bridge*
*7 The Grove Heaps*
*8 Woods nr Allensford*
*9 Oakey Park, Stanley (AT)*
*10 St Cuthberts Chapel, Ushaw College (YG)*
*11 Harperley Heath*
*12 Burnhope War Memorial (CFW)*

13 Middle Street, Consett (CFW)
14 Red Menace (MC)
15 St James Church, Burnopfield (CFW)
16 Ushaw College (YG)
17 Civic Parade 2008 (CFW)
18 Heaps in Winter
19 South Moor Banner (JH)
20 Winter view nr Satley (CFW)

# Chapter Eight
# Partnerships

*DurhamNet, Infonet; Derwentside Homes, Video Pods, Council still involved, Careline; Leisureworks, Stanley Blues Festival, Lamplight Arts Centre; Smiling Dave, Charlie's Angels; Economic Development; Regeneration; Community Safety; Revenues & Benefits; Land & Property; Derwentside Training; Procurement; You can get the Staff; Looking after the Money; Organisation & Administration; On the Lighter Side.*

*Alan Hodgson, DurhamNet boss*

## DurhamNet

Bringing Broadband to Derwentside sooner than any other district took foresight and determination, but the Council could not have achieved it on its own. Perhaps the most significant partnership entered into by the Council was DurhamNet, with Durham County Council. DurhamNet, which went on to provide internet services across the region, had its beginnings in 1995 when DDC did a deal with Telewest to link up the district with their base in Team Valley, Gateshead, and bring Broadband to the area. A £1m grant from the RDC took the network into Langley Park, Lanchester, Leadgate, Craghead and Burnhope at a total cost of £4m. The Stanley Infonet became the Derwentside Infonet, 27km of fibre optics, launched by welfare minister Frank Field MP in 1998.

DurhamNet eventually provided internet facilities in all schools in County Durham, plus libraries and hundreds of community and voluntary groups. Derwentside inspired this project, designed to meet the needs of the technology revolution for people throughout the district, initially via a partnership proposal with all seven district councils in the county, plus the county council. The result was a partnership between Derwentside and Durham County Council. Apparently, the other six district councils thought it was too risky. They were asked to put up £50,000 each but declined. DurhamNet has now been networked region-wide and is contributing a "profit" of £700,000 to the General Fund each year. The operation grew dramatically as the network expanded. By 2008, DurhamNet was providing internet services to 750+ Schools in Northumberland, Durham, Gateshead and Sunderland, 70+ community venues, 110+ businesses – including 10 business centres, 300+ homes in the AB@H Project, 300+ remote users, home workers and support staff, ten local authorities, and NHS Trusts. In all DurhamNet supported more than 1,500 sites across the North East with over

200,000 users. DurhamNet brought high quality ICT jobs to the area. In its first ten years, the number of staff employed within the organisation rose from nine to 34 and consistently offered apprenticeships to young people. Derwentside's pioneering success stirred interest in government and European circles. The video conferencing facility attracted interest from Germany, Italy and Spain as well as from the NHS, and DurhamNet has advised the British cabinet. "Our initiative has had far-reaching, knock-on effects," said Deputy Leader Cllr Malone. Alan Hodgson and his team have given presentations in Durham, London and Brussels. To take advantage of European funding, DurhamNet has found partners in Italy, Germany, Portugal, France, Spain and the Czech Republic.

By 2006 the CCTV system had been extended throughout the District. There were 22 local partnerships across the Council's 22 wards, each involving local people to determine their own priorities and help bring about improvements. There were ethnic focus groups, including one for Japanese mothers. 615 dogs had been micro-chipped, and 406 new houses built – 73% on brownfield sites. Overall crime rates were down to 84.5 per thousand population, compared with 89.2 in County Durham and 117.4 in England as a whole. Life expectancy in Derwentside was still less than the national average, 75.5 years for men (76.6 national) and 79.5 for women (80.09 national). Long-term sickness and economically inactive rates were still higher than national figures, but in all cases the gaps were closing.

*DurhamNet offices, Rivergreen Centre, Aykley Heads, Durham*

**Derwentside ICT**
Leading In Europe

## Derwentside Homes

Monday 4th December 2006 was much like any other Monday, but the day marked a fundamental change for thousands of Council tenants – they had a new landlord. On that day, 6,840 Council houses, including 2,800 elderly persons bungalows and flats, were transferred from the Council to Derwentside Homes. This meant the not-for-profit housing organisation replaced Derwentside Council as the biggest landlord in the district. A large majority of tenants had voted for the change. Prior to the ballot vote, DDC Chief Executive Mike Clark wrote to every Council tenant: 'the Council has come to the conclusion that the only way to provide good quality housing for all its tenants and overcome its housing problems is to transfer all the Council's homes to a newly created housing association, Derwentside Homes Ltd.' Derwentside Homes would be able to borrow and invest £117m for improvements to homes and services, including expenditure of around £67m of this for repairs, modernisations and improvements by the end of 2011, and £15m on home improvements for the elderly in its first five years. Rents would be kept at affordable levels in accordance with government policy and therefore would be no different from rents charged by the Council. The "right to buy" would be retained for transferring tenants and Housing Benefit would not be affected.

The LSVT (large scale voluntary transfer) took place in Derwentside, as in many other local authorities, primarily because councils were restricted on how much money they could borrow to finance improvements to their houses. Thousands of new homes built after WW2 all needed upgrading at around the same time. With strict limits on PSBR (public spending borrowing requirement) local councils like Derwentside simply could not raise the cash to bring their houses up to date. Councils also faced restrictions on how they could use "capital receipts", such as the money they received from the sale of Council houses under the right to buy. No such restrictions apply to housing associations, so the transfer made sense. In the event, Derwentside's Council tenants agreed to the transfer by a large margin. 66% of tenants took part in the ballot in December 2005, 76% voting "yes". Mike Clark: 'the vote means the Council's homes are on course to

*Geraldine Wilcox, chief executive, Derwentside Homes (DH)*

*Derwentside Homes in action (below)*
*1 Roofers*
*2 Insulation*
*3 Fitting new bathrooms*
*4 Fitting new kitchens*

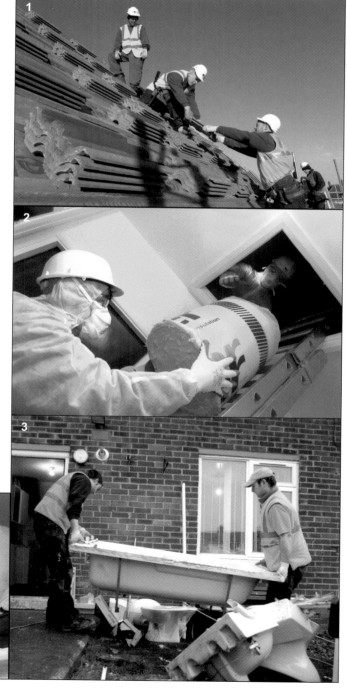

transfer next year, unlocking £117m investment in repairs and improvements to tenants' homes in the first 13 years after transfer'.

On taking over, Derwentside Homes – motto "affordable, attractive homes in strong, safe communities where everyone is valued" - promised that by 2011 all their homes would meet the government's "Decent Homes" standard, and more than 2,000 homes would get new fitted kitchens, bathrooms, doors, windows, central heating and be fully rewired. In its first two years the company spent over £26m improving homes, and said they would spend three times as much on home improvements as DDC could have done up to 2010/11. A key priority for Derwentside Homes was to deliver the promises made to tenants prior to the transfer ballot. As well as significant investment to upgrade tenants homes, the company promised to improve services, including those for the elderly - half their tenants were now over pensionable age – and improve the quality of life for tenants by working with key partners to tackle anti-social behaviour, and through community initiatives to help support neighbourhoods. The company launched its Handy Van service to help older tenants with minor household jobs such as fitting curtain rails and shelves, and extended the free gardening service to over 300 elderly and disabled tenants. DH kept its promise to invest in new aids and adaptations in tenants' homes by spending £500,000 a year and completing over 500 adaptations.

*Partnership is a serious business for Council Leader Alex Watson*

## Video Pods

Following extensive consultation with tenants, Derwentside Homes restructured its housing services by closing under-utilized neighbourhood offices to enable the creation of a telephone and estate-based service that tenants wanted. In 2009 DH planned to pilot a Tele Talk project in partnership with DDC and DCC, aimed at improving customer access to services through strategically-placed video pods. These enable customers to contact the company's customer service centre through a touch-screen TV and see who they are speaking with via the webcam, as well as allowing them to input application forms direct. Derwentside Homes is monitored and regulated by the Tenant Services Authority. This was previously done by the Housing Corporation who in July 2008 awarded DH three "green lights", the highest classification possible for meeting standards in financial viability, good governance and management. DH was one of seven major housing providers across the North East in the Spirit Development Partnership, and aimed to build at least 50 new homes for affordable rent and/or low-cost home ownership - market conditions permitting - in Derwentside by 2010. In 2008 DH had 210 employees, including skilled tradespeople, and had recruited two trainee quantity surveyors and five trade apprentices. At the end of 2008, Chief Executive Geraldine Wilcox said: "Derwentside Homes has got off to a good start". Geraldine was previously Assistant Chief Executive of the Tees Valley Housing Group. She graduated from Newcastle University with a degree in social administration and had worked in the housing field ever since. The DH board of 15 members: five Council nominees (Carl Christer, Olga Milburn, David Llewellyn, Bob Alderson, Watts Stelling), five Tenant Board Members (Ann Manley, Glynis Benson, Jill Te-Aho, Ann Parker, Derek Robson); five Independent Members: (Karen Stoker, Amy Redpath, Denise Taylor, Mark Davies, Steve Errington).

## Council still involved

The transfer of all its Council houses to Derwentside Homes still left Derwentside Council with considerable responsibilities for housing, particularly with regard to the homeless. The Council had an arrangement with DH to have emergency accommodation available at all times. Families can be made homeless for any number of reasons, such as fire and flood, as well as the less sudden but equally traumatic circumstances such as having their home repossessed. At such time the Council's experienced housing staff were on hand to give help and advice. The Council retained its broader role in allocating home improvement grants, dealing with private landlords and private developers. Choice Based Lettings was a way of allocating housing through choice, giving applicants a greater say. Durham Key Options is the name of the partnership developing Choice Based Letting for County Durham. Derwentside Homes maintains and administers a housing register for rented housing, and acted as agent for DDC in maintaining the Council's housing waiting list.

"Our aim is to ensure a balance of all different types of housing, including affordable homes," said Kath Heathcote, the Council's Head of Housing. Based at the old Stanley UDC offices in Front Street, Kath headed a staff of 25 who were still the first port of call for people with housing problems. Originally from Leicestershire, Kath studied psychology and economics at Sunderland Poly and Durham University. Her first job was as a youth worker with the Banks of the Wear organisation, which local MP Hilary Armstrong had a hand in starting. She moved on to work for Durham County Council, with special responsibilities for Derwentside, before joining DDC in 2005. Mary Forster had worked in the DDC Housing Department for nearly thirty years and Shirley Robinson for nearly twenty. They had seen profound changes in the service in their time, not least with record keeping. When they first started, everything was recorded by hand in huge, leather-bound ledgers. Every Monday night the books had to be balanced, and this led to staff often having to work late. Over the years, "right to buy" and demolitions reduced the number of Council houses in the district from 14,500 to 8,000. OAP bungalows were much in demand, and both staff and residents wanting a bungalow would keep a close eye on the obituary columns in the local paper. If it said the dear departed was husband or wife of their "late" wife or husband, there would be a rush of applications for that particular bungalow. One elderly gentleman regularly used to come into the Council offices in his "mourning suit." He was always on his way to or from a funeral, and his handkerchief was often brought out as he dabbed the tears from his eyes to reinforce the effect. People could wait anything from eight to twelve years before getting a bungalow. Now, youngsters as young as sixteen could apply for their own accommodation, instead of "living in" with parents for several years as used to be the norm.

Council clerk Gilbert Green spent many hours in long and tedious Planning Committee meetings, so to keep his concentration, he started to record the funny and peculiar things that councillors would say from time to time. Over the years, his record of the off-beat ran to scores of pages.

*The Clock at Potts' big store in Middle Street, Consett, never told the right time. This gave rise to the saying "as much use as Potts's Clock." When Mr Potts died, the clock stopped, giving rise to the saying "you're like Potts' clock, you've stopped!" Potts' Clock was mounted on a massive cast-iron frame. Its gilt-decorated dial was 3ft in diameter. By coincidence, the Potts family of clock-makers originated in the North East and specialised in making turret clocks for churches and public buildings, so they may well have made Potts' Clock.*

## Careline

One legacy DDC planned to leave by the end of March 2009 was to have all 3,500 elderly Council house residents wearing a pendant or wrist alarm so that they could summon help immediately in an emergency such as a fall. These were to replace the pull-cords which clearly had their limitations, and also cost more to install and maintain. The Careline system, introduced in 1991, had already undergone two big changes. Derwentside Homes had taken over most of the Council's houses, and since May 2007 the control centre had been run by Sedgefield Council on behalf of themselves, Wear Valley, Teesdale and DDC, yet another example of local councils doing things jointly and so saving Council taxpayers' money. Lee Spraggon, Head of System Integration, was responsible for 17 staff, including Careline Operations Manager Bernie Malone. In 2008, DDC was directly responsible for seven residential courts. Wardens, based at Morrison Busty, were available for emergencies 24 hours a day, as well as visiting their elderly charges on a rota basis to check on their welfare.

Careline was the District Council's Community Alarm and Mobile Warden Service, linked to all older person's bungalows. Every new tenant was visited and the service explained. Careline was also available to Council tenants living in general needs housing, owner-occupiers, Housing Association tenants, and people living in private rented accommodation. Anyone who felt they were vulnerable or at risk for whatever reason, regardless of their age, could be linked to the service. Derwentside Careline was easy to use. In most older person bungalows and sheltered flats it was operated by means of a pull cord, although eventually these were to be phased out and all Careline tenants given a pendant or wrist alarm which links to Careline via a telephone line. The service was available 24 hours a day, seven days a week. Tenants could use the service if they felt unwell, anxious or needed reassurance, if they experienced problems with vandals, prowlers or suspected bogus callers, or – most importantly – if they fell and needed assistance. Callers were answered by a Control Centre Operator who then took the necessary action, such as sending out a Mobile Warden, or calling the emergency services. In 2008/09, Careline completed 2,500 visits per month, responding to an average of 500 emergencies and 2,000 welfare visits. "What other service gives so many people the confidence to live safely and happily in their own homes?" asked Council Leader Alex Watson.

*Proud man – boxer Glenn McCrory shows his world championship belt to Council Chairman Cllr Mary Armstrong.*

## Leisureworks

In 2008 the Council's leisure services were being run by Leisureworks, an independent trust. The change from direct Council control to a trust was controversial, but Council Leader Alex Watson insisted the move gave the public a better service as well as saving cost to the Council taxpayers. The Council's Leisure Department, incorporating parks, swimming baths and sports centres, had been set up in 1989. It took on the unusual if not unique role in promoting local boxer Glenn McCrory's world title fight at the Louisa Centre, Stanley, on 3rd June 1989. Another task was to create and manage a large display at the 157-day National Garden Festival at Gateshead, May to October 1990. The Derwentside garden featured a water fountain sword garden,

showing the district's connection with the swordmakers of Shotley Bridge. It also included a Victorian Bandstand, borrowed from the Beamish Museum, with live performers every day. Some 600,000 people attended the Festival.

Derwentside Leisure Ltd, a not-for-profit organisation, was launched on the 5th July 1999. Some years later, it was decided another change was needed and Leisureworks (the Derwentside Trust for Sports and the Arts) was launched on 1st June 2007 with Paul Fiddeman as Chairman and Lindsay Tuck as Chief Executive. Leisureworks Arts Development Manager Martin Weston joined DDC in 1989, shortly after a Council re-structure which had brought together a

*Stanley Blues Festival*

number of arts, sports and recreation facilities together as a Leisure Services Department. Weston was the Council's first Arts Development Officer. This new initiative was driven by some newly-elected members and supported by the Regional Arts Board, Northern Arts. A generous budget from the Council, supplemented by Northern Arts grant, resulted in a programme featuring new concerts and professional theatre and dance performances, artist-in-residence projects with local schools, a dance and music residency for adults with learning difficulties, holiday activity workshops, and a grants scheme to support arts, community and voluntary organisations. When the arts grants budget was wound up in March 2002, the Council had provided grants to over 250 organisations across the district.

## Stanley Blues Festival

The early 1990s saw the start of new outdoor festivals and events, the two biggest being Allensford Show and the Stanley Blues Festival. The Allensford Show became a three day Music Festival, featuring a range of music, dance and other performance, displays, stalls and a craft marquee. It included the Allensford Rock and Roots Festival, produced by Northern Recording Ltd. Allensford ran from 1992 to 2000, and in 1999 was attended by over 12,000 people. The Stanley Blues Festival was programmed and promoted by Northern Recording with Council support from 1993 to 2004. For the next three years it ran as an independent festival owned and managed by Stanley Blues Ltd with financial support from the Council and others. At its peak the Blues Festival attracted approximately 15,000 people. In its 15 years, Stanley Blues Festival exploded from an afternoon session which attracted 400 people to become the most popular blues event in the region. Over the years, headline bands included Chicken Shack, Otis Grand, Zoot Money, Wilco Johnson, Mick Taylor R&B Allstars, Paul Lamb & the Kingsnakes and Peter Green Splinter Group who in 2002 played to the Festival's biggest ever audience of 15,000 people. In 2005 the attendance was 12,000, still a big audience. Other stars who played Stanley included former Rolling Stone Mick Taylor, ex-Fleetwood Mac guitarist Peter Green, The Blues Band, Stan Webb, the Yardbirds, the Climax Blues Band and former Dr Feelgood guitarist Wilko Johnson.

*Rock'n'Roots Festival, Allensford Park 1999. An appreciative audience.*

*Lamplight Arts Centre (AT)*

opening event on 13th July 2002. This arts programme has featured collaboration with Mad Alice Theatre Company with four outdoor Shakespeare productions; annual brass band concerts and other music events featuring rock, world and classical music; and involvement in a range of events, small and large. On 1st June 2007 arts development along with other Council Leisure services was transferred to Leisureworks, the new Derwentside Trust For Sport & The Arts. A new chapter had begun. Also, the Hobson Golf Club has transferred to the club members, and DDC has transferred a large area of land at South Moor to the Great North Forest, taken over by GroundWork to be developed into a nature reserve.

### Lamplight Arts Centre

Weston's appointment unfortunately coincided with the public controversy around a perceived threat to Stanley Civic Hall. Following some rather uncomfortable public meetings, the Council agreed to invest in the building, and a major refurbishment was carried out in 1990/91. This saw greatly improved technical facilities, new tiered "bleacher" seating in the auditorium, full re-decoration throughout and other improvements. Another very important feature of the work in the mid-1990s onwards was the support the Council was able to provide to new professional and community arts organisations which set up in the district - Theatre Cap-A-Pie, Busy Ape Arts, The Cobweb Orchestra. SNUG (Special Needs Unity Group), creating opportunities and social inclusion for people with learning disabilities, was formed. The Council also supported Kalapremi, a locally-based charity which promoted and celebrated the arts and culture of India and South Asia.

In recent years there has been a greater emphasis on formal partnership working. Major projects have included the complete modernisation and upgrading of the Empire Theatre (2002-03); further investment in Stanley Civic Hall, and its re-naming in 2002 as The Lamplight Arts Centre; and a substantial new outdoor arts programme based in Blackhill & Consett Park, following the restoration of the park and subsequent

### Smiling Dave

When Dave Barratt first took over as manager of Consett Civic Hall in 1987, it was clear this facility – built as an extension to the Civic Centre in Medomsley Road – was underused. The Council introduced a profit-sharing scheme and the hall really took off with functions most days of the week. Takings doubled in the first year alone. Barratt was working 80-90 hours a week, making him one of the Council's highest earners. Every day the Hall Manager would be there, resplendent in his dickie bow and dinner jacket, to make sure everything ran smoothly. Barratt, who originally worked as a builder, had always been an entertainer. He played drums in his own three- or four-piece band at the pub he ran, the "Back o' the Shaft" at Leadgate. Barratt decided to retire in 2001 but was soon called back as Bar Manager. In 2008 Barratt was still running the hall on behalf of Five Star Catering who hold the lease. By 2009 the long-term future of the hall was in doubt, as it was looking its age and was in need of refurbishment - a decision for the new Durham County Council.

*Ruth Reed (on left) with her Civic Hall staff, Ann D'Northwood next to her (RH)*

*"Smiling Dave" – Civic Hall Manager Dave Barratt*

*InPrint, opening new production centre at Hownsgill Trading Estate in 2006, Council Leaders Alex Watson (Derwentside) & Fraser Reynolds (Durham City) to the fore. (IP)*

## Charlie's Angels

The story of InPrint is the story of Charlie Stephenson. Born in Shotley Bridge, Charlie went to Benfieldside School before starting a five-year apprenticeship with local printers Ramsden Williams whose printing works was in the centre of Consett. Ramsden Williams published the much-loved local newspaper the Consett Guardian, but in 1968 he had sold out to the Westminster Press who incorporated the Guardian into the Durham Advertiser series. Having promised Westminster Press not to publish a rival newspaper, there was nothing to stop Williams printing one for another publisher. At Williams from 1970, Charlie worked on the Consett Post, the town's first free newspaper, one of six local free papers published by Durham Free Press and printed by Williams. In December 1978 Charlie was appointed Print Manager with Derwentside Council. 'There was just me and four girls, who naturally got to be called "Charlie's Angels"', he recalled with a grin, 'we printed minutes, committee reports, agendas and the civic lottery tickets'.

It was clear to Charlie that the Council's printing machinery was very much under-used, so he looked around for ways of bringing in more business to his small department and making better use of the

equipment. Experienced litho operator David Barker, who had learned his trade with Blackhill print firm Andrew Douglas , was brought in as temporary maternity cover – one of "Charlie's Angels" was expecting. David proved so useful he was kept on as a permanent employee until his retirement in 2006. As the DDC print unit gained more and more business from neighbouring local councils, new machinery was bought and the staff expanded to eleven. In 2006 Derwentside went into partnership with City of Durham Council to provide a shared servce design and print facility  under the name InPrint, now based in refurbished premises on the Hownsgill Trading Estate which incorporates a design studio. As well as high-volume digital printing of all kinds, InPrint also undertake direct mail operations. 'InPrint is totally self-funding,' said Charlie, 'regular benchmarking proves we are cheaper than a commercial equivalent.  Last year our turn over was just under a million pounds with 40% of the surplusses being retained for development and the balance going straight back to the two councils'.

*Deputy Chief Executive's Department (l-r): Peter McDowell (Head of Economic & Community Development), Darren Knowd (Head of Corporate Procurement), John Pearson (Deputy Chief Executive), Lisa Wall (PA), Ian Ferguson (Head of Revenues & Benefits), Gerard Darby (Head of Land & Property) (CFW)*

## Economic Development

The Council has a strong history of working in partnership to promote business and job creation. This includes a long-standing partnership with DIDA and its predecessor British Steel Industry but the Council has worked closely with other organisations in delivering a range of initiatives that have helped reduce Derwentside's unemployment rate to the national average – a remarkable achievement given the extraordinarily high levels experienced during the 1980s. This work has included the development of over 150,000 sq. ft. of new office and modern production "Business Centre" space in Consett and Stanley that has helped create scores of new businesses and hundreds of new jobs. One of the Council's most important partnership initiatives in recent years was with Easington, Sedgefield and Wear Valley District Councils. A joint bid was submitted for "Local Enterprise Growth Initiative" funding from the Government. Having been short-listed, a joint presentation in London by John Pearson of Derwentside and Richard Prisk of Easington to a "Dragons' Den" panel of business people and civil servants secured an offer in early 2006 of £30 million of Government funding over a ten year period to promote enterprise and economic development in the most deprived parts of the four Districts.

One of the initiatives that helped to win this Government funding was further development of the Council's "Emerge" imitative that has helped over 150 new businesses to start up and grow in Derwentside. This initiative provides a flexible package of advice and funding linked to business ICT development and has been driven forward by Peter McDowell, the Council's Head of Economic Development, and his Principal Development Officer, Ross Bullerwell. Apart from being a key part of the Local Enterprise Growth Initiative, Emerge has won regional and national recognition for its success in substantially increasing the rate of business start-ups in Derwentside and increasing the levels of employment of Derwentside residents to above the national average.

## Regeneration

Another important part of the Council's Economic and Community Development Division is the Regeneration Team led by Marie Moore. This team has been instrumental in helping to establish and develop 22 Community Partnerships in Derwentside, covering all of the District's electoral Wards. These Partnerships have brought together local residents and community groups to create Local Visions, develop and deliver local projects and secure funding from the Lottery, Trusts and other sources to support area regeneration. Over £15 million has been secured from Lottery Funding alone to assist social and economic regeneration projects across Derwentside. The Regeneration Team has also led on developing Single Regeneration Budget bids for both the Consett and Stanley areas. These "SRB" Programmes have secured some £50 million of Government and other funding to support local regeneration, managed by partnerships between the public, private and voluntary sectors.

The Team has also had a key role in raising and managing a range of other funding, winning £3.5

million in resources to establish the Green Corridor Neighbourhood Management Pathfinder, successfully managing £8 million of Neighbourhood Renewal Fund allocations from the Government, successfully bidding for £1 million in Rural Challenge funding to support ICT development in Derwentside, Wear Valley and Teesdale Districts and winning well over £20 million in other European and Government regeneration grants.

## Community Safety

The Council has worked in partnership with the Police, the Fire Service and the Primary Care Trust for many years and was one of the founder Members of the Derwentside Community Safety Partnership that has helped to make Derwentside one of the safest communities in the country. The Council's work in this field has included substantial commitments to creating a state-of-the-art CCTV network, helping vulnerable households to install additional security measures, rapid responses to fly tipping and graffiti and supporting measures to reduce Domestic Violence and Anti-Social Behaviour.

## Revenues & Benefits

The Council's Revenue and Benefits Division is one of its key areas of interface with the public. This includes the collection of Council Tax and Non-Domestic Rates as well as payment of Housing and other benefits. This involves dealing with thousands of customers and managing millions of pounds. Some ten years ago it was recognised that the service needed to be improved in order to meet the expectations of both the Council and its customers. Significant changes were introduced. The Council's current Head of Revenues and Benefits, Ian Ferguson, was recruited in 2003 and, under his management, the Team has achieved national recognition for its work and won several awards, the most recent one being in 2008, when it won an Institute of Revenues Rating and Valuation Performance Award for working in partnership to introduce a Voice Risk Analysis system to speed the processing and assessment of Benefit claims. This has involved working with Sedgefield, Chester-le-Street and Durham City Councils on the sharing of systems and processes, as well as working with private sector suppliers and local organisations.

## Land & Property

The Land and Property Division manages a substantial estate on behalf of the Council and engages with a range of organisations from the public, private and community sectors in seeking to optimise use of the Council's assets. In recent years a major part of the Division's work, under Head of Land and Property Gerard Darby, has been reviewing the Council's asset portfolio and disposing of, or transferring, those that are either surplus to requirements or can be better utilised or developed by other organisations. This has included transfers of land and property to Derwentside Homes and supporting the creation of Leisureworks to manage the Council's Sports and Arts Centres. The disposal of surplus assets, largely for housing development, has had

the twin benefits of generating capital for the Council to re-investment in local infrastructure and new facilities as well as seeing the development of hundreds of new homes to accommodate new families, increase local spending and consequently help to sustain and grow local services and jobs.

When Council Leader Joe Rhind gave a helping hand to the Consett Junior Brass Band, there was an unexpected spin-off for his family. "The band was invited to visit our German twin town, but was short of cash. So, instead of us going by plane, we went by coach and invited the band to come with us," he said Joe's son Alistair, whose building & plastering business was suffering along with many others at the time, was asked by a German friend to take his tools with him. In true "Auf Wiedersehen" fashion, Joe found work, married a German girl and settled over there.

*Agresso, the Council's new finance system, went "live" on 25th November 2003.*

The Hownsgill Viaduct, known as the Gill Bridge, was built in 1856 to cross the ravine. It was designed by Thomas Bouch and built by John Anderson. Sailors were employed to erect the scaffolding. 2,655,000 bricks were used, supplied by Peases of Crook at £1.65 per thousand.

*At the Council's annual meeting on 22nd May 1985, Police Sergeant Harry Stephenson and Constable Henry Moses were presented with Royal Humane Society Testimonials for their attempt to save a life at Causey Arch on 3rd October 1984.*

Population Figures: 1947 - 100,130; 1974 - 91,478; 1981 - 86,995 ; 1991 - 86,046; 2001 - 85,065; 2006 - 86,500.

*The only toilet in the old Empire Theatre was right behind the stage, so it could not be used during performances – the audience would have heard the flush.*

The New Stanley Civic Restaurant was opened by Cllr Mrs E Brass on 5th May 1949. It closed after only 18 months and was taken over by the Council Surveyors and Housing Departments.

*After WWI, the five Reed brothers joined with Harrison and Richardson to jointly run Venture and Reed Brothers Ltd. This became Venture Transport Ltd in 1938.*

In 1956 Consett entered a team of local artistes to compete in the BBC's Top Town competition, winning the North regional final in Blackpool.

*Apprentice class.*

*Training can be fun*

### Derwentside Training

Derwentside Training, based at Consett Business Park in Villa Real, was founded in 1981 by Derwentside District Council to support the regeneration of Derwentside after the closure of Consett's British Steel Works. It has developed and run many youth and adult training schemes, working with the Learning and Skills Council, Jobcentre Plus, local employers, residents, voluntary organisations and further education establishments to provide educational and work-based training and is a highly successful training provider. Over the years the organisation has successfully developed many youth and adult training schemes working with local employers, residents and community associations to provide educational and work based training, helping individuals in the Derwentside area to access employment or further training.

At midnight on Friday 18th December 1959, Dr Barbara Moore, who had started a walking craze, passed through Castleside on her attempted marathon walk from Edinburgh to London.

*House builders Barratt angered residents when it sent in contractors to cut up a giant crucible used in the smelting process that had stood on the Genesis site for more than 120 years. It looked into hiring a crane to move it but found it would cost about £220,000, so instead it agreed to clean and mount the remaining, smaller crucible at a cost of more than £20,000.*

One initiative that failed to flourish was the education enterprise initiative. "Derwentside Council took a lead from the government and set up a centre on the Tanfield Estate," Cllr Llewellyn explained, "a government minister came to open it, and there were three to four thousand visits a year by children using the facility. But government funding dried up and the education authority did not give it sufficient support, so after four years it had to close."

### Procurement

Procurement is just a fancy word for buying stuff. Every Council spends millions each year buying what it needs, from paper clips to bin wagons. It makes sense to shop around and buy in bulk, with consequent savings for that Very Important Person, the Council Taxpayer. It makes even more sense for small, local councils in the same area to band together and order materials and equipment jointly, making even more savings for the VIP Council Taxpayer. So Derwentside, Chester le Street and Sedgefield Councils pooled their resources to boost their buying power. The man in charge of this process was Head of Procurement Darren Knowd, who in 2008 was also heading up the county-wide procurement team paving the way for the Durham unitary authority to take over on 1st April 2009. Knowd, described by Cllr Michael Malone at a conference in Gateshead's Hilton Hotel as 'the best thing to happen to Derwentside in procurement terms', was only a recent recruit to local government, joining DDC in 2005 after a career in automotive industry purchasing with General Motors Liverpool and Nissan Europe. The tie-up between Nissan and French car manufacturers Renault took Knowd to Paris for a two-year stint which he endured with his customary stoicism, or so he claimed. Darren is one of many people who have moved into the area who have found the lifestyle very much to their liking, as does his wife Lisa who is also from Merseyside. 'The quality of life is fantastic, we have stability and good educational prospects for our two children who were both born in Durham,' was his verdict.

### You can get the Staff

Any council is a partnership between councillors and staff, and Derwentside Council members have always taken great pleasure in congratulating long-serving Council employees. On 5th May 1987 14 members of staff, each with 38-47 years service, were given long service awards. In 1990 long service awards were given to 22 council employees, each with 30-37 years service. In 2001 Chairman Les Vaux presented engraved wrist watches for 25 years' service to Allison East, Richard Huggins, Paul Robson and Christopher Robb. Next year Cllr Vaux presented watches for 25 years service to Sandra Stewart, Malcolm Hole, Paul Roscoe, Williams

*Darren Knowd (Head of Corporate Procurement) with his key staff Ian Williams (left) and Kelly Stewart (CFW)*

1967, and another Chargehand Mason, David Byers, since 1969. Clearly, doing a hard physical job outdoors in all weathers is good for the constitution – if it doesn't kill you first. Other long-serving staff had transferred to other organizations such as Derwentside Homes and DurhamNet.

The 26-strong "roll of honour": John Appleby (street cleaning operative), Ronald Bennison (highways operative), David Byers (chargehand street mason), Peter Cain (facilities manager), Raymond Chetter (chargehand street mason), Malcolm Clark (building technician), Graham Davison (senior environmental health officer), Austin Dial (gardener), William Eccles (street cleaning operative), David Errington (senior environmental health officer) Keith Errington (public protection manager), Heather Hansom (InPrint client support officer), Austin Hodgson (tractor driver), Richard Huggins (allotment & service development officer), Malcolm Jefferson (highways inspector), William Johnston (mechanical sweeper driver), Peter Reynolds (Director of Environmental Services), John Shepherd (Deputy Head, General Services), John Snaith (chargehand highways operative), George Stanyer (kerblayer), Rennie Turnbull (highways operative), Alan Turner (mechanical sweeper driver), Henry Vaux (highway maintenance manager), Keith Walker (Rapid Response driver), Alan Ward (benefits officer), Trevor Watson (engineering assistant).

Gerrans, James R Lee and John Watson. Later that year new Council Chairman Cllr David Llewellyn presented personally engraved wrist watches for 25 years service to: Gordon Peel, Mike Bonser, Paul Donkin, Leta Dickson and Billy Wilkinson. In all that year, 22 employees got personally engraved wrist watches for 25 years of service – over 500 years in total! In 2004 it was the turn of Chairman Cllr Denise Bennett to present watches to Charlie Stephenson, Alan Parker and Edward Panting. In 2005, 25-year awards went to Peter Alderson, Malcolm Allaker, George Cameron, Joseph Dawson, Desmond Gowland, David Hancock, Joseph McGuigan, David O'Neill, Paul Quarzi, Geoffrey Smith, Doreen Burdon, Grethe Bell, Mary Forster, Susan Gettings, Pamela Harrison, Linda Murphy and June White.

Stan Green and Gilbert Green – no relation - had 80 years of Council service between them. Stan Green retired as Chief Administrator in 1992 after sixteen years with DDC and a lifetime, 41 years, in local government. He started with Consett UDC as a 16-year old Clerical Assistant and had 16 years there. Stan then worked for Whickham UDC and Gateshead Borough before returning to what was now Derwentside Council in 1976. Born in Leadgate, Gilbert Green spent the whole of his working life, 39 years, with Consett UDC and Derwentside DC. Starting as a 15-year old Junior Clerk, he retired in 1993 as Principal Administrator and Principal Licensing Officer in the Environmental Services Department.

**Long & Loyal Service**
No fewer than twenty-six staff who joined Derwentside Council in 1974 were still there in 2009. Tractor driver and Leadgate lad Austin Hodgson started work with Consett UDC in 1963 as a 15-year old apprentice. He moved on to grass cutting before becoming a tractor driver, and job he did for the next 35 years, completing 45 years' service and beyond. Chargehand Mason Raymond Chetter had been in the employ of the local Council since 1966, street cleaner John Appleby since

**Looking after the money**
Dave Watson, the Council's Head of Financial Services, was born and brought up in Hexham. He left school at 18 to start work as a Trainee Accountant with a local firm, later getting a job with Tynedale District Council as he gained more qualifications. He joined Derwentside Council in 1987 as Accountancy Assistant and worked his way up to become Head of Finance in January 2007. Dave's first boss at Derwentside was Brian Shields, who was followed in turn as Treasurer by Keith Robinson and then Alan Smith. 'Shields had his finger on the pulse, he knew every aspect of finance," said Dave, 'but Alan Smith was my mentor. I was his Accountancy Manager and took over from him when he went to Sedgefield Council'. In the changeover year 2008/2009 before the new County unitary authority was to take over from Durham's seven district councils, Smith was the lead officer on the county's Finance Working Party which had the unenviable task of amalgamating the budgets of eight separate councils. Watson's department now covered accountancy, audit, risk & insurance. revenues and benefits came under Deputy Chief Executive John Pearson.

'When I first started, accounts were still being recorded by hand in huge ledgers,' recalled Dave, 'now most

1 Building inspector Steve Elder checking traffic noise.
2 Paddling Pool, Allendale Park (IP)
3 Industrial pollution, Elm Park Farm outfall 1987
4 Pollution, Howden Burn 1983
5 Issuing Bus Passes
6 Water sampling
7 Environmental Health Officer Keith Errington checking temperatures.
8 Friendly Reception (l-r): Grethe Belle, Anthony Page, Pat Mein, Vivien Brame (CFW)
9 Organisational Development (l-r): Iain Herdman, Lesley Allison, Christine Jarvis, Ian Jones (Head of Department), Wendy Nichol, Alison Cranney, Graeme Smith (CFW)
10 Mountsett Crematorium staff (l-r): Michael Chipperfield, Ian Staplin (Supervisor), Neil McCrory, Neil Baker.
11 How can we help? (CFW)
12 Planning Department staff, December 2008 (CFW)
13 45 years service - tractor driver Austin Hodgson, who started work as a 15-year old with Consett UDC in 1963 (CFW)

transactions are done electronically and much less paper is used'. The decision of the Council to keep Derwentside's Council Tax rise to zero for the final four years of its existence gave Watson a major headache. 'With the budget being set in January, the previous July or August we would put up a position paper," he explained, 'we always got a long wish list from the spending departments of what they would like to do, and inevitably most of these were knocked back. At the end of the day, the budget had to balance'. With local councils having relatively little discretion on how they can spend their money – most of which is determined by government decisions – Watson rates the Member initiatives as a success. Each councillor was allocated £2,000 a year to spend on facilities for his/her ward. On top of that, the Council introduced an additional scheme of £20,000 a year in capital expenditure per councillor, decided by each set of ward councillors.

It hasn't been all plain sailing for DDC. In common with many local councils, Derwentside has sometimes had difficulty recruiting qualified staff in some areas. Where there was a shortage, richer councils could offer higher salaries than the agreed standard rates. In 1990 DDC found itself short of qualified accountancy staff, resulting in an adverse report from the District Auditor. This in turn led to a critical editorial in the North Echo. Susan Oliver, a qualified accountant, was looking for part-time work. She read the editorial, contacted Derwentside Council and completed a job application. She knew from her previous experience working for Durham County Council that they paid part-timers only at the lowest grade, regardless of qualifications. Not only was Susan taken on straight away by Derwentside, they paid her at the qualified rate, pro rata. But there was more. While working for a large county authority is largely remote from the public, at Derwentside Susan enjoyed being much closer to the people of the district she serves. 'It's nice to be dealing with things like grant applications, knowing something about them makes you feel more involved. It's a pleasure to come to work,' she said. Another reason why Susan stayed with DDC for all of nineteen years was the happy working relationships within a small team, most of whom have also been there for years. 'When there's a job needed to be done, we all pull together,' she said. Susan, full-time Principle Accountancy Assistant, is grateful to her first boss, Chief Accountant Catherine McCormick for her help when she first joined the Council staff.

*Pictures, left*
*1 Consett rail bridge, overlooking C2C cycle way (CFW)*
*2 Terris Novalis*
*3 Cycle Maze*
*4 Transformers, or Iron Robots (YG)*
*5 Beamish Short Horns (YG)*
*6 Hot metal carrier, cycle way nr Gill Bridge (CFW)*

*Salt Barn, Morrison Busty*

He stayed on to get his PhD, and then started work in the Economic Development Department of Newcastle City Council. He stayed there ten years before moving on to Gateshead as Head of Policy. He "came home" to Derwentside Council as Head of Corporate Strategy in 2001 before assuming his current role in 2004. Elliott's department covered policy and performance, customer services, licensing, printing and servicing councillors and Council meetings. The department administered such things as the youth project SPICE, Careline, town twinning and the Local Strategic Partnership. Elliott had two spells as the Council's Monitoring Officer and had responsibility for Public Health for four years, 2003-2007. During his time in charge of the Council's administration, Elliott has seen waiting times for telephone callers considerably reduced. Callers to the Council number had three options to choose from instead of nine, and 80% of callers were put through to the person they wanted first time. Elliott was proud of the fact that Derwentside was the first Council to "go smokeless", ahead of government legislation. 'Fifty per cent of all the silver and gold smoke free awards given to businesses in the North East came to Derwentside,' he said proudly, 'and the Council has won four Beacon Status awards as national innovators'.

Head of Organisational Development Ian Jones worked his way up from a 17-year old Filing Clerk with Durham County Council. After 22 years with DCC, he joined the Probation Service as

*Salt Barn opening: DDC Leader Cllr Alex Watson with Durham County Councillor Don Ross.*

## Organisation & Administration

Gordon Elliott, Director of Corporate Administration & Policy, is another local lad who chose to make his career locally. Born in Corbridge but brought up in Winlaton, Gordon went to Hookergate School in High Spen before taking a degree in town planning at Dundee University.

Personnel Manager and then moved to Derwentside as Personnel Manager in 1999. His department dealt with personnel, health & safety, staff welfare, payroll as well as staff and member training. 'Our biggest task in recent years has been dealing with changes facing the Council, including the creation of Derwentside Homes and the

Leisure Trust', he said, 'staff have needed to become more flexible and multi-skilled to be better able to meet changing circumstances and this will hopefully help them as they move forward into the new council. We strive to be an employer of choice and try to offer opportunities for staff to progress within the Council, examples being Peter Reynolds, John Pearson and John Shepherd who have progressed to senior management positions after joining the Council several years ago at a much junior level'.

### On the Lighter Side

Tea ladies Jean Walls and Julie Hobson have over thirty years' experience in the job between them. Officially entitled "Refreshment Assistants", the two Js – together with colleague Neville Rose - provide the cup that cheers to the DDC Civic Centre staff and for meetings with councillors and visitors. Both Jean and Julie have a great sense of humour, which is perhaps just as well. For years they had to put up with the jokes and quips of Wages Clerk Frankie Bowes, who died in 2008. Frankie would sometimes hide the tea trolley, and he would always have something to say, such as 'how long are your Curly-Wurlies?' and 'give us a Twirl'. Cheeky Frankie was perhaps lucky to get away with non-PC comments like 'I could hear your jugs rattling from here', 'are your Ripples hard?' and 'have you got any Snickers on?'

*The Tea Team (l-r) Julie Hobson, Jean Watts and Neville Rose (MW)*

Former tea lady Hilda Ashby, who also died in 2008, did the job for many years despite her tea and coffee sometimes tasting funny. This could have been due to her habit of boiling the dirty dishcloths in the same boiler in which she made the hot drinks, or because she would scrape up any spilled tea or coffee and put it back into the pot. Hilda was an ardent Communist, and as a young woman she actually went to Moscow – a rarity in those days. Another former staff member no longer with us is Electoral Officer Mike Bonser. He is fondly remembered by Jean and Julie not only for getting them a fully-equipped kitchen, replacing the "pokey little corner" they had previously, and cutting the ribbon at the official opening of the new facility in 2002. Also fondly remembered, at least by the male staff, was the succession of teenage Italian girls who came each year for a fortnight's training in English and

administration. The blokes would find any excuse to go into the Admin Section to ogle the foreign crumpet. When one of the girls – Lucia - had her 18th birthday, Jean got her a birthday cake. Having run out of candles, she got some on her way to work. Unfortunately, they were the self-lighting variety. Not only did they re-ignite each time the birthday girl blew them out, they set off the smoke alarms and everybody had to be evacuated from the building. Police cars and a fire engine duly arrived to find there was no emergency and no fire to put out. The one consolation for Jean was that the Council's Health & Safety Section found the whole event a useful exercise, identifying a gap in the fire alarm procedures, and the firemen were very good looking. A calendar of handsome firemen adorns the kitchen wall to this day.

Another amusing episode occurred when a book club customer opened up a play tent that was also on sale but decided not to buy it. Julie and Margaret Edwards struggled and struggled to get the tent back into its bag, but all their efforts were in vain. With the two women almost helpless with tears and laughter, the unassuming Neville came to the rescue. Within seconds he folded up the cussed tent and calmly placed it back in its bag – clearly the work of an origami champion. Moral: men do have their uses, sometimes. The efforts of the Council to get their staff to eat more healthily were met with strong resistance. One day a month, all chocolate and crisps were banned from the tea trolley which instead carried a healthy selection of fruit and nuts. With customers deprived of their twice-daily "fix", kind Jean smuggled much-needed chocs to the ones who really could not get through the day without them. The Council drew back from asking staff to drink water instead of tea and coffee – the consequences of caffeine deprivation among the higher ranks being too grisly to contemplate. Besides, it would have put Jean, Julie and Neville out of a job.

*Environmental Health Department, Civic Centre (CFW)*

*Full Council (MW)*

*The lads & lasses who work on the ground: Environment Dept, General Services Division (Engineering, refuse collection, recycling, grounds maintenance, street cleaning, highways maintenance, Managers and Admin support staff) at Morrison Busty depot. John Shepherd (Head of General Services) is standing front left, next to Cllr Ossie Johnson in front of Cllr Dennis Lavin. The staff are gathered around a Scarab Minor road sweeper (CFW)*

*Refuse Collection team (l-r) Geoff Smith (Refuse Supervisor), Stephen Darroch (loader), Malcolm Wall (driver), David Wilson (loader) (CFW)*

*Twin-Bin Wagon*

# Chapter Nine
# Community Action

*The Derwentside Partnership, The Vision; Credit Union; Local Democracy Week; Question Time; Citizens Panel, Children's Panel, "Ellie" the Youth Bus; Stanley Town Council; Testimonials; New Village Hall; Hedleyhope Fell.*

## The Derwentside Partnership

Twenty years after the closure of Consett Steelworks and 20-40 years since almost all the pits had closed, there was still much to do, and to do it, people had to be involved at the grass roots. Derwentside was one of first councils in the North to establish a Local Strategic Partnership (LSP). The Derwentside Partnership was set up in November 2001 with Council Leader Alex Watson as Chairman. There was no doubt as to the size of the task they faced. 'This history of heavy industry has left a legacy of poor health, high youth unemployment, low levels of enterprise, skills and educational attainment,' said a Council report, 'there is significant deprivation with much of the population living in some of the most deprived wards in England'. But as well as seeing the problems, the Partnership also had a vision of the future. The Derwentside Partnership and community vision for 2010 was this: 'The community believes in itself and knows that working together can build a district people want to live in and be proud of'. Decision-making would involve the whole community, including youth. The six strands of the strategy were headed: democracy, health, economy, lifelong learning, community safety, environment. By 2007, this had expanded to seven strands.

## The Vision

**Employment:** Derwentside needs to create more jobs, promote enterprise and aspirations, enhance business support; **Built & natural environment:** regeneration of towns, villages & town centres, sustainable construction & design, housing provision to match needs, promote the benefits of open space, clean local environments, protect landscape, promote alternative energy, increase recycling, improve transport links; **Health:** encourage people to stop smoking, better mental health, improve access to playground activities, better support in pregnancy & early life, support vulnerable groups, better access to health services; **Strong communities:** involve more people in decision-making, improve communications, information sharing, better access to facilities; **Lifelong learning:** raise aspirations, multi-agency approach for older people; **Children & young people:** better access to health & mental health services, promote healthy living, eating & lifestyles, combat substance abuse, early intervention, safe in the home, safe in the community, identify individual needs, recognise aspirations & achievements, promote life skills, better transport links to education & training, promote social, emotional & intellectual well-being; **Community safety:** promote safety in public places, reduce race hate & homophobic crime, increase

*Local resident makes his point about South Stanley regeneration.*

*Community Strategy – Youth Forum youngsters get involved (MW)*

crime detection, reduce domestic violence, tackle drugs & alcohol problems, reduce crime & the fear of crime, reduce road accidents.

Local Community Partnerships were set up in every part of the District, involving ward councillors and local residents. These partnerships played a major role in encouraging and enabling improvements at grass roots level. 'At first people were unsure about the Partnership,' recalled Delves Lane ward councillor Eric Edwards, 'now they are fully on board'. In 2002, Street Wardens were introduced in Havannah ward, Stanley, for a 12-week trial period. Derwentside Crime & Disorder Partnership teamed up with security firm Delta One to provide the service, based in the Shield Row communal rooms. One useful and enjoyable scheme Cllr Ian Agnew (Consett South) helped was the initiative by the YMCA to collect and recycle second-hand furniture to be given to families facing hardship due to poverty, fire or flood.

*Credit Union, oldest & youngest members 1998. Lawrence Dominic Coady of Lanchester, born 25th March 1918, holding Jamie Philip Robinson of Leadgate, born 28th April 1998. Lawrence was 80, and young Jamie "joined the union" when he was just seven days old!*

## Credit Union

Another manifestation of local action is the Credit Union office at The Grove, Moorside. The West Derwentside Community Credit Union was set up in 1997 with the help of former councillor Doreen Anderson. In its first year it gained a membership of 250, with more than £20,000 in assets. Features of the scheme were a simple savings system and easy access to low-cost loans. Credit unions have been set up all over the country to combat loan sharks who prey on the poor and vulnerable. They are rooted in the community and provide a valuable service for local people.

*Community Strategy launched, Lamplight Theatre, Stanley, 31st March 2004. Alex Watson (right) with Peter Hanley of GO-NE (Government Office, North East) (MW)*

## Local Democracy Week

In 1999 Derwentside Council set out to modernize its workings and to get the public more involved in decision making. The process was launched with Local Democracy Week, 13-19 September 1999, designed to "open the door" to local government in Derwentside. The new system, introduced in April 2000, saw the Council adopt its first Corporate Plan. The old committee system was scrapped and replaced by a "Cabinet and Leader", similar to government at Westminster. An essential of the process was the formation of Scrutiny Committees, some chaired by opposition members, to take a close look at Council decisions. The public was able to get involved through the Citizens' Panel, the Youth Panel and the Children's Panel. Local communities were encouraged to get involved through Community Appraisals and Area Regeneration Partnerships which looked at what needed doing in each area and how improvements were to be funded. As well as the Council newspaper "Inside Derwentside", delivered to every house in the district, there was the Council's website with the ability to make complaints "on line", and the community website (Infonet). The district's 55 elected councillors had a dual role, letting their constituents know what was going on as well as listening to people's views on local matters.

## Question Time

DDC gave members of the public in Derwentside the opportunity to ask questions of the Council and of individual councillors, including Executive Members and the Leader. The public could table virtually any questions they wish for the relevant councillors to answer. The whole system was designed to encourage members of the public to take an interest in how the Council was run. Leader of the Council, Alex Watson said: 'I have always been proud of our culture of openness at Derwentside. All of our Council Meetings have always been open to the public. We have always sought to try and engage our communities as much as possible in the democratic process and I see this initiative as an extension of all of the good work that we have been doing in this area. I hope that this will help to reinvigorate peoples' interest in local democracy and I am really looking forward to seeing our residents take full advantage of this opportunity'.

## Citizens Panel

The Derwentside Citizen's Panel was founded in May 1998 and started off with 700 local residents. Over the years, the membership grew to 1,700 and was largely representative of the district, including all the different communities and covering all ages from 18 to 88. The panel was consulted on a wide variety of issues over the ten years of its existence, including the provision of leisure, street cleanliness, new political structures, customer services, anti-social behaviour, the SPICE programme, Council housing, car parking, refuse and recycling collections. Best Value performance indicators and Community Strategy performance indicators to name but a few. Panel members were involved in thirteen major postal surveys over the years. After each round of consultation, all Citizens' Panel members received an 'Inform' newsletter with an introduction by the Leader of the Council, thanking members for their valuable and much appreciated feedback. The results of these surveys were used to inform Council strategy and aid performance monitoring and the newsletter advised panellists of any action taken as a consequence of their feedback. As well as the formal postal surveys, panellists were also invited to take part in other forms of consultation from time to time, for example focus group discussions and public meetings on a specific subject matter. Recent examples of this kind of participation and involvement by Citizens' Panel members was in the naming of he new leisure trust for Derwentside 'Leisureworks' in 2007 and the setting up a Shotley Bridge Hospital support group in 2008.

### Children's Panel

Launched at the start of 1998, the Council's Children's Panel involved 80-100 children aged 5-14 years, a cross-section from all parts of the district. Over the years the youngsters gave a valuable insight into things affecting them, such as facilities in local parks and crime and disorder issues. In 2001, twenty-three young people from Derwentside, aged 5-15, who made up SPICE (Special Project to Implement Children's Elections) were given a £10,000 budget by the Council. With youngsters from New York and Athens watching on the Internet, the new Youth Council discussed the merits of various projects and then voted on them. They decide to build a skate park and three "Hang-out Stands" in the district and to share the rest of the money equally between Derwentside's 50 schools. As there was only enough money in the budget to build a small skate park, the youngsters decided to try to get additional funds to build a big one. The debate was chaired by Cllr Lyn Boyd, Cabinet Member for Community & Culture. 'The young people were absolutely amazing,' she said, 'the searching questions they asked and the quality of the debate was of a very high standard and a credit to them all'. SPICE Project Officer Sharon Robinson said the involvement of over 12,000 young people in the district and observations from schools in America and Europe made it "a very special and unique project." The first meeting of Derwentside Young People's Forum was held in 2003. In 2004 alone, over 1,000 young people in the district benefited from the 17 grants awarded by the Young People's Forum through the Spice Project.

*Jill Stephenson and Cllr Tony Donaghy*

*Youth Parliament – Jill Stephenson is "Madam Speaker"*

*Youth Parliament, on the one hand…..*

*…..on the other*

## "Ellie" the Youth Bus

Youth Bus "Ellie" had her official launch on Saturday/Sunday 16/17th April 2005, at Stanley Kings Head Fields on the Saturday, and on the Sunday at Consett & Blackhill Park. The launch was a huge success with approximately 550 young people attending and enjoying activities which were on offer, including: magicians, clowns, circus skills, live singers, police dogs Jet & Ben, face painting, football competitions, art and craft workshops, balloon launch, Police Road Team and all the activities on board the bus. 'Ellie', a DDC project, came about following consultations with young people who identified the need for a mobile youth provision in the district. Following successful funding and partnership working, the bus operated four nights a week in four target areas, Blackhill, Consett town centre, Burnopfield and Stanley town centre. During the nightly sessions the bus offered young people the opportunity to access the internet through laptops, use of DJ equipment, playstations, tv and videos and a wide range of games. The aim of the project was to target wards within Derwentside that had limited youth provision or high statistics of youth nuisances. The bus was also used to consult with young people in the district as well as provide sessions on the bus around issues that affect young people. In the next few months awareness session have been planned around sexual health, drugs, anti-social behaviour and healthy eating.

*"Ellie" the Youth Bus (MW)*

*Inside "Ellie" the Youth Bus (LW)*

Films shown at Stanley Civic Hall in 1975 included "Battle for the Planet of the Apes","Willie Wonka and the Chocolate factory","Jesus Christ Superstar","Young Winston","Live and let Die","The Red Baron" and "The Quiet Man." The Pavilion Cinema, Stanley, known as the "Piv", had a three-manual theatre organ.

*"It's a Knockout" was filmed at Beamish in May 1975. Derwentside competed against Darlington and Berwick.*

*Singer Susan Maughan, of "Bobby's Girl" fame, was born in Consett, as were former Sunderland chairman Bob Murray and England & Newcastle Falcons rugby union player Matthew Tait.*

*Stanley town centre (CFW)*

### Stanley Town Council

Parish and Town Councils – they have exactly the same powers – are the grass roots of democracy. With the new unitary Durham County Council taking over from Derwentside DC and the other district councils in the county from 2009, it may well be that these very local councils will take on more responsibilities. In 2008 there were nine Parish Councils in the District, plus the newly-formed Stanley Town Council. The parishes are: Burnhope, Cornsay, Esh, Greencroft, Healeyfield, Hedleyhope, Lanchester, Muggleswick and Satley. The twenty members of the new Stanley Town Council were elected on 1st May 2008, the same day as the unitary council elections. The line-up: nine Derwentside Independents, nine Labour, two Liberal Democrats. At the inaugural meeting on Thursday 15th May, Independent Cllr and DDC member Tom Pattinson was elected as Chairman. He had been a member of the steering group for a Town Council set up in 2005. Tom, a retired project engineer, was anxious to put past disagreements behind. "That's water under the bridge," he said, "we felt the referendum set up by the District Council was not a fair test of public opinion, and the percentage of people who returned their ballot forms was very low, but we need to draw a line and move on." As no precept had been applied in advance for the Town Council, as has happened elsewhere, the District Council loaned it £100,000 to meet its first year's running costs. DDC was also providing clerical support until the appointment of a Town Clerk who was expected to be in post by January 2009. One of the first tasks the Town Council set itself was to draw up a "Parish Plan", and to this end public meetings were called in all seven wards.

### Testimonials

At the council's annual meeting on 22nd May 1985, Police Sargeant Harry Stephenson and Constable Michael (Mick) Moses were presented with Royal Humane Society Testimonials for their efforts to save a life at Causey Arch on 3rd October 1984. Both men were known to now retired Police Superintendent Stan Hegarty who is proud of his record of serving at every rank in the Derwentside area. Hegarty, originally from Hartlepool, started as a local bobby in Ebchester . He was promoted to Sargeant at Stanley, then became Section Sargeant at Blackhill before moving back to Stanley as Inspector. Hegarty retired in 1998 with the rank of Superintendent as Derwentside Division Commander and still lives in Shotley Bridge.

*Craghead Village Hall opened by DDC officer Fergus Mitchell, 25th November 2000.*

*Craghead Village Hall (CFW)*

### New Village Hall

Craghead Village Hall is one of many throughout the District. The village newsletter "Canny Crack" described the official opening thus: "Craghead's New Village Hall Opens At Last! At 2pm on Saturday 25th November 2000, the whole village (well, almost the whole village), turned out to see Craghead's new Village Hall officially opened. Fergus Mitchell, an officer from Derwentside District Council, was chosen unanimously by the Village Hall Committee to do the honours, as he has lived and breathed our new building since it was no more than a twinkle in a lottery chief's eye! After listening to Rev. Austin Johnson bless the new Village Hall, the huge crowd in the hall and the foyer heard Fergus declare the building open, and then watched a performance by the Craghead Children's Variety Group. The first Christmas Fayre was then held, and afterwards most people took the opportunity to have a look at the rest of the building while tucking into the buffet and champagne. Santa's Grotto was in the new Business space, but for many of the older children the IT (Information Technology) room was the place to be. There is also a training room as well as a new base for Groundwork West Durham, who have carried out so many of the environmental improvements in our area. As usual, our local businesses came up trumps and donated prizes and gifts - many thanks to all of you. Thanks must also go to all members of the Village Hall Committee who have worked so hard to make the dream a reality, especially Betty Stout, Eileen Cox and Janice Docherty, who have no doubt endured many a sleepless night over the last few months!"

### Hedleyhope Fell

Hedleyhope Fell is home to several heath species of heather, including common heather (Calluna vulgaris) which is favoured by beekeepers hoping to reproduce the illustrious "heather honey". Heather honey is generally a dark reddish/orange colour, very different from the golden honey seen in the shops; it tends not to crystalise over time; it has a high protein content, much higher than normal honey, giving it a gelatinous nature; it is sweet, but has a rich and mature flavour unlike other honeys. Billy Crozier is beekeeper of the Hedleyhope bees. Hedleyhope Fell lies alongside the B6301, the road from Tow Law to Cornsay Colliery.

*Hedleyhope Fell in winter (CFW)*

## Chapter Ten
# Sport, Recreation & the Arts

*The Empire, Gala performance, International Folklore Festival, Film Matinees, Friends of the Empire; Lamplight Arts Centre; Pitman Poet; Sculptures; Swimming, Olympic glory, Soccer, Rugby, Golf, Derwentside Heritage Centre, Bowls, Tennis, Dragon Boats, Hunting, Pigeon racing; Beamish Museum; Miners Gala at Burnhope; Juvenile Jazz Bands; Young Achievers, Blackhill & Consett Park.*

### The Empire

The Empire Theatre stood empty and neglected in 1974 when Derwentside Council came into being. Reckoned to be the finest theatre in North West Durham, the Empire was destined to be replaced by shops or even a car park. In 1975 it took courage, boldness and foresight – not qualities you normally associate with a local authority – for Derwentside Council to buy the empty building and restore it as a theatre and cinema. The three councillors who spearheaded the move were a mixed bunch: firebrand Deputy Leader Selby Walker and Norman Seymour, both Labour men from Stanley, and businessman, choirmaster and Independent councillor Willie Westgarth from Consett. But the Empire was rescued from oblivion and is now the oldest working theatre in County Durham. Once again the Empire, with its fine acoustics, became the venue of choice for the local operatic societies, drama groups and choirs.

### Gala performance

The 500-seat Empire Theatre in Consett's Front Street was built in 1885 as a variety hall. Comedy duo Laurel & Hardy were among the many stars who played there. In 1912 the Empire was converted to show films as well as stage productions, and in more recent times it had became a bingo hall before being closed. After refurbishment the Empire was re-opened in Jubilee Year with a gala performance on 11th July 1977. Cllr Norman Seymour, Council Chairman, declared the theatre officially open. Cllr Willie Westgarth proposed the vote of thanks, seconded by Cllr Sid Dixon, Council Vice Chairman. Many local artists and musicians performed that night, including the Benfieldside Folkdance Group (Director Malcolm Doughty), Consett, Blackhill & Shotley Amateur Players Society (Producer Keith Little, Musical Director Pat Boustead), Consett Citizens Choir (Conductor William E Westgarth MBE), Consett Junior Brass (Bandmaster David Jackson), Greencroft Comprehensive School (Headmaster S Borrell BSc), Lanchester Male Voice Choir (musical director Mark Monroe). Former Theatre Manager Ruth Reed, now Ruth Harrison: 'Derwentside Council should really be praised for taking the initiative and buying the Empire. I was very proud to be the first Manager employed by the Council, and I also took on the job of managing the Consett Civic Hall as well. Two of our first shows at the Empire were Derek Batey of "Mr & Mrs" fame, and the Nolan Sisters. Later there was a memorable performance by Ken Dodd. "Doddy" kept the audience back until 11pm but nobody left'. Ruth Hume was born in Shotley Bridge in 1922, the eldest of five children. Her father had been a master upholsterer but was unable to work due

*Empire Theatre (CFW)*

to wounds received in WWI. Her three brothers, including long-serving DDC Councillor Derek Hume, were all involved in amateur stage productions.

### International Folklore Festival

After the grand opening night at the Empire, the first Derwentside International Folklore Festival, 16-23rd July 1977, was also a huge success and a fitting first major show for the refurbished theatre. The Durham Constabulary band led the parade from Consett town centre to the Belle Vue football ground for the opening ceremony. Festival Management Committee Chairman Cllr Lawrence Brown did the welcome, Council Chairman Norman Seymour the opening, previous Council Chairman Billy Bell the vote of thanks. The anthems of the "Assembled Nations" were played, followed by entertainment, a free-fall parachuting display and the Ever Ready Junior Band. There were groups from Belgium, Czechoslovakia, the Faroe Islands, Germany, Hungary, Italy, Luxembourg, Norway, Sweden, Yugoslavia, Scotland, Ireland and England. Some of the foreign

*St Cuthbert's Youth Choir, Willie Westgarth standing, far right (LHA)*

*David Jackson (white shirt, left) with the Consett Junior Brass (RG)*

groups had taken part in the Consett International Festival in 1971. Hosts Benfieldside Folk Dance group had been to Luxembourg in 1976 and had played two concerts at the Aldeburgh Festival in 1970. Other local groups involved: Stanley Choral Society, Consett Citizens Choir, Annfield Plain Gleemen, Leadgate Gleemen, Lanchester Male Voice Choir, Greencroft School Choir, Consett Junior Brass, Consett Steelmen, Lads o' Derwent, Amoco Band, and other local artistes including Keith Gregson. There were performances at the Empire Theatre and Stanley Civic Hall, plus open-air performances. Chief Executive Terry Hodgson was the Festival Controller and Malcom Doughty, Director of the Benfieldside Group, was the Festival Director. Doughty was also on the national executive of the English Folk Dance & Song Society. The Festival was supported by Northern Arts, Durham County Council, Stockton Borough Council, the British Council, the Tyne Division of the Royal Naval Reserve, the British Army and staff at Consett Technical College.

### Film Matinees
Films were also restored to the Empire, but new equipment was needed. Ruth Reed: 'We went to London to sort out all the equipment needed to show films at the Empire. We visited several film companies: Rank, Warner Bros and EMI and it was EMI who supplied us with all the sound equipment to turn the Empire into a first-class cinema. We put on children's film matinees, and at first it was very tough. Many of the kids had never been in a cinema before, and there they were in this beautiful building, boisterous, throwing things around, shouting and yelling. I had to employ four usherettes,

*1997 Triple Trophy winners, the Brighouse and Rastrick Band.*

and I was the Gestapo, patrolling the aisles. Any child who misbehaved, I would haul out of their seat and put them out of the theatre. The only way I would let them return was if they came back to say sorry and promised to be good in future. Years later, a man told me that he was one of the naughty ones I ejected, and when he went home, his mother clipped his ears! After three weeks, everything calmed down and we had no bother whatsoever since. I chose the films, and occasionally one of my choices would be criticized by a particular councillor, but I was filling the cinema and that's what counted'. When Ruth left in 1987, her Secretary Ann D'Northwood took over as Theatre Manager.

### Friends of the Empire
The Council could afford only minimal improvements to the Empire, so in 1978 Willie Westgarth, Pat Holmes and Ruth Reed formed the Friends of the Empire. DDC Chief Executive Neil Johnson helped by providing secretarial support. By 2008 the Friends had 1,200 members and had raised £63,000 for the theatre, paying for new lighting, sound equipment and no fewer than three new pianos: grand, upright and electronic. The Council also played its part. A nine-month refurbishment programme in 2003 cost £1m, of which DDC paid £0.75m. The work included new seats with extra leg room, an expanded bar and foyer, a new sound system and stage lighting. The film projector was upgraded. The Empire escaped destruction in 2007 when the Decades nightclub next door suffered a major fire. It took 30 firefighters and six appliances to bring the blaze under control.

Willie Westgarth started the Consett Citizens Choir in 1949. They used the old Citizen House, a building in Front Street. When it was demolished, Citizen House moved to its present location in the old Station Yard. Pat Holmes – perhaps better known as Pat Boustead – in 2008 still lived in the house in Medomsley Road bought by her parents Fred and Peggy in 1935 for £434. Fred Boustead sang in various local choirs, and Pat had piano and singing lessons from an early age. She trained with Dr John Hutchinson in Newcastle and became a professional singer and was still entertaining well past seventy after recovering from a series of serious operations for cancer in her thirties. She also conducted local choirs and operatic societies for many years. In 2008 she conducted a 270-strong joint choir in Durham Cathedral, and she also conducted the Leadgate

*Lamplight Arts Centre, Stanley (YG)*

Gleemen. Soprano Pat won a singing festival at the age of 17, also taking part in a performance of Merrie England put on by Consett UDC at the local football ground for the Queen's coronation in 1953.

Amateur productions have always flourished in Derwentside, with churches, schools, youth groups, community associations, theatre and operatic groups and choirs providing an outlet for local talent and entertainment for all. Just one example: in 2003 the Villa Real Special Needs School put on a production of Joseph and the Technicolour Dreamcoat. Inside Derwentside Editor and photographer Mark Wilkinson saw the show and said he was 'tremendously impressed with the amount of effort put in by the youngsters and the dedication of the staff'. Stanley Civic Choir – Hon Sec Ralph Powton – won the Mixed Voice class at the Blackpool Choral Festival in October 1974. The choir was started in 1962 – Cllr Selby Walker in the chair – and its

*Carnival Cinema at the Empire, Consett (LHA)*

*"The Piv" – Pavilion Cinema, Stanley (JH)*

first conductor was Norman Williams. They gave their first public performance in March 1963 at a concert in Stanley Civic Hall shortly after it had opened. Derwentside is famous for its bands. The first ever Salvation Army Band was formed in Consett in 1879. Leading bands of recent times include the AMOCO Blackhall Band, the Craghead Colliery Band (for some years the Ever Ready Band), Langley Park Colliery Band, Consett Whitbread Trophy Band, Lanchester Village Band and Consett Junior Brass Band. The Consett Junior School Band played numerous concerts after being formed in 1973, and visited the Rhineland in 1975. The Brighouse and Rastrick Band, 1997 National, All England & European Champions, played the Empire 13th March 1999, and on two other occasions. Consett Junior Brass, supported by Derwentside District Council, have promoted over 30 concerts in the Empire Theatre. These concerts have featured Championship Section bands including Black Dyke Mills Band, Grimethorpe Colliery, Leyland, Brighouse & Rastrick, Fodens and Yorkshire Building Society. Two very famous brass groups have also been featured: The White River Brass (from Black Dyke) and the James Shepherd Versatile Brass.

**Lamplight Arts Centre**
The refurbished Lamplight Arts Centre in Front Street, Stanley, is another flourishing Council theatre and cinema. Built in 1960 as the Stanley Civic Hall, it was first opened to the public on 7th January 1961. Rehearsal rooms were added in the early 70s. In 1990/91, DDC, helped by the EEC's RECHAR grant scheme for former coalfield areas, carried out a complete refurbishment programme. Since then, there have been further improvements to the auditorium, bar and foyer. Renamed as the Lamplight Arts Centre in 2003, the venue includes a flexible main hall seating between two and four hundred, a large and well-furnished function room, a gallery space, two rehearsal rooms and a daytime café. The Lamplight has excellent access for people with a disability. There is an orchestra pit at auditorium floor level, with removable top floor sections revealing a stepped orchestra pit. The auditorium can accommodate up to 410 people on a retractable bleacher seating system, arranged in rows of 20 seats. A more intimate format for smaller productions can be set up, seating between 100 and 330. The Lamplight has a "reasonable" baby-grand piano, plus a Technics digital electric piano, and a "serviceable" upright piano in the two rehearsal rooms. There is a self-contained function suite on the first floor, with a small dance floor, small bar and kitchen. Around 60,000 people a year visit the Lamplight. In 2005, it was the venue for the BBC's seminal programme "Question Time", hosted by David Dimbleby.

The Theatre Royal, Stanley, opened in 1903 with a seating capacity of 1,400. It was destroyed by fire in March 1930. The Victoria Theatre in Front Street, Stanley, opened on 29th June 1893. Gracie Fields, Bud Flanagan and Charlie Chaplain are all said to have appeared there. In 1935 it was replaced by the Victoria cinema, which in 1948 became the Essoldo and in 1970 the Classic. It closed in 1976, and the building was demolished in 1999. In 1949 there were eight cinemas in and around Stanley: the Victoria, New Pavilion, Albert Hall, Kings (Annfield Plain), Tivoli & Arcadia (South Moor), Regal (Tantobie) and the Empire (Dipton). The Arcadia cinema in South Moor opened on 24th March 1914 and closed in 1962. The Pavilion cinema in High Street, Stanley, opened in April 1923 and closed in 1966. In the 1940s and early 50s you could go dancing at the Stanley Palais ("the new trend in modern ballroom"), the Hibernian Hall, Stanley Co-operative Hall, Castle's Ballroom, Catchgate, and many smaller local halls. The Stanley Inn, the first public house to be built in Stanley, opened around 1860. It was better known as "Paddy's Rocks". It was demolished in the 1970s. The Queen's Hotel in Front Street, Stanley, built in 1898, was demolished in 1971. Stanley Market Hall was opened in 1924.

*Terris Novalis (CFW)*

### Sculptures

Project Genesis worked closely with Sustrans to help fund and locate the Tony Craggs sculpture Terris Novalis near Morrisons as a landmark for Consett on the world famous C2C cycle route.

### Pitman Poet

The area has a great tradition of story-telling, songs and poetry. The "Pitman Poet" Thomas Armstrong (1848-1919) lived in Tanfield Lea. Tommy was a miner whose songs and poems tell life as it was in the pit villages at that time. He wrote *"Wor Nanny's a Maizor", "The Oakey Strike Evictions", "The Trimdon Grange Disaster", "The Skuil Board Man"* and *"The South Medomsley Strike"*. Of the Oakey strike, Tommy told of the "candymen" who were used by the mine owners to evict striking miners from their homes.

*"It was in November and aw never will forget*
*How the polisses and the candymen at Oakey Houses met*
*Johnny the Bellman he was there squintin' roond aboot*
*And he put three men at ivvery door te' torn the miners oot*
*And what would a dee if aw had the power mesel'*
*Aw would hang the twenty candymen and Johnny whe carries the bell"*

The Trimdon Grange Colliery explosion occurred on February 16th 1883. Tommy wrote:

*"Men and boys left home that morning*
*For to earn their daily bread*
*Little thought before that evening*
*That they'd be numbered with the dead*
*Let us think of Mrs Bumett*
*Once had sons but now has none*
*By the Trimdon Grange explosion*
*Joseph George and James are gone"*

*Swim kids (SW)*

*New Pool here soon! One lad can't wait (LW)*

*Olympics 1996 Vicky Horner (left) and Marion Nadine*

*Nicola Jackson with coach David McNulty*

*Joanne Jackson (right) on the podium with her 2008 Olympic bronze medal; gold winner Rebecca Adlington on left.*

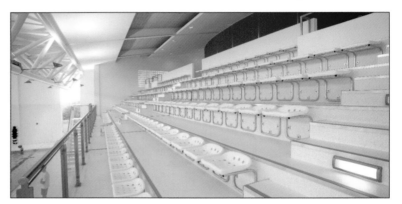

*New pool, Stanley, seating (MW)*

*Old Burns Pool, Stanley (LW)*

*New Pool, Stanley (MW)*

*Treadmill, Louisa Centre (MW)*

*Louisa Centre gym (MW)*

## Swim, swim, swim

In 1974, the new Council was very proud of its swimming baths in Stanley and Consett. Stanley once had open-air swimming baths, which opened in the early 1900s and closed around 1938. Construction of Stanley Baths, which cost £200,000, started in April 1963 when Cllr Ralph Powton removed the first turf at the Kings Head field. Opened on 21st August 1965 and later known as the Burns Leisure Pool, the Baths had to be closed in December 1996. Repairs would have cost £1m and upgrading a further £3m, so it was decided a new pool would be the better option. In 1998 the Council appealed against the rejection of a £4.5m National Lottery bid for a new swimming pool for Stanley. Council Leader Alex Watson said:'After two years dialogue with the Sports Council we felt we had submitted a strong bid which met the criteria required. Everyone involved, especially the people of Stanley, feels let down by this decision. We will simply not accept this rejection and intend to contest the points raised by the Sports Council.' The new pool at the Louisa Centre was finally opened by Cllr Watson and local ward councillor and Executive Member Cllr Anne Taylor on 2nd November 2004.

Anne Jervis, Margaret Maughan, Janice McCulloch, Robin Richardson, Carol Sharp, Glenda Smailes, Moira Smith, Carolyn Wilson. Lunch followed at the Freemasons Hotel in Front Street. Consett ASC held its first gala on 14th June 1963.

As with most sports, swimming can be likened to a pyramid – a broad base involving people of all ages and capabilities, leading up to the peak of athletic performance, the Olympics. Getting swimmers to four successive Olympics would be a huge achievement for any swim coach, but to do it with a small club like Derwentside was an even more remarkable achievement for Chief Coach David McNulty from Stanley. In 1996, Vicky Horner made the GB 400 metres freestyle. Marion Madine also got to Atlanta, making the Irish team in the 200 butterfly. At the Sydney Olympics in 2000 Nicola Jackson was a member of the GB womens 4x200 freestyle relay team that made the final, finishing sixth. In the 2004 Games in Athens Nicola's younger sister Joanne, only 17 and the youngest member of the UK swimming team, qualified in two events, the 400 freestyle and the 4x200 freestyle relay, in

*Cllr Lyn Boyd with Mike Clark (left) and Cllr Alex Watson, announcing Lottery Fund bid (LW)*

Consett swimming baths were opened by Cllr Mrs Irene Williamson, Chairman of Consett Urban District Council, on Saturday 11th August 1962. The six-lane main pool was 100ft x 42ft, 3ft 0in at the shallow end and 8ft 6in at the deep end. There were diving platforms with 3m and 1m springboards, and seats for 198 spectators. The small pool was 46ft x 20ft. The main pool held 220,000 gallons of water and the small pool 17,000 gallons. The baths were heated by two coal-fired boilers with automatic stokers. Harbour & General were the main contractors. The structural steelwork, 100 tons of it, was supplied by the Consett Iron Co. To build the baths, 6,000 tons of earth was excavated, 2,500 tons of cement used and 40,000 bricks laid. It took over a year to complete. At the opening ceremony, the Rev D Moxon, Vicar of St Ives, Leadgate, offered prayers. Cllrs F Agar (Parks Committee Chairman), GH Howatt (Baths Committee Chairman) and SW Smith also took part in the opening ceremony, but the stars of the show were the 17 local children who had the honour of swimming the first lengths of the new pool: James Arden, Geoffrey Baird, Geoffrey Carlill, Harold Cornforth, Jeffrey Davison, Malcolm Douglas, Colin Eade, Linda & Robert Gardner,

the latter helping GB to fifth place in the final in a British record time. In 2008 Joanne made her second Olympics in Beijing, claiming the bronze medal in the womens 400 freestyle behind Britain's double gold winner Rebecca Adlington who also took the 800 crown.

### Olympic glory

It was on 11th August 2008 that Joanne Jackson won her 400 freestyle bronze, the first Olympic medal for a Derwentside swimmer, to make it two British girls on the medal rostrum. In Beijing's Water Cube pool, Jackson paced herself perfectly to come through in the closing stages for third place. Pre-race favourite, American Katie Hoff was leading until the very last stroke when she was overtaken by Adlington whose more decisive finish gave her victory by a mere 0.07 seconds in 4min 3.22 sec. Just 0.30sec separated gold and bronze – Jackson clocking 4min 3.52sec. "Joanne has been my most successful swimmer, winning medals at World, Olympic, European and Commonwealth Games," said McNulty, who was himself a top competitive swimmer with Chester le Street ASC and a member of the GB squad. He just missed out on qualification for the 1988 Olympics.

At 20, McNulty decided to give up competitive swimming and make a career as a professional swim coach. He took charge of the Derwentside Swimming Development Scheme at its start in 1990, and ran it for 18 years before becoming a British Swim coach in April 2008. After five months helping prepare the GB Olympic squad for Beijing, McNulty became Head Coach at Bath University, a GB centre of excellence for the sport. In 2006, Joanne won two silver medals at the Commonwealth games in Melbourne. Another local swimmer, Alyson Duffy represented England at the Commonwealth Games in Auckland, New Zealand in 1990. Derwentside's first Commonwealth swim medalist was Keith Walton, a member of Consett ASC. Keith won bronze at the 1974 Commonwealth Games in New Zealand as a member of the England 4x100 metres freestyle relay team.

## Soccer

Football has been an enduring part of the Derwentside story for at least 150 years. More than just a sport, the local football team has very often been the heart and soul of its town or village. As well as the area's "senior" clubs of Consett and Annfield Plain, many other teams have flourished over the years. In addition, the district's wider soccer loyalties have been split between Sunderland and Newcastle United. The Derwentside Football Development Scheme, in partnership with Sunderland AFC, has flourished. In 2002, attendances reached a total of 15,500 between the two sites at the Belle Vue Leisure Centre in Consett and the Louisa Centre, Stanley. By 2003, 17 young soccer players from Derwentside had signed for the Sunderland soccer academy, three for Hartlepool United and one for Newcastle United. A Tanfield Comprehensive School pupil, 15-year old Carly Telford, was picked to play in goal for England against France in Paris in October 2002. England lost, but it was a great experience for Carly who played for Sunderland AFCW. She became a goalkeeper by accident – she just happened to be wearing a goalie's jersey when she went for trials at Chester le Street at the age of eleven. In 2003 two teams of special needs children from Derwentside competed in the Millenium Youth games in Boccia, Italy. They were from Villa Real School, Harelaw, and Tanfield Lea Juniors who won the under-11 trophy.

## Rugby

Consett rugby club, who provided a place for the Council to meet in its early days, got a substantial grant from DDC to upgrade the facilities at the club in 2003/04. The pitches were regraded and re-seeded, new fencing put up, new floodlighting installed, and an all-weather training pitch built. A new car park was constructed. The Council also helped with the administration of the contract.

## Athletics

Glorious morning sunshine on a snow-covered hillside provided the perfect setting for the Great North Cross-Country, held at Berry Edge, Consett on Saturday 30th December 2000. The event was covered by BBC television, attracting a peak audience of 3.1m viewers. The expansive tv and newspaper coverage was estimated to be worth over half a million pounds in advertising terms. This was one of a series of six major events for the European CrossCup. Olympic athlete Paula Radcliffe stormed home to win the women's 6k race ahead of her old rival, Ethiopia's Olympic 10,000 metres gold winner Deraru Tulu by a minute and 15 seconds. 'Radcliffe at the peak of her prowess,' said Brough Scott in the Sunday Telegraph. 'Radcliffe produced a brilliant performance of power,' said Richard Lewis (Sunday Express). There were also men's 4k and 9k races, plus the Great North Winter Run and Junior Run which together attracted over 600 runners. Paul Kosgei of Kenya, world cross-country bronze medalist, collected the Energiser Cup as the men's 9k winner, while Irishman Gareth Turnbull retained his international 4k title. Irish prime minister Bertie Ahern, after Éamon de Valera the republic's second longest serving Taoiseach, was there to watch.

*Paula Radcliffe leads the way at Berry Edge, 2000*

Local running club Blackhill Bounders were very much involved in the event, assisted by Council staff who turned out on a holiday weekend to ensure everything "ran" smoothly. At short notice the club, which had previously hosted harrier league events on the Genesis site, was called in to assist with the organisation of the international cross-country event at Berry Edge when it had to be switched from its usual venue at Durham. At Radcliffe's request, the course was not cleared of snow. Radcliffe said she liked running on snow, and an icy surface would be dangerous. Blackhill Bounders had hosted the 1998 and 1999 North East Counties cross-country championships, held at Berry Edge. In 1998, Minister of Defence Doug Henderson MP took part along with 1,200 runners aged nine years upwards. This was the first time the event had been held in the area since 1926. In 2005, the Council sponsored three days of cross-country running events: the North Eastern Harrier League with 4,000+ competitors; and a primary school fun run and a comprehensive school race involving 3,000 children from 30 schools. In 2005 Lanchester St Bedes, representing Derwentside, won the under-13 team title in the national schools athletics

*Senior men's race 1999, Stewart Bell (runner 70) from Moorside with the leading group*

championships in Southampton. DCC hosted the Great North Walk at Berry Edge on 8th September 1990. 8,000 people took part.

*Fun Run, Berry Edge, 28th January 2005. 32 schools and 2,200 youngsters took part. (IP)*

*Hobson Golf Club (CFW)*

## Golf

There are 18-hole golf courses at Consett, Beamish and South Moor, plus the municipal golf course at Hobson which was opened in 1978. Consett is the home of Harry Ashby, English Amateur matchplay champion in 1972 and 1973. In 2002 the Council-owned Hobson club was handed over to its members to run and develop the course.

## Derwentside Heritage Centre

At the time of writing, arrangements were being made for the official opening by Cllr Mike Malone of the Derwentside Heritage Centre in Blackhill & Consett Park in March 2009. The Heritage Centre will include full access and facilities to a £150,000 resource centre and classroom equipped with state-of-the-art technology. In a television interview when the Park was re-opened by Sir Bobby Robson in July 2002, Cllr Malone expressed a desire that it would develop as a "Park for the People". "The completion of the Heritage Centre is the last piece of the jigsaw in achieving this," he said.

*Ladies who golf*

*Consett Park Bowls Ladies, National Rink Champions 2002*

## Bowls

In 2002, Consett Park Bowling Club ladies became the English Women's Bowling Association national rinks champions, defeating teams from Cumbria, Hampshire, Hertfordshire, Huntingdonshire, Dorset and Devonshire before beating Cornish champions Penryn in the final. The team was Margaret Robson from Leadgate, and Maureen Gowland, Edna Stokoe and Gillian Jones, all from Blackhill. In 2006 Consett Park Ladies BC again became national champions, beating Bridport BC from Dorset in the final at Torquay. The tournament lasted five months in all and involved 850 clubs. There are indoor bowls centres at Stanley and Consett. Fine Fare, later to become Asda, opened a store at the bottom of Stanley Front Street in 1961. They moved to their present premises – with indoor bowling green above – in 1977. The World Bowls Tour and Professional Bowls Association UK national qualifiers was held at Stanley Indoor Bowls Centre in September 2003. Local club member Brett Arkley qualified for the third year in succession. Carol Ashby, the women's world indoor bowls champion, beat six men to become the first woman ever to qualify for a World Bowls Tour ranking event.

## Tennis

The first Derwentside tennis championships were played in October 1974. Jane Collinson (Blackfyne School & Shotley Bridge LTC), won both the girls under-16 and under 18 titles. Other winners: boys u18 Keith Dodd (Tanfield School & Burnopfield LTC), u16 John Lucy (St Bedes School), u14 Richard Collinson (Blackfyne School & Shotley Bridge LTC); girls u14 Pamela Jameson (St Bedes School). Derwentside tennis coach Christine Heppell won several awards in 2004, including Sport England National Female Community Coach of the year, which she received from Clive Woodward, Head Coach of the England rugby union team.

## Dragon Boats

DDC Environmental Health Officer Tracy Dodds was a member of the GB dragon boat crew – the "Serpents" - that won two gold medals and one silver at the 2002 European championships in Poznan, Poland.

## Hunting

The district is hunted by the North Durham Foxhounds, the Braes of Derwent Foxhounds, the Northern Counties Otterhounds and the Weardale Beagles. The famous Braes of Derwent Hunt was officially formed in 1854, but had operated before that under other names, perhaps as early as 1743. The Weardale Beagles were formed in 1950.

## Pigeon Racing

Thanks to a £4,000 grant from the Council's "Awards for All" Scheme, in 2004 Shotley Bridge Homing Society was able to buy computerized clocks and two printers. New technology has increased interest in the sport of pigeon racing.

*Stanley Indoor Bowls Centre (CFW)*

*Local derby*

*Consett Park Bowling Club Ladies, 2006 national champions: (l-r) Jackie Rogan, Trudy Kitto, Anne Bernard, Sheila Shaw, Dorothy Summerson, Edna Stokoe, Gill Jones, Maureen Gowland, Rose McCormack, Pat Armstrong, Pearl Calvert. (IP)*

## Beamish Museum

The world-famous Beamish Open Air Museum lies mainly in Chester le Street district and only partly in Derwentside, but includes two reconstructed buildings from the area, Annfield Plain Co-op and Rowley railway station. Beamish tells the story of the people of North East England at two important points in their history – 1825 and 1913. The museum stands in 300 acres of beautiful County Durham countryside and is not a traditional museum. Most of the houses, shops and other buildings have been dismantled, brought to Beamish and rebuilt. Some - Home Farm, Pockerley Manor and the Drift Mine - were there already. All of the buildings are filled with furniture, machinery and objects, real artefacts from designated collections. The story is told not by labels but by costumed staff who are proud of their heritage and happy to share their knowledge with visitors. Founder of Beamish and its first Director, Frank Atkinson, was appointed Director of the Bowes Museum at Barnard Castle in 1958. Frank realised that the North East was changing dramatically, the old industries of coal mining, shipbuilding and iron and steel manufacture were disappearing along with the

*Rowley Station – now at Beamish (AP)*

## Miners Gala - at Burnhope

During the 1926 General Strike, it was decided to cancel the Durham Miners Gala because the organisers believed there would be poor attendances due to the fact that there was no public transport. The miners of Burnhope Lodge however felt aggrieved that their day of pride, when they could proudly march behind their banner into the "Big Meeting" was being denied them, so they decided to organise it in Burnhope. And so the Durham Miners Gala of 1926 took place at Burnhope, the only time in the history of the Gala that it has been held outside Durham City. Thousands of miners and their families descended on the small village, proudly bringing with them their lodge banners. The miners were addressed by their respected leader AJ Cook, probably his last public appearance as he was terminally ill with cancer of the oesophagus. In 1986 a Jubilee Miners Gala was organised under the auspices of Cllr Joe Wilson to celebrate the sixtieth anniversary of the Burnhope Gala. This again attracted several thousand miners along with their families, bands and banners, some coming from as far away as Kent. The miners were addressed by their leader Arthur Scargill. Whilst primarily a miners' meeting, the 1986 event focused on the history of the mines, the Gala, the village and its heritage. In order to give children first-hand

*Annfield Plain Co-op – now at Beamish (AP)*

communities that served them. He was most concerned that the region was losing its identity, and its customs, traditions and ways of speech were dying out. Atkinson and his small band of colleagues first came to Beamish in 1970. The idea was to establish an open-air museum of the Scandinavian type. Frank proposed that the new museum would vividly illustrate the way of life of the ordinary people, and would attempt to make the history of the region live. Frank adopted a policy of unselective collecting. "You offer it to us and we will collect it". The imagination of the people of the region was captured and they donated objects of all sizes, from steam engines to shops and sewing machines. Beamish is now established as a major museum with outstanding collections of national and international importance and is one of the major tourist attractions in the North of England.

*Beamish Hall (YG)*

*Burnhope memorial (CFW)*

experience of vehicles of the era, Cllr Joe Wilson and Robert Atkinson organised a short road run in the hope of attracting vehicles that may have been around during the 1926 General Strike. Twelve vehicles entered that first run which was won by Ken Spencer from Northumberland. The road run was a side show from the main event of the Gala which turned out to be an overwhelming success. Without realising it, the one-off side show became an annual event. As Cllr Ossie Johnson, one of the other organisers said: 'it's a good day and takes no organising'.

### Juvenile Jazz Bands

At one time there were at least eleven juvenile jazz bands in the district: Leadgate Spartans (formed 1972), Stanley Spectrons (formed 1968, secretary Mrs E Bewick), Stanley Forrestors and the South Moor Homesiders, both formed from the Forrestors in 1971, the Consett Deltones (formed 1970), the Sundowners (formed 1972 as the Flint Hill, Leazes & Burnopfield Toreadors), the Dipton Hussars and the New Consett Jazzmanians (both formed 1971), the Bridgehill Lancers (formed 1972), the Langley Park Overlanders – secretary B Tulip, trainer R Shorton - (formed 1973), the Pontop Pike Grenadiers (formed 1969).

### Young Achievers

The Council's "Young Achievers" awards started in 1981. Two businessmen in London heard a radio programme about the devastating effects of the closure of Consett steelworks. They donated the money to set up the Colburn Trophy for outstanding

achievement by a girl and the Farquhar Trophy for a boy. All young people in the District were eligible, up to the age of nineteen. Awards could be given for sporting achievement, in recognition of courage and determination in overcoming handicaps, in helping others, or in outstanding acts of bravery. Former winners include boxer Glenn McCrory, swimmer David McNulty, and Durham County cricketer Neil Killeen.

*Young Achievers 1st March 1988: front row (l-r): Gareth Clegg (Farquhar Trophy, boys), Glenn McCrory (British cruiserweight champion), Cllr Michael Brough (Council Chairman), Mrs Mary Brough (Chairman's Lady), Joanne Williamson (Colburn Trophy, girls).*

Derwentside Youth team (LW)

Badminton ladies

Canoe lads

Fishing at Greencroft
Industrial Estate (YG)

Youth sport 1997, Chairman Tony Donaghy &
Vice Chairman Richie McArdle congratulate girls
& boys

Stanley Indoor Bowls

Whippet racing, Belle Vue Park (AP)

Louisa Centre, Stanley (YG)

Adventure playground – having a great time!

Oakey Park, Stanley (CFW)

## Blackhill & Consett Park

The Grand Opening Celebration of Consett Heritage Park – since reverting to its original name of Blackhill & Consett Park - took place on Saturday 13th July 2002, supported by the Council and the Friends of Consett Park. Hundreds of people attended. PC Richard Scott, splendidly arrayed in 19th century Police uniform, led the parade, along with Cllr David Llewellyn, Chairman of the Council, and his wife Carol. The new bandstand was christened with a concert by the Glendale Choir with Leadgate Gleemen, and the entertainment included an Aboriginal dancer. The day ended with the Grand Finale, a terrific display of fireworks.

*Opening Day Concert in the Park*

*PC Richard Scott in period costume*

*Fireworks, opening of Blackhill & Consett Park (LW)*

*Robson & McCrory meet Beckham! Bobby Robson & Glenn McCrory with young dancer Claire Beckham at the opening of Blackhill & Consett Park (LW)*

*Leading the procession (from right): PC Richard Scott, DCC Chairman Cllr David Llewellyn, Mrs Carol Llewellyn and Claire Beckham (LW)*

*Choir, opening of Blackhill & Consett Park*

*Staff Christmas Party 2008 (MW)*

## Chapter Eleven
# Members of Parliament

*David Watkins, Ernest Armstrong, Hilary Armstrong, Giles Radice, Kevan Jones.*

### David Watkins

A toolmaker by trade, David Watkins from Bristol was MP for Consett from 1966 until 1983, and was previously a Bristol City councillor. In 1983 there were boundary changes, and Watkins lost out to Ernest Armstrong in the selection to be Labour candidate for the new North West Durham constituency which combined Consett with Crook, Willington and Weardale, while Stanley joined with Chester le Street in the new North Durham seat. Always a back-bencher, he was said to have "fought for the rights of the British working people". Watkins was sponsored by the AUEW and was secretary of the AUEW parliamentary group 1968-77.

Watkins called his political biography "Seventeen years in obscurity – memoirs from the back benches", an ironic reference to a well-used journalistic cliché. He was a member of two Commons Select Committees (on Standing Orders and Unopposed Bills), and of the Chairmen's Panel of senior back-benchers who chair Standing Committee in the detailed scrutiny of bills and at times chair the House of Commons during debate on the Finance Bill, when by tradition the Speaker is not allowed to preside. Watkins had the rare distinction of successfully introducing and guiding through two Private Member's Bills which became law: the Employer's Liability (Compulsory Insurance) Act 1969 and the Industrial Common Ownership Act 1976. The first, which has since been added to by successive governments, protects employers and employees against large compensation claims; the second gave properly defined legal status to workers' co-operatives for the first time.

Watkins became an internationally-recognized authority on Palestine and the Middle East. This expertise once enabled him to confound Mrs Thatcher during Prime Minister's questions, a rare event indeed. Years later, when Labour Leader Michael Foot put Watkins forward for elevation to the House of Lords, Mrs T vetoed his nomination along with most of the other Labour MPs on Foot's list. Watkins never neglected his constituency, and is remembered as a hard-working local MP. He lobbied government minister Dick Crossman MP to give loan approval for Consett UDC to build the Civic Centre. Prior to that, Consett Council had met in the town's rugby club. After leaving parliament, Watkins became full-time Director of the Council for Arab-British Understanding, retiring in 1990. Since then he has written a number of books with political themes, plus his first novel "Class & Consequence" which came out in 2007. As 2009 approached, the 83-year old former MP was as active as ever and still taking a close interest in national and international politics.

Passengers on the Derwent Line Railway had to get off at Blackhill (Blackfyne) Station and walk or take the bus to Consett, as passengers were not allowed to travel on the line through the Ironworks.

*David Watkins MP (BGP)*

### Ernest Armstrong

Ernest Armstrong was the youngest of nine children. His father John was a miner and a Durham County councillor. In his youth Ernest played centre half for Stanley United (Stanley, Crook) in the Northern League and later became a referee. During WW2 he served in the RAF, returning to teaching after the war to become a headmaster in Seaham and Washington. He was also a member of Sunderland Council. Ernest was first elected as MP for North West Durham in 1964. At that time Consett was a separate constituency. When the boundaries were redrawn prior to the 1983 election, Armstrong won the nomination and was duly elected for the new NW Durham seat. Ernest was a government whip 1969-70, an opposition whip 1970/73, a junior minister for education (1974/75) and the environment (1975/79). He was made a Privy Councillor in 1979, and

*Ernest Armstrong MP*

finally Deputy Speaker of the House of Commons 1981-87. He was also Vice President of the Methodist Conference 1974/75. In 1987 he stood down and was succeeded as North West Durham MP by his daughter Hilary. He died in 1996. Former Speaker George Thomas described Ernest as 'a man whose reliability was as solid as Durham Cathedral'.

## Hilary Armstrong

Hilary Armstrong set something of a record when she was first elected as North West Durham MP in 1987 – she succeeded her father Ernest in the job. Anyone who thought they were getting Armstrong Mark II was in for a shock. Not only did Hilary greatly increase her father's majority, she proved to be very much her own woman and with a more direct approach than her more easy-going Dad. Not for nothing did Tony Blair appoint no-nonsense Hilary as Chief Whip 2001-2006 – only the second women ever in the post and one of the longest-serving Chief Whips. She was a Minister on either side of that. In 1997 Hilary was made Minister for Local Government & Housing, and in 2006 she became Minister for Social Exclusion, remaining in the cabinet as Chancellor of the Duchy of Lancaster. She stepped down from front-line politics in June 2007. Even before she was elected as MP, Hilary was well aware of Derwentside's problems as a Durham County councillor and assistant to her father Ernest. Following the closure of Consett steelworks in 1980, the Gartcosh steel mill in Scotland was under threat, and Hilary well remembers the protest march by Scottish steelworkers that passed though the North East on their way to London in the winter of 1985/86.

'The closure of Consett steelworks in 1980 was the biggest single challenge facing the Council,' said Ms Armstrong, 'the Council had to take action to secure the economic regeneration of the area. Huge resources were needed, requiring substantial government and European funding. New companies, like Derwent Valley Foods, were brought into the District. The Genesis Project was a hugely ambitious attempt to redevelop the former steelworks site. It has been only partly successful, and the original idea of it being a focus for sustainability and renewable energy has not taken off. But the Council did establish a new and better relationship with the private sector'. Hilary and her fellow Derwentside MP, North Durham MP Giles Radice, both joined the board of Genesis. Radice was first elected as MP for Chester le Street in a bye-election in 1973. He continued as MP from 1983 when Stanley and Chester le Street were combined in the one constituency, stepping down in 2001 when he was made a life peer. Kevan Jones took over as North Durham MP. 'One of the problems of Genesis was that it was based on the Newcastle Business Park, which had also been developed by Dysart Developments,' said Hilary, 'in my view too much was put in the hands of the developers, such as the appointment of architects, and the 25 years they were left in charge of the development I felt was too long. But Genesis has still brought considerable benefits to the area'.

Armstrong praised the Council's achievements for the youth of the district, such as the Youth Bus and the SPICE project. 'It's great to see young people debating in the Council Chamber, deciding how to allocate the funds the Council has given them,' she said. Another big plus was International Women's Day – 'very inspiring'. As a former Housing Minister, Armstrong recalled that Derwentside was being ranked one of the best two or three local authorities in the region in this field. She is also proud of her own role in encouraging Council house tenants to take more responsibility for managing their estates. She quotes the improvements in Lily Gardens, Dipton, as a good example where a run-down area has been much improved by a combination of Council action and active tenant participation.

Another area of participation Armstrong strongly supports is with the Council's leisure services, now run by a not-for-profit management company. After initial difficulties due – in her view – to Council staff not having sufficient business experience, the introduction of people from the private sector has made for success. 'We must get away from the old culture in this region of dependency and paternalism,' said Armstrong, 'so-called ordinary people are perfectly capable of running their own affairs, provided they have the necessary support'. As a government Minister, Armstrong could not show special favours to her own constituency, but the measures she brought in were, she believes, very much to Derwentside's benefit. 'Neighbourhood Renewal and Local Strategic Partnerships have been particularly beneficial,' she said, 'and, without changing the rules, we were able to widen the parameters so that areas where the pits had closed years ago could take advantage of Coalfield Communities grants.

'Derwentside is remarkable in that, when its basic industries of coal and steel collapsed, the community did not break up as has happened in other areas. It did go down to some extent, but that has largely been recovered. This district was built on coal and steel, and

"Cover Britain in Crocuses" (l-r, front): Hilary Armstrong MP, Mrs Carolyn McArdle, Council Chairman Cllr Richie McArdle. Alex & Mike to the rear.

although those industries have gone, the communities they created have remained largely intact'. Health issues Armstrong has worked hard to bring to the fore include the high levels of diabetes, chest complaints and heart conditions in the district. She supported research into the cluster of throat cancers instigated by Dot Atherton, a District Councillor and well-know community activist and worker, in the Consett area. 'Although we could not prove this was caused by working in the steelworks, it drew attention to the problem,' she said. From Hilary's point of view, what was the legacy of Derwentside District Council? 'They made sure that Consett did not die,' she said.

### Giles Radice

Reflecting on his time as North Durham MP, Giles Radice – now Lord Radice – said: 'The difference between Derwentside as it is now and how it was when I first became MP for the new North Durham constituency in 1983 is quite outstanding - there is full employment, thanks in part to what the government has done, but also in large measure to the efforts of the District Council. I have been particularly impressed with the local development body DIDA. The problem that Derwentside Council had from the start was how to weld together two different parts of the district, Consett and Stanley, which have always been traditional rivals

All smiles: Hilary Armstrong MP and husband, Professor Paul Corrigan

*Investors in People Award 1995 (l-r): MP Giles Radice with (l-r) Vicky Kirkley, Kim Cramb, Barbara Claspor*

and to some extent still are. When Stanley was brought into my constituency in 1983, I was struck by the contrast with Chester le Street which I had represented since 1973. Whereas Chester le Street was even then a relatively prosperous area, and is more so now, there was substantial unemployment and many areas of deprivation in the Stanley area. It was my policy to concentrate my efforts on these areas of need and try to persuade government to give them a high priority'.

A two-up, two-down terraced house in Tanfield provided a local base for Radice and his wife Lisanne for several years. Radice had regular surgeries in the constituency, including the areas of high deprivation, and worked closely with local councillors. The opening of a new community centre at Dipton was a highlight. Radice officially opened the Derwentside Community Action Centre in the Lousia Centre offices in Stanley in 1998. A wide range of local groups use the centre, now located at the Tommy Armstrong Centre, which is also an Infonet access point.

### Kevan Jones
Not many MPs can change a set of tyres in double-quick time, but North Durham MP Kevan Jones can – and he's proud of it. It's a skill he learned as a teenager, and it has never left him. But instead of becoming a "quick-fit fitter", Kevan made his career in the world of politics and is now an MP and government minister, appointed Under-Secretary of State for Defence and Minister for Veterans in November 2008. Born the son of a miner in a little village in North Nottinghamshire, Kevan's childhood home was No. 74 The Common, Shireoaks, so in a very real sense he has moved from the Common to the Commons. He came to the North East as a student at Newcastle Poly, gaining a degree in government & public policy. As part of his course, Kevan spent six

months at the University of South Maine in north east USA, studying American politics. 'It was during Ronald Reagan's years as President, when the US invaded Grenada, so it was very interesting, and a quite different culture,' recalled Kevan.

After four and a half years as parliamentary assistant to Newcastle East MP Nick Brown, Kevan had a 13-year career with the GMB union. He started as political officer, then became regional organiser and finally senior national organiser. For a period, he was also the GMB's legal officer. Kevan led his union's campaign to support the victims of asbestos and setting up the Asbestos Register. A Newcastle City councillor for eleven years, Kevan was chief whip of the controlling Labour Group for ten of those years, and also deputy leader, committee chairman and cabinet member. He was elected as MP

*Two Derwentside MPs, Giles Radice & Hilary Armstrong*

*No Place and Sleepy Valley – amused local MP Kevan Jones (CFW)*

for North Durham in 2001 and immediately made an impact as an active and outspoken constituency MP, but also as a member of the Defence Select Committee. 'In my maiden speech I described the constituency as being rural with urban problems,' said Kevan, 'I found areas of severe deprivation, with levels of poverty as bad as anything in a big city like Newcastle, but masked to a certain degree by the wonderful countryside we enjoy in Durham.

'After the closure of the Consett steelworks in 1980, I think there tended to be a concentration on the town of Consett, when in fact it affected the whole of the District. Many of the people who lost their jobs at the steelworks came from the Stanley area, and even

*Kevan Jones MP*

before then there had been the steady closure of the pits. Add to that, some of the new industries that had come in like Ever Ready were themselves closing down'. Kevan praised the efforts of the community to help themselves. 'Craghead is a shining example where local

people really have made a difference. Craghead lost its pit in the 1960s and its clothing factory in the 1980s, but the villagers themselves led the way in community regeneration. The Craghead Partnership was formed in 1996 and won support from Europe and the Single Regeneration Budget. It now has a new and modern village hall, which offers Internet access - a focal point for all villagers,' he said.

As the local MP, Jones supported the setting-up of Stanley Town Council. 'With the introduction of a single unitary council for the whole of Durham, something I have always supported, I believe town and parish councils should play a much more significant role in the future,' said Jones, 'to me it makes sense for services like street cleaning, street lighting, footpaths, play areas and recreation grounds to be administered at a very local level. These may seem minor matters to some, but for many residents they are very important. In meeting the chief executive and Leader of the County Council, I have advised them to devolve these types of services to town and parish councils, and for the County Council to concentrate on strategic decision-making'. On becoming the MP, Kevan was much amused to find he was representing No Place and Sleepy Valley. 'I've asked lots of people, but no-one can tell me exactly how these places got their names,' he said.

*Craghead Village Hall, next to Post Office (CFW)*

## Chapter Twelve
# Famous Visitors

*Prince Charles, Princes Anne, Tony Blair, Mo Mowlam; Visitors Book; David Bellamy; Women in Action.*

Prince Charles visited Derwentside three times, in 1982, 1984 and 1998, a rare accolade for a small District. On his first visit on 3rd December 1982, he came by special train (the line had recently been closed) and was met by Lord Barnard, Lord Lieutenant of County Durham at Consett's old railway station where he unveiled a plaque. The Prince was taken by coach to Integrated Micro Products and Paul Loughran, then walked to the Civic Centre for a buffet lunch. The official party included Sir Charles Villiers, DDC Chief Executive Terry Hodgson, DIDA MD Laurie Haveron, Mark I'Anson (Integrated Micro Products) and Arthur Loughran. The guest list for lunch at the Civic Centre included: BSC(I) Chief Executive John Dunbar, the Chief Constable of Durham, Durham County Council Chairman Bill Firby, DDC Chairman Joe Walker, Consett MP David Watkins, DCC Chief Executive DCC Peter Dawson, DDC Leader Billy Bell, DDC chief officers Bill Hetherington (planning), & Malcolm Davies (technical), Industrial Development Officer John Carney, and all seven members of the Industry Committee: William Coates, Vince Kelly, Ken Robson, Bill Stockdale, Joe Walker, Selby Walker, Willie Walton. Prince Charles' visit on 2nd July, 1998 was for the official opening of International Cuisine Ltd at their new factory on the Hownsgill Industrial Estate, part of Project Genesis. Princess Anne opened the Delves Village Hall on 11th February 2000.

Charles was not the first Prince of Wales to visit the district. The future King Edward VIII, who broke protocol by visiting miners' families in their homes and publicly voicing social concerns, visited Stanley on 29th January 1929 and again on 6th December 1934 when he laid the foundation stone for the Stanley Social Services building. Unemployed men were put to work building these social centres, the materials often paid for by prosperous southern towns who "adopted" a northern town or village. HH Princess Marie Louise opened the three-day YMCA Royal Fair at Consett in February 1924. General Booth visited the Salvation Army barracks in Stanley High

*Meeting the Prince in 1982 (l-r) DDC Chairman Joe Walker, DCC chief executive Peter Dawson, DDC Chairman Bill Firby*

*Chairman Brian Charlton gives Prince Charles, on his 1984 visit, a warm handshake as DDC chief executive Terry Hodgson looks on.*

*Opening of International Cuisine factory, Hownsgill, 2nd July 1998. Chairman Richie McArdle greets Prince Charles.*

*Pair of cannon presented by DDC to the Prince & Princess of Wales on their marriage in 1981*

*A cannon for the Prince & Princess of Wales, married on 29th July 1981. DDC Chairman Sid Dixon with the Council's wedding gift.*

*Hands in pockets, Charles chats to Edith (MC)*

*Royal train approaches Consett 1984. PC stands guard (left), dog not impressed (right) (CO)*

Street in 1911. He died next year aged 83. In the 19th century, Charles Dickens and his associate, hunting author Robert Smith Surtees, who lived at Hamsterley Hall, came to Shotley Spa, as did Prime Minister William Gladstone. Future Prime Minister Tony Blair opened the Victoria Centre, Consett on 21st July 1995.

*Princess Anne opens Delves Lane Village Hall 11th February 2000. Cllrs Bill Stockdale & Alex Watson in close attendance (WS)*

It is claimed that Oliver Cromwell took refreshment in the Three Horse Shoes pub in Maiden Law near Annfield Plain in the 1640s. Likewise, he is said to have visited the Pack Horse in Tanfield.

The Omagh
Glass Sculpture

Mo Mowlam MP with youngsters

Cllr Mike Malone meets the much-admired Mo Mowlam (MM)

## Mo Mowlam

Much-loved Redcar MP and former Northern Ireland Secretary, the late Mo Mowlam was the star guest at a presentation 23rd April 1999 to mark the link between Derwentside and families affected by the Omagh bombing. Mo handed over a glass sculpture created by local artist Maralyn O'Keefe. Local MPs Hilary Armstrong and Giles Radice were also present. The ceremony finished with a prayer for peace by representatives of all faiths in the district. Maralyn was inspired by the Northern Ireland peace talks in which Mo Mowlam played a crucial role as Secretary of State for Northern Ireland. The sculpture consisted of three hexagonal panels, red, white and blue, and is based on the Giant's Causeway. The colours depicted the varying scenery as well as the Union flag; each panel is

Omagh visit to Derwentside, (l-r):Cllr Richie McArdle (Derwentside DC chairman), Hilary Armstrong MP, Maralyn O'Keefe (artist), John McKinney (Omagh chief executive), Dr Mo Mowlam MP, Cllr Alan Rainey (vice chair Omagh DC).

*Tony Blair meets the people after opening the Victoria Centre, Consett on 21st July 1995*

*Blair meets "the Don", County Cllr Don Robson. Happy Hilary on left, pensive Mike Malone in centre*

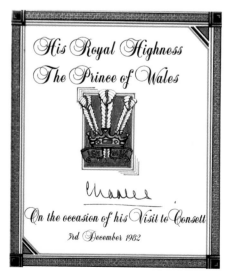

*Charles signs just one of his names for the DDC Visitors' Book*

split from top to bottom to represent peoples' differing ideals, and the barbed wire motif evokes not only terrorism, barricades and security measures, but also the crown of thorns worn by Jesus on Good Friday.

**Visitors Book**
The official DDC Visitors Book records that the 1977 International Folklore Festival, organised by Cllr Willie Westgarth, attracted visitors from Germany, the Netherlands, Luxembourg, Yugoslavia, Sweden, Czechoslovakia, Norway, Belgium and Italy. Stanley Lions organised a Commemorative Luncheon for the Port Stanley Civilians Appeal on 25th September 1982, attended by the Earl of Derby. Sports Council Chairman Dickie Jeeps was guest of honour at the Derwentside Recreation Scheme Seminar on Thursday 4th October 1984. ISTC General Secretary Bill Sirs headed a party from the Iron & Steel Trades Confederation which gave a presentation to the Council on 18th December 1984. Patrick Jenkin MP, Secretary of State for the Environment, inspected the reclamation work at the BSC site on 19th April 1985. Frank Field MP, Minister for Welfare Reform, visited the district in 1998 as part of his regional tour. Derwentside was chosen to see the improved service delivery methods introduced by DDC using new technology.

*David Dimbleby at the Lamplight Arts Centre, Stanley, for Question Time in 2005 (IP)*

*Old Pals reunited: Cllr Larry Thomas (right) meets Speaker of the House of Commons George Thomas MP, later Viscount Tonypandy, in 1982. They were at school together in Wales (BT) [see Chapter 8]*

*Duke of Gloucester (left) meets with Cllr Denise Bullivant, DDC Leader Billy Bell, Cllr Vince Kelly, Cllr Ken Sessford (right)*

*Environmentalist Dr David Bellamy launches Watling Wood in January 1995 with Cllr Terry Richardson (left) and Cllr Kevin Earley (WS)*

### Bellamy wood planting

In January 1995, famed environmentalist Dr David Bellamy, with Cllrs Terry Richardson and Kevin Early, started the planting of "Watling Wood", a new community woodland at Leadgate. The name of the wood was chosen by pupils at nearby Leadgate Junior School and was taken from the Roman road that passes close by. The project, by the local environmental charity Consett Acorn trust, involved the planting of over 40,000 coniferous and broadleaved trees on 40 acres of old spoil heaps from former collieries and ironworks. In 2005, the Lamplight Arts Centre in Stanley was the venue for the BBC programme "Question Time", hosted by David Dimbleby.

### Women in Action

Actress Denise Welch, Diana Lamplugh OBE, Founder/Director of the Suzy Lamplugh Trust, and GMB official Dari Taylor – later to become a North East MP - were guest speakers at the Derwentside Women in Action Week, 6-10th May 1995, at the Stanley Civic Theatre. The event was set up to coincide with International Women's Day. "Agony Aunt" Denise Robertson, who has appeared regularly on the "Richard & Judy" tv show, spoke at the same event the following year.

*Pictures (right) from International Women's Day in Stanley 7th March 2008*

*General William Booth, Salvation Army founder, on his visit to Stanley in 1911 (AP)*

*Preparing for lift-off (MW)*

*Radio presenter Judie McCourt (MW)*

*Away they go! (MW)*

*Hilary makes a point (MW)*

*Consett Junior School. Thumbs up, girls. For boy on left, it's thumbs down.*

*Hilary in eye-catching coat.*

*Three formidable ladies (l-r) Cllrs Anne Taylor, Olga Milburn, Sue Rothwell (MW)*

## Chapter Thirteen
# Ambassadors & Heroes

*Bobby, Denise, Angela, Susan, Glenn, Bob, Terry & Kevin, Pat, Owen, Karl, Arnold, Michael, Sadie et al.*

Derwentside folk are understandably enormously proud of people from the District who have achieved national and international fame in their chosen professions. Their success has helped raise the profile of the North East in a positive manner, and they have become in reality ambassadors for the District. Derwentside District Council has formally recognised the value of these high-achieving individuals who were born in, live, or have a strong family connection with the District, honouring them by bestowing on them the formal title of "Ambassador of Derwentside".

*Ambassadors of Derwentside (l-r): Roger McKechnie, Angela Bruce, Glenn McCrory, Susan Maughan, Bob Murray (MW)*

*Graeme Danby*

*Lyn Miles*

*Paul Collingwood*

*Alun Armstrong*

*Terry Deary*

*Mark I'Anson*

*Sir Bobby Robson*

*Sadie "the Bra Lady" Ayton*

Bobby Robson – later to become Sir Bobby – was appointed as one of Derwentside's first official Ambassadors in Millenium Year 2000, along with actresses Denise Welch and Angela Bruce, and singer Susan Maughan. Boxer Glenn McCrory, singer Ian McCallum, and businessmen Bob Murray and Roger McKechnie followed. In 2005, cricketer Paul Collingwood, actor Alun Armstrong, author Terry Deary, opera singer Graeme Danby, company bosses Lyn Miles and Mark I'Anson, and Sadie Ayton "the Bra Lady", were added to the illustrious list. All have strong local connections. An "investiture" took place at a short ceremony at an Ambassadors' Dinner in the Civic Hall, Consett on Friday 27th May 2005. During the ceremony each Ambassador was presented with a parchment recording the Council's decision and a pendant to be worn on formal occasions. Guests representing all sections of the community were present to welcome the new Ambassadors.

The last two Ambassadors to be created by Derwentside Council were Olympic swimmer Joanne Jackson and former Durham County Council Leader Don Robson, former Chairman of Durham County Cricket Club and Deputy Lord Lieutenant of County Durham. At the final ceremony to celebrate the District's Heroes and Ambassadors at the Civic Centre on Friday 21st November 2008, Joanne Jackson's father Barry said: "we live in Yorkshire, and we have been coming here for 13 years, using the facilities at Consett and Stanley baths, so something must be good." Don Robson said: "I can't disguise it, I'm a lad from Winlaton. When my wife and I moved here to live in Medomsley, we didn't know what to expect. Here in Derwentside, you are a different sort of people, quite unique. People will greet you, they will help you, and it is a great privilege to be one of you. And in the Empire Theatre coffee shop they serve the best cherry scones in the world!".

**Alun Armstrong** was born in Annfield Plain and went to Consett Grammar School, Currently starring in the tv series New Tricks, he spent nine years with the Royal Shakespeare Company. Made his film debut in 1971 in "Get Carter." His notable television appearances include the 1996 BBC drama series "Our Friends in the North" and, most recently, "New Tricks." In 1994 Armstrong won the Laurence Olivier Award for Best Actor for his

*Ian McCallum (second on left) with Stiff Little Fingers*

**Ambassadors of Derwentside**

Alun Armstrong actor
Sadie Ayton "the Bra Lady"
Angela Bruce actress
Paul Collingwood international cricketer
Graeme Danby opera singer
Terry Deary children's author
Mark I'Anson businessman
Joanne Jackson Olympic swimming medallist
Ian McCallum rock guitarist
Glenn McCrory former world champion boxer
Roger McKechnie businessman
Susan Maughan singer
Lyn Miles businesswoman
Bob Murray CBE businessman
Sir Bobby Robson top soccer player & manager
Don Robson CBE leader in politics & sport
Denise Welch actress

*Don Robson becomes an Ambassador of Derwentside. Council Vice Chairman Cllr Susan Rothwell does the honours (MW)*

*Sir Bobby Robson, then manager of Newcastle United, receives his Ambassador Award from Council Leader Alex Watson at St James Park, 2000 (MW)*

*(l-r) Neil Killeen, DDC Chairman Liz Coulson, Paul Collingwood (MW)*

*Denise Welch*　　　　　*Joanne Jackson*

performance in the title role of the stage musical Sweeney Todd. **Sadie Ayton**, or Sadie the Bra Lady, as she is better known, opened her first shop in Consett in 1970. She now has 63,000 customers and outlets in Darlington, Sunderland, Ashington, Thirsk and Scarborough. She has won the Underlines Shop Award, the top award for the lingerie industry, as National Lingerie Retailer of the Year. Actress **Angela Bruce** was born in Leeds but brought up in Craghead. Played Janice Stubbs in Coronation Street, Sandra Ling in Angels, prison officer Mandy Goodhew in Bad Girls and Foreign Secretary Ruth Chambers in Spooks. Bruce has also appeared in Prime Suspect, Red Dwarf and Only Fools and Horses, and in many other tv roles. Durham and England cricketer **Paul Collingwood MBE** was born and brought up in Shotley Bridge and played for the local club, forcing his way into the under-13 side at the age of nine. He went to Blackfyne Comprehensive School, now Consett Community Sports College. Collingwood made his first-class debut in 1995, played his first one-day international in 2001 and made his test debut two years later. He was England one-day captain 2007/08 and is Vice Captain of Durham. He was named one of the five Wisden Cricketers of the Year in 2007. International opera singer **Graeme Danby** was born in Consett. He studied at the Royal Academy of Music in London and is Principle Bass with the English National Opera. In 2006 he was awarded an honorary degree by Northumbria University, along with his wife Valerie Reid. "Horrible Histories" author **Terry Deary** has written nearly 200 books, mainly for children and teenagers. In 2007 the Daily Telegraph described him as 'the most influential historian in Britain today'. His books have won numerous awards and have been translated into 39 languages. He also writes for tv, theatre and radio. Born in Sunderland, he lives in Burnhope. Businessman **Mark I'Anson**, former Chairman of DIDA (Derwentside Industrial Development Agency), is Managing Director of Integrated Micro Products which he set up in Consett in 1982. **Joanne Jackson** came through the Derwentside Swimming Scheme to win medals at Commonwealth, World and Olympic level – her greatest achievement to date a bronze medal in the womens 400 metres freestyle at the Beijing Olympics in 2008. Now for London 2012! Rock guitarist **Ian McCallum** plays for Stiff Little Fingers, a punk band from Belfast. He has also been associated with folk-rock group Lindisfarne. Born in Newcastle, he is now based in Los Angeles. **Glenn McCrory** from Stanley, the only North East boxer ever to win a world title. Since retiring from the ring, McCrory has shown remarkable versatility as an actor, scriptwriter and tv pundit. 'Although my job takes me all over the world, I am still very much a local lad who is proud of his roots and the traditions of the North East'. Businessman **Roger McKechnie** rose from Marketing Manager to Managing Director at Tudor Crisps. He founded snacks company Phileas Fogg in 1982. When he sold out to United Biscuits twelve years later, the company had a turnover of £25m. More recently he has been Chairman of Pride Valley Foods and founded The Samling, a luxury retreat for businessmen in Cumbria. Singer **Susan Maughan** reached No. 3 in the UK pop charts with "Bobby's Girl" in 1962 and has remained popular ever since. She was born in Consett where her father Vin still lives. **Lyn Miles** is Managing Director of Consett-based glass specialists Romag who supply photovoltaic panels and glass and glazing products to the renewable energy, architectural, safety/security and transportation markets. Consett-born **Bob Murray CBE** is a businessman and former Chairman of Sunderland Football Club. An accountant by trade, he made his fortune through the growth and sale of the Spring Ram kitchen manufacturing company. He became Chairman of Sunderland AFC in 1986, replacing the motor magnate Sir Tom Cowie. 'As an Ambassador of Derwentside I am inspired by the area and its people who, as I learned in my formative years, embody the qualities of which the North East can be justifiably proud'. **Bobby Robson**, or **Sir Robert William Robson Kt CBE**, to give him his full name and title, was born in Langley Park in 1933, played for Langley Park Juniors, and was a professional footballer for nearly 20 years. In all that time Robson, an inside forward, played for just three clubs: Fulham, West Bromwich Albion and (briefly) for Vancouver Royals. He won 20 England caps, scoring four goals. As manager, he twice took Ipswich to the league runners-up spot, and won the FA Cup in 1978 and the UEFA Cup three years later. In his 13 years at Ipswich, Robson signed only 14 players from other clubs. As England manager, he took the national side to the semi-finals of the 1990 World Cup. Then followed great success in Europe in charge of PSV Eindhoven, Sporting Lisbon, FC Porto and Barcelona, winning league titles in Holland (twice) and Portugal (twice), and national cups in Holland, Portugal and Spain. In 1997 Robson led Barcelona to a cup treble, the European Cup Winners Cup, the Spanish Cup and the Spanish Super Cup. From 1999-2004 Robson was manager of Newcastle United where he is still held in high esteem. Bobby has received many honours, including being knighted in 2002, given an honorary doctorate of Newcastle University in 2003, made a Freeman of the City of Newcastle in 2005 and of Ipswich in 2008. He has been inducted in the English Football Hall of Fame and is the Honorary President of Ipswich Town. In 2007 he received the BBC Sports Personality of the Year Lifetime Award. He said: 'Derwentside is a proud, closely-knit and very picturesque part of North East England'. **Don Robson CBE,** Deputy Lord Lieutenant of County Durham, was the youngest ever Chairman of Durham County Council. After boundary changes in 1974, he became Deputy Leader of Tyne & Wear Council. He returned to County Durham to become Leader of Durham County Council and in 1997 was awarded the CBE for services to local government. Many people think his greatest achievement came in 1990 when he brought first class cricket to Durham. Actress **Denise Welch** was born in Ebchester and went to Blackfyne Grammar School. Her many television appearances include Auf Wiedersehen, Pet (1986), Byker Grove (1990-1991), Spender (1991-1993), Soldier Soldier (1993), and Coronation Street (1997-2000). Her stage roles include that of Sandy in the musical Grease. Since 2005 Denise has been a regular panelist on ITV1's topical chat show Loose Women. Has been married to her second husband, actor Tim Healy, since 1988.

## Heroes

Uniquely in Durham, the Council introduced "Heroes of Derwentside", an idea suggested by Cllr Mike Malone, to celebrate the contribution of ordinary people to the community, voluntary sector and charities. There are 52 Heroes of Derwentside: Joan Armstrong, Adam Shaun Barker, Goff Bates, Cecilia Bell, Joanne Bennett, Michael Bragan, Ryan Bragan, Marie Carr, David Collingwood, Mrs. Christina (Chrissie) Coombes, Mavis Coulson, Tom Cowan, Rosalie Coyle, Christine Creegan, Doreen Cummings, John Cunningham, Margaret Darroch, Kevin Dinsdale, Ian Andrew Fenwick, Kathleen Grogan, Harry Guildford, Jack Hair, Ann Hall, Joan Harley, David Jackson, Harry Jeffery, Trevor Jones, Margaret Jopling, Mrs Ethel Kerswell, Carole Livingston, Jim McCrory, Hugh Malone, Aileen Mantle, John O'Connor, Thomas Palmer, David Parker, Alan Parnaby, Mrs Vera Parnaby, Brian Roberts, Mrs Gail Roberts, Cyril Robinson, Dorothy A Robson, Rose Mary Robson, Ann Rogers, Jim Ruddick, Richard Salkeld, John Short, Mrs Ruth Thompson, Alan Turner, Sadie Walton, John Robert Whaley, David (Jock) Williamson.

## Bob Liddle MBE

When multiple sclerosis forced Bob Liddle to take early retirement from his job teaching computer programming with Derwentside ITEC Unit in 1996, he found a new role with the launch of the Council's Infonet Project. With the encouragement and help of DDC Director of Corporate Development Alan Hodgson, Bob took on the job of creating hundreds of web sites for community groups and local schools, bringing the benefits of the internet to thousands of people around the world. He never charged for his services, and in 2000 he was awarded the MBE. Bob was diagnosed with MS in 1990. He said: "my world was at an end and that was it. I had done everything I was going to do with my life. I was going to the day centre at Stanley and getting very depressed, thinking 'oh my God, this is my life from now on.' Now I realise that as this door closed, another door opened". In 1998, Bob worked with the Council's infastructure client manager Steve Hodgson to set up Britain's first on-line job centre. Bob said:'Derwentside Infonet has opened up new horizons for me to contact people all over the world, including New Zealand, Australia, Canada and the USA, as well as with the UK. Through the medium of the Internet, I have an enormous source of information and communication at my finger-tips. I have made friends, been involved with educational programmes, and 'chatted' with people in real time. The potential is there for 'virtual classrooms' for schools via Internet Relay Chat, to share valuable teacher resources, as well as for research. I cannot over-emphasise the difference this has made to me, and I feel that this is too valuable and important to all the community to be ignored or allowed to fail'.

*Special people (l-r): Christine Creegan, Joanne Bennett, Cecilia Bell are made Heroes of Derwentside in 2008 for their work in helping people with special needs (MW)*

*Bob Liddle MBE*

*Heroes on stage (MW)*

*Derwentside Hero Jack Hair (MW)*

*DDC Chairman Cllr Denise Bennett and more Derwentside Heroes 2003 (MW)*

*A night for Heroes, 21st November 2008. Harry Guilford (centre) to the fore (MW)*

*Bosnia Aid, Terry (left) and Kevin.*

**Terry & Kevin - aid to Bosnia**
In 1995 and again in 1997 Terry Scarr and Kevin O'Rourke, both workers with Derwentside Council's Direct Service Organisation, drove a wagon to Bosnia with much-needed aid. The 5,500 mile round trip took three weeks and delivered ten tonnes of food, medical supplies and clothing to a refugee camp near Tusla. Both aid trips were supported by Council staff and members, as well as the people of Derwentside.

*Bosnia Aid, local youngsters lend Terry a hand*

*Pat Holmes (CFW)*

### Singer, conductor

Pat Holmes – perhaps better known as Pat Boustead - still lives in the house in Medomsley Road bought by her parents Fred and Peggy in 1935 for £434. Fred Boustead sang in various local choirs, and Pat had piano and singing lessons from an early age. She trained with Dr John Hutchinson in Newcastle and became a professional singer and was still entertaining well past seventy after recovering from a series of serious operations for cancer in her thirties. She has also conducted local choirs and operatic societies for many years. In 2008 she conducted a 270-strong joint choir in Durham Cathedral, and she also conducted the Leadgate Gleemen. Soprano Pat won a singing festival at the age of 17, also taking part in a performance of Merrie England put on by Consett UDC at the local football ground for the Queen's Coronation in 1953.

### Local lad flies high

Owen McFarlane is Managing Director and Chief Executive of CAV Aerospace. The company's three divisions are involved with aerostructures, ice protection and manufacturing small component machinery. After attending Whinney Hill Secondary Modern School in Durham, McFarlane served his engineering apprenticeship with NEI and Clark Chapman Marine in Gateshead, becoming NEI Production Manager at the age of 27. During his time with NEI he was able to continue his education, gaining OND and HND qualifications leading to a degree in management. He moved on to work as Operations Manager for Haltwhistle-based Killfrost who produced ice protection systems, and was part of a three-man management buyout with MD Geoff Cross and Brian Humphries. The new company set up in brand-new premises in Annfield

Plain in July 1990. At that time just ten people were on the payroll. By 2008 CAV had a £6m annual turnover and employed a 700-strong workforce worldwide, 450 at the company headquarters on the No 1 Industrial Estate, Consett. The company had other manufacturing sites in Leicester, Poland and the USA. "Derwentside District Council had the foresight to make facilities available," said McFarlane, "we were able to move straight into a 20,000 sq ft factory. Not only that, we were made to feel so welcome. The service and support we have had from the district council has been second to none". In 2003 McFarlane became Chairman of DIDA – Derwentside Industrial Development Agency – and oversaw its change to DEA – Derwentside Enterprise Agency – in September 2008. This was the merger of three organisations, DIDA, the Derwentside Business Network and the Derwentside Engineering Forum. "DIDA always was a broad church," said McFarlane, "Its focus has been on creating jobs, particularly high value, high technology jobs. DEA now includes the Council, business, banks, lawyers and education. With changes in local government, it is essential that the loyalty and goodwill built up over the years is not fragmented".

### Blackhill soldier wins Military Cross

The award of the Military Cross to local soldier Karl Jackson in 2007 was recognised by Derwentside Council, possibly the first local authority in the country to honour our fighting forces in Afghanistan. The civic reception and hospitality given to L/Cpl Karl Jackson and his young comrades from the Third Battalion the Parachute Regiment helped to turn the tide of public opinion which previously had been largely indifferent if not overtly hostile to the men and women putting their lives at risk in our name.

Jackson, from Bridgehill, then a 24-year old private, was awarded the MC for gallantry in Helmand province between 2nd July and 29th August 2006. The Colonel Commandant, General Sir John Reith, summed up Karl's actions. He said: 'Your actions in Sangin during July and August were outstanding and you clearly displayed strong courage and leadership in the face of a determined enemy. Your bravery in going forward under fire to repel an enemy attack and retrieve vital combat stores in one contact and later your total selflessness in exposing yourself to rescue your stricken Platoon Sergeant were in keeping with the highest traditions of the Regiment.'

Karl told the News of the World: 'The Taliban were giving us a real fight. We were on top of a two-storey building when 40 of them charged to at-tack a position on our left. We hit them with eve-rything we had - two ma-chine guns, a grenade launcher and two Minimi machine guns. I reckon 80 per cent of them were killed or seriously hurt. But as they regrouped and tried to sneak up on us Paddy [Sgt Caldwell] was shot through the neck. The bullet was so close it made me flinch. I knew straight away he was in big trouble. I grabbed him by his webbing and dragged him down off the roof and on to my shoulders. He was unconscious but I checked his airways and they weren't

Cpl Karl Jackson with MC at Buckingham Palace (GD)

(l-r) Cllr Tom Clark, Cpl Karl Jackson MC,
Cllr Mike Malone (MW)

Paras past and present. Karl Jackson, standing fifth from
left (GD)

Remembrance Day Parade 2008 (MW)

3rd Bt Parachute Regiment Seated at front (l-r): Cpl Jake Bourne (instructor), Capt Dave Richardson (Platoon
Commander), Cpl Karl Jackson MC, Cpl George Scott (instructor) (CFW)

bad. The bullet had obviously missed his jugular and spine. Then the medics arrived. I didn't think for a minute I'd get a medal'. Sgt Caldwell later made a good recovery back in the UK.

In another incident, Karl Jackson led his men under intense Taliban attack as his unit fought its way through the streets of Sangin to re-supply the beleaguered garrison in the district centre. On Wednesday 23rd February 2008 Karl, by now a Lance Corporal, went to Buckingham Palace to receive his medal from the Queen. Karl, a former pupil at Blackfyne School, told the Durham Advertiser that he had not been afraid as he faced the Taliban, but he had been nervous at meeting the Queen. Two days later, 25th February, Karl and 15 of his comrades from 3 Para, plus Major Keith (Ned) Cameron, also from Consett, were the guests of honour at a civic reception in Consett Civic Hall. They were also the guests of the Council at the four-star hotel Derwent Hotel that night. This hospitality was very much appreciated by the soldiers, who had expected only a "pie and a pint" and basic overnight accommodation. In addition, all members of the Durham Branch of the Parachute Regimental Association were invited. The Council also paid for Karl's grandmother to attend from Bedfordshire. Major Cameron's mother still lives in Blackhill – three doors away from where Karl's mother used to live.

Durham PRA branch member George Devanney said many of the guest were astonished by the number of medals the soldiers wore, the majority of whom looked like they should still be in the sixth form. "The graceful acceptance, the demeanour and the gentlemanly behaviour of the young soldiers representing 3 Para that evening gave all our members something to be proud of," said George. The Council had framed a copy of LCpl Jackson's citation and presented Karl with a statuette. A further statuette was presented to the Corporal's Mess of 3 Para. The prime mover for the event, said George, was Council Deputy Leader, Cllr Mike Malone, who instructed DDC Public Relations Officer John Davis to "clear his desk and pull out the stops." "Nothing was too good for the soldiers of 3 Para," said George. Another chapter was added at the 2008 Remembrance Day, on 9th November. A squad of 3 Para, including Cpl Jackson, took part in the parade through Consett for the service at the Civic Centre. This was the last such occasion to be hosted by Derwentside Council, so there were presentations by Council Chairman and Cllr Malone at the reception afterwards. The only thing missing was the regimental mascot, a pony, which had been promised but which failed to make it.

### Four generations at The Works
Arnold Parkin was a "roller" at the CIC Slab, Bloom & Billet Mill – "the top job in the Mill" was his proud boast. He later became Production Foreman, but lost his job with everyone else in 1980, or rather "the steelworks left me" is how he put it. Arnold and his son David, father Stan and grandfather Richard Parkin all worked for the Consett Iron Co or British Steel, a four-generation family record that was common if not typical. The closure of the

*Sadie Walton gets her award from Council Vice Chairman Cllr Susan Rothwell (MW))*

steelworks was announced on 5th December 1979. The last steel was made on Friday 13th September 1980, and the works officially closed on the Saturday. Although steel production ceased on the Friday, the men were entitled to a full week's pay and were expected to work until the end although there was nothing they could be expected to do. As the Foreman on the last Friday night shift, Arnold's worry was to keep everybody safe and make sure they all got away without incident. When it was realised that the fight to save the steelworks had been lost, the emphasis then was on how much redundancy each worker would get. Christmas 1980 was a bonanza for the local shops. Big redundancy cheques made it a Christmas like no other, before or since.

Always a keen photographer, Parkin took it up full-time. He had previously been a freelance photographer with the Consett Chronicle. With persistent rumours that the steelworks would close one day, Parkin made sure he had another string to his bow. From 1948-56, Parkin was full-time projectionist at the Empire, Consett, as well as doing holiday relief at the Olympia Cinema in Blackhill. At that time there were six cinemas in Consett, the Empire, Town Hall, Plaza, Rex, the Roxy in Leadgate and the Olympia. All but the Rex - the poshest of the lot - were owned by

*Sadie Walton (centre) enjoys a joke as the champagne is poured to honour her son Keith (second right, holding trophy) after his medal-winning success in the 1974 Commonwealth Games (SW)*

Consett Cinemas Ltd. The introduction of the "big screen" with stereophonic sound at the Empire made extra work for the staff. Raising the huge screen to switch from cinema to theatre shows had to be done by hand and took a full day. After the 2002/03 refurbishment, the screen could be raised and lowered at the touch of a button, allowing film and theatre shows on the same day.

### Brickie on the march

Michael Curran was working as a bricklayer with CIC when the blow fell. It was traditional for brickies to seek an indoor job at the steelworks during the winter, and the last time Michael did this, he stayed four years. He had started with Consett UDC and was there for ten years before going to work for private construction firms. Michael took part in the march and demonstration in London. 'We caught the train from Durham to Kings Cross, and marched from there to the Houses of Parliament,' said Michael, 'there were too many of us all to go inside, but hundreds did and they lobbied the MPs'.

### The last apprentices

Gerard "Ged" Smith started as a craft apprentice at Consett Steelworks in September 1979 in the last intake of apprentices. Nearly thirty years later [20th September 2008] he organised an emotional reunion at the Consett Steel Club of the 35-strong band, many of whom went on to have successful careers in the steel industry elsewhere and abroad. After an initial 18 months general training, the apprentices went into one of three specialities: electrical, mechanical and boiler-making. Hundreds applied for these plum positions, so only the best gained places. On venturing out from the relative calm and safety of the training centre, the apprentices were introduced to the 'daunting, dangerous and visually exciting' world of steelmaking. 'To see the molten metal from the blast furnace being tapped, and experience the heat, the noise and the smell, is something you can never forget,' recalled Smith.

### Swim Coach Sadie

Life-long swim coach Sadie Walton – 81 in 2008 – has spent a lifetime coaching young swimmers. She was a founder-member of the amateur-run Consett Swimming Club in 1963 and held various positions over the years, finishing up as the club's long-serving President. Consett Baths, built with the help of a fund-raising campaign, opened in 1962. Previous to that, the nearest swimming baths were at Durham. Sadie's father

James Haley learned to swim in the River Derwent at Shotley Bridge. Sadie's children Marjory, Keith and Helen enjoyed family holidays with an aunt at Luton where there was a fine open-air pool. Keith became a champion swimmer, winning a bronze medal at the 1974 Commonwealth games in New Zealand as a member of the England 4x100 metres freestyle relay team.

### Big Brother

Anthony Hutton from Consett won Big Brother series 6. Aged 23 when he entered Big Brother, he has worked as a postman and a dancer, has played in panto and has made a keep-fit DVD. Anthony, who used to play soccer for Annfield Plain FC, played for the Celebs against the Legends on Sky 1's The Match in 2005 and 2006. He was "Man of the Match" in 2005. After his Big Brother victory, Derwentside District Council made Anthony an "Ambassador for Young People". Council leader, Alex Watson said: 'Anthony has certainly put Consett on the map'.

### Fond memories for Angela

Actress Angela Bruce came to Craghead at the age of three, purely by chance. Born in Leeds, she was sent to the Barnardo's children's home in Newcastle and was brought to the village by one of the nurses who were allowed to take a child home for the weekend. The nurse's family treated Angela so kindly, that when it was time for her to go back to Newcastle, she turned and said 'bye-bye, Mummy and Daddy'. The Bruce family just could not let her go, so they took off her coat and she stayed, never to return to the children's home. The nurse became Angela's adopted

*Angela Bruce*

sister. Angela has very fond memories of Craghead and the people who lived there. Angela was probably the first black person most Craghead residents had ever seen, but incidents of racism were rare. One such was at a school netball match. Someone from the visiting school tied a black plastic doll to a goalpost. The Craghead lads did battle on behalf of "our Angela" and the netball match had to be abandoned. Angela moved away 1970, but she has never forgotten the kindness of the people of Craghead.

Angela Bruce first came to notice in the stage musical "Hair", and since then has taken leading roles in many tv programmes including Angels, Dr Who, Holby City, Coronation Street and Lovejoy. Deputy Council Leader Mike Malone, in common with a lot of other councillors, has a favourite scene in "Only Fools and Horses" which involves Angela. Our intrepid pair, Del Boy and Rodney, dressed as Batman and Robin, accidentally burst on the scene, emerging through the mist just as a local councillor (Bruce) is being mugged by some young thugs. On seeing this apparition approaching at a run (the lads were late for a supposed fancy dress party due to their Reliant Robin breaking down) the would-be muggers take flight. The councillor lady, Chair of the local Planning Committee, is suitably grateful and – remember, this is fiction – in return does Del Boy a favour over a planning application. Of course, this could not possibly happen in real life(!).

## Honorary Aldermen

On Tuesday 17th March 2009, thirty-four present and former Members of Derwentside District Council were to be made Honorary Aldermen: Ian Agnew, Mary Armstrong, Walter Armstrong, Alan Atkinson, Colin Bell, Denise Bennett, Lynn Boyd, Michael Brough, Joanne Carr, Brian Charlton, Ronald Dodd, Tony Donaghy, Kevin Earley, Eric Edwards, Robert Telford Gardener, Janet Temperley Greener, Jim Griffiths, Henry Shaw Guildford, Derek Hume, Jean Huntley, Dorothea Khamis, Dennis Lavin, David Gwyn Llewellyn, Michael Malone, Olga Milburn, John Pallas, John Pears, Terry Richardson, Bill Stockdale, Anne Taylor, Joseph Toner, Eric Turner, Ken Walker, Alex Watson.

*Aldermen to be: Back row (l-r) Cllr David Llewellyn, Cllr Mike Malone, Cllr Ossie Johnson, Mike Clark; front row (l-r) Cllr Dennis Lavin, Cllr Alex Watson, Cllr Anne Taylor, December 2008. All, apart from Cllr Johnson and Chief Executive Mike Clark, were to be made Honorary Aldermen of Derwentside in March 2009 (MW)*

## Chapter Fourteen
# Beacon Awards

*Outstanding Achievement, Social Inclusion, Supporting New Businesses, Engaging with Youth, Shining Example, Improving Health; Quality Management; Planning Excellence; Broadband Innovation; Green Awards; Investors in People; Alex OBE.*

### Outstanding Achievement

Four Beacon Status Awards in six years is a remarkable achievement for a small district council. These awards are given for "clear vision, outstanding achievement and genuine excellence". Beacon Status is a national scheme launched in 1999 to recognise excellence and innovation in local government. The idea is to share good practice and improve the performance of others, the object being to deliver high-quality services to all. The first of Derwentside's four Beacon Awards, for social inclusion, came in 2003. Two years later DDC won Beacon Status for helping new businesses, and in 2006 there was a third award for "youth engagement". Then in 2008 it was a fourth Beacon Status Award for the Council, for reducing health inequalities.

### Social Inclusion

The Council's first Beacon Council Award for Social Inclusion through ICT (information communications technology) in 2003 came with a rare government accolade: "Derwentside has set out an agenda for change which is recognised not only regionally but nationally and internationally. The authority has shown leadership in spheres normally outside its control". Ministers and senior civil servants were impressed not only with the Council's initiative in bringing an IT network to the whole of the district, but also with the number and extent of its applications. Executive Director Mike Clark: 'projects such as SPICE, SWIFT, the Derwentside Infonet and the Network have all been strong factors in the award of Beacon Status'. Local and Regional Government Minister Nick Raynsford presented the award. The Council even got its own Beacon Status flag. On being told by the Office of the Deputy Prime Minister that there were no Beacon Council flags, DDC commissioned AA Flags of Consett to make one of their own.

### Supporting New Businesses

In 2005, Raynsford handed over DDC's second Beacon Award, for supporting new businesses, after a successful presentation in London. Cllr David Llewellyn, Economy portfolio holder: 'this is a real coup for the area and justly recognises the huge efforts that have been put in place to support the growth and competitiveness of existing companies and the setting up of new businesses under the Emerge Scheme'. The presentation was made in London on 21st March. The Council had presented its case to the Advisory Panel for Beacon Councils back in January when they went through to the final stage of the bidding process. Cllr Llewellyn, Economy Portfolio

*Celebrating the Beacon Award for Positive Youth Engagement 2006 (MW)*

Holder for the Council was there with staff from the business support team to receive the award from the Minister. This was round six of the Beacon Council Scheme coordinated by the Improvement and Development Agency (IDeA). It started with 210 applications from local authorities all over the country, but only three other councils in the country were awarded Beacon Status for Supporting New Businesses. The No.1 Industrial Estate became famous nationwide through television adverts as the home of Phileas Fogg snacks, made by Derwent Valley Foods. The adjacent 13-acre Consett Business Park site is another of DDC's success stories. Originally a municipal council depot, the site was reclaimed by the Council in the 1990s With the aid of  One NorthEast and EU funding, over 70,000 sq ft of modern production and office facilities were developed, creating over 200 new jobs for the area. This was one of the initiatives that led to Derwentside Council being awarded Beacon Status for supporting new businesses. Only four councils throughout the country gained this accolade. Derwentside was the only council in the North East to win this award and the only district council – the other three being large unitary authorities.

*Beacon Council Award for Social inclusion through ICT 2003: Pic shows (l-r) Executive Director Mike Clark, Council Leader Alex Watson, local government minister Nick Raynsford MP, Cllr Jean Huntley, IT director Alan Hodgson*

*Beacon Award 2005, Supporting New Businesses (l-r): Cllr David Llewellyn, Maria Antoniou, Local Government minister Nick Raynsford MP, deputy chief executive John Pearson, head of economic development Peter McDowell (LW)*

*Beacon Award for Tackling Health Inequalities 2008 (l-r) Mike Clark (Derwentside DC), Verna Fee (Derwentside Primary Care Trust), Colin McBride (Derwentside Leisure)*

## Engaging with Youth

In 2006 DDC was one of just eight authorities across the country awarded Beacon Status for "Positive Youth Engagement". A panel of experts from the Office of the Deputy Prime Minister reported: "Derwentside District Council have delivered exceptional results through a strong vision, political commitment and resources, enabling the young people of the district to involve themselves in their Council and community in a wide range of ways". Nick Tzamarias, Policy Manager: "the Beacon application was based on our award winning SPICE programme which has an impressive record of working with thousands of young people across the District." SPICE stands for Special Programme to Implement Children's Elections.

Much of the credit for DDC gaining Beacon Status for Youth Inclusion went to Cllr Anne Taylor, Executive Member and Portfolio Holder for Strong Communities, whose work was recognised by the Office of the Deputy Prime Minister (ODPM). In pitching for the award, the youth of Derwentside showcased their talents to a panel of judges in London in 2006. DDC was one of 11 councils short-listed for Beacon Status for its work with "Positive Youth Engagement". They were pitching for a first prize of £50,000 to continue the Council's work in engaging young people in real decision making in their own

communities and they won! Derwentside Youth Forum Chair Phillip Marshall (14), and members Natalie English (16), Toula Tzamarias (14), Nicola Penrose (14) and Philip Howard (14) impressed the judges with an articulate presentation of their achievements. Judge Wasim Akhtar said he was "bowled over by the enthusiasm of the young people." Cllr Anne Taylor, Cabinet Member for Strong Communities: "SPICE is helping young people get involved in real decision-making with a real budget, giving them a true voice in matters that affect their lives."

### Shining Example

Derwentside District Council's pioneering work with young people also won recognition at the first ever local government awards for the North East. The Council's SPICE project won the Engaging with Young People Award at the glittering ShiNE (Sharing best practice in the North East) Awards ceremony held at the Newcastle Gateshead Hilton Hotel on 26th October 2008. Commenting on Derwentside's outstanding contribution the judges said: 'the SPICE campaign generated positive responses and ensured young people felt they had been really listened to and successfully engaged with'. The ShiNE Awards recognise the achievements, performance and improvement of the region's 25 ouncils and four fire & rescue services. The awards reflect the commitments, policies and work of North East local government. The awards were organised by the Association of North East Council (ANEC), the political voice for local government in the North East. Cllr Mick Henry, Gateshead MBC Leader & Chair of the Association, said: 'the ShiNE Awards showcase how the region's local authorities make a positive difference to the citizens and communities they represent'.

Since SPICE was launched in 2001, more than 10,000 young people and nearly 50 schools had been involved in the inspirational programme. Highlights over the previous four years included a referendum and three children's elections, leading to the launch of the Young People's Forum; a campaigning body uniting 58 elected members with a budget of £10,000 to spend on youth projects. 'We are building the foundations for a new generation of young people who really care about their communities', said Cllr Anne Taylor, DDC Cabinet Member for Strong Communities, 'SPICE is helping young people get involved in real decision making with a real budget, giving them a true voice in matters that affect their lives'. The Council's SPICE team won the prestigious Public Management Leadership Award in

2004. The team was nominated by the Derwentside Young People's Forum for its work with the youth of the district. The team was Nick Tzamarias (Senior Policy Officer & team leader), Eleanor Seed (Young People's Officer), Val Hill (Smartcard Administrator) and Sharon Robinson (ex-SPICE Officer & honorary member).

## Improving Health

In 2008 Derwentside District Council won yet another prestigious national Beacon Status Award, this time for its work in reducing health inequalities. The awards were announced at an Oscar-style ceremony at the Royal Horticultural Halls in London. Communities and Local Government Minister, Parmjit Dhanda, who presented the awards, said: 'I would like to congratulate Derwentside District Council on being awarded Beacon Status. This authority is leading the way in their use of new ideas and methods, and is ideally placed to drive change throughout the sector, helping to improve public services for everyone. The most important product of the Beacons is the real improvements to everyday public services that can be seen in the remit of every one of the winning authorities, and the sharing of new ideas and best practice that the Beacons promote will lead to improvement across the board'.

Council Leader Alex Watson said: 'this is another piece of fantastic news. It recognises our excellent work in health, together with the PCT (Primary Care Trust) and other partners. It's also further proof that we are one of the best district councils when it comes to excellence. This is our fourth Beacon award and we are very proud'. Derwentside District Council and the PCT had worked in close partnership for some years. This involved carrying out lifestyle surveys and a "health equity audit". Through this work, Derwentside was one of only a few districts on track to meet the government target to reduce the gap between the local and national averages of life expectancy. In addition, Derwentside had already surpassed the 2010 government target to reduce the gap for deaths from circulatory diseases. Dr Tricia Cresswell, Director of Public Health for County Durham & Darlington, said: 'Derwentside District Council has been a community leader in health matters'. Marianne Hood, chair of the Beacons Panel, said: 'being awarded Beacon Status means that Derwentside District Council will receive recognition from central government and other authorities for its expertise in tackling health inequalities'.

## Quality Management

Over the years, DDC gained many awards. In 1995 Durham North MP Giles Radice presented the Council with a BS5750 certificate. This British Standard award was judged by Lloyd's Register Quality Assurance who assessed the Council's Quality Management System. DDC's Technical Department was believed to be the first in the country to achieve certification for a multi-disciplined technical department. No outside consultants were used as Chief Technical Officer Malcolm Davies and his staff designed the system and its procedures from scratch. For the technically-minded,

BS5750 is now BS EN ISO9000. Also in 1995, Derwentside Training, the Council's training organisation, gained the County Durham TEC Training Provider Award. It was presented by polar explorer Robert Swan. In 1996 Derwentside Council became the first authority in the North East to gain an "Investors in People" award. On being re-tested at three year intervals, DDC repeated the accolade each time since then. Also in 1996, Annette Hendry from Blackhill, an Audit Assistant with DDC, won a competition set by CIPFA, the professional organisation for accountants. Annette, who was studying at Derwentside College, based her project on the feasibility of extracting water from below the Council depot at Morrison Busty near Annfield Plain. Derwentside Council Apprentice Carl Nevin won the 1997 IMI Copper Tube award as Top Apprentice in the Northern Region. Carl had joined the Council's Direct Service Organisation in August 1993, meanwhile attending New College Durham where he gained NVQ levels 2 and 3. He worked on installing bathroom suites, central heating, lead work and trained on gas servicing. 'This young man is an excellent example of the high standards that can be achieved by the youth of our District,' said Cllr Neil Gregory, Chair of the Council's Contracting Committee.

In 1997 Derwentside Council's Housing Division was rated in the top ten in the country for letting houses quickly, according to government watchdog, the Audit Commission. "This is good news, but we still want to do even better," said Cllr Terry Richardson, Chair of Community Services. And it's not often that a local council gets an award for Council Tax, but that did happen in 1998 when the DDC Council Tax team won a national award sponsored by banking system company BACS Ltd for recording the greatest increase in take-up of Direct Debit payments of Council Tax. The team received a trophy and a cheque for £500 which they donated to the Council Chairman's charity fund.

## Planning Excellence

In 1999 the Council's Planning Service was recognised as a centre of excellence by Planning Minister Richard Caborn. "We were also one of only two district councils that were shortlisted that year for a Planning Beacon

*Stanley Health Centre*

*Apprentice pays close attention*

Award. We didn't get that award, but hey we were close," said Director of Environmental Services Peter Reynolds. Reynolds is another local lad. He was born and grew up in Stanley, joined DDC straight from school in 1974 as a trainee technician in the planning department, and rose through the ranks to become Head of Planning Services in 1995. The following year Derwentside became the first local authority in the country to win three national risk management awards given by the Association of Local Authority Risk Managers (ALARM) for demonstrating integrated risk management: first in 1995 for introducing a comprehensive approach to loss control; then highly commended second place in 1997 for the development of in-house claims and risk management software system. The design of doors and windows is important for several reasons. In 2002, Durham Chief Constable George Hedges presented Derwentside Council with the Certificate for Secured Design for the joiner's shop door sets and new specification windows at the Morrison Busty Depot on Wednesday 30th January 2002.

While the Council continued to raise its standards, the 2002 Comprehensive Performance Assessment (CPA) showed areas where improvement was still needed. In a self-assessment exercise, the Council identified as its strengths: knows where it wants to go; set aside money to finance priority initiatives; a community leader, championing local causes; works well with other agencies. The Council scored highly with 78% of citizens satisfied with services provided; 97% urgent repairs completed within government time limits: 67% people satisfied with clarity of Housing Benefit forms; 91% satisfied with waste collection service; 100% population with kerbside recycling collection; 89% planning applications within government time limits; 86% satisfied with planning service; 100% standard searches carried out within 10 days. The weaknesses identified were: poor mechanisms for internal leadership, poor project management, poor performance management (now being addressed); still trying to get to grips with

arrangements for overview and scrutiny. The Council performed relatively poorly (bottom 25 per cent of councils) with: invoices paid within 30 days; Council Tax collected; no. of days lost to sickness; proportion of rent collected; average times to re-let Council houses and processing Housing Benefit claims. There were no women in senior positions and only one in 400 ethnic minority employees.

### Broadband Innovation

In 2003, Derwentside Council's IT Section gained the Broadband Britain Challenge for the North East public sector award for "outstanding innovation" using broadband technologies for their work in education and the community. David Spoors, DDC's IT systems engineer, picked up the award at the Life Conference & Banqueting Centre, Times Square, Newcastle. David then went on to the national finals in London to receive the National Challengers award (public sector) on behalf of the Council. The Council also won a national award for risk management and reduced insurance premiums.

### Green Awards

Blackhill & Consett Park won two awards in 2005: the Green Flag standard and the Green Flag Heritage Award. Work on the park was a team effort involving Leisure Services and Grounds Maintenance. Also in 2005, the Finance Directorate won a Charter Mark award for financial services. Among its achievements were successful implementation of the Agresso finance management system, improving collection rates, benefit

*Housing Seminar 28th June 1996 (l-r): Cllr Alex Watson, minister Nick Raynsford MP, Mike Clark*

processing times and benefit take-up resulting in over half a million pounds being paid out to customers. In 2006 Derwentside Council gained no fewer than three major awards: a Charter Mark for its financial services, Beacon Status for youth services and a Green Award for its Local Strategic Partnership. Add to all that a zero increase in Council Tax, and it was no surprise when the Audit Commission pronounced that DDC was on a 'positive direction of travel'. At that time DDC was the only council in County Durham to win three Beacon awards, and one of only eight in the country. DDC also gained a Green Flag Heritage Award – for the second year in succession - for the comprehensive renewal of Blackhill & Consett Park. The Council's planning website gained maximum points for e-government.

*Direct Debit: DDC Chief Financial Officer Keith Robinson with Cllrs Dot Atherton and Janet Greener behind the wheel*

### Investors in People

The Investors in People standard was originally attained for the whole of the Council in 1995, when Derwentside District Council was the first Local Authority within Co Durham to obtain accreditation. Since then, the authority retained the standard on being assessed every three years by meeting national standards set by Investors In People and inspected locally by Assessment North East. There was also a Best Value award in 2004 for human resources. DDC pioneered "Peer Challenge" in 2005, the only District Council in the region to do so. DDC has a strong commitment to staff development and has collaborated with Chester le Street and Easington councils and the trades unions to develop the KAT (Knowledge and Training) project which has had both regional and national recognition. In 2007 the Council received both the GO (Government Office) award itself and the national award for partnership working in recognition of the joint work that had been undertaken through the KAT project. DDC won a Council tax award in 1998 thanks to the work of Finance Director Keith Robinson and his team. Cllr June Armstrong was Chair of Finance) and Cllr Dot Atherton vice chair. In 1996 Delves Lane Junior School won the Robert Swan award for schools environmental projects. Every week the school collected newspapers, cans and old clothes. The cash raised was used by the Acorn Trust for a new community woodland near the school.

In 2007 DDC Chief Executive Mike Clark and Head of Organisational Development Ian Jones stepped up on behalf of the Council to receive the national award for partnership working, given in recognition of the joint work done through the KAT (Knowledge & Training) project. The first step was to win the GO Local Government Award, described as "your Authority's first step to achieving your Skills Pledge". The

*Investors in People (l-r): MPs Hilary Armstrong & Giles Radice, DDC chief Executive Neil Johnson*

Council was tested by the IDeA, the government-backed Improvement & Development Agency, for its action plan to promote Skills for Life. Derwentside Council's GMB Union learning rep Mac Waters said: 'We have had a phenomenal response. Staff working in all departments have wanted to join in, it hasn't just been about the so-called manual workers. It's great to see the progress made. We had one person who could hardly read and write: he came forward. Did the course and has really come on'.

### Alex OBE

Long-serving Council Leader Alex Watson was awarded the OBE in the 2007 New Year's Honours List for his services to local government. Cllr Watson said: "I am honoured to receive an award of this magnitude. I am extremely pleased, and also very grateful to all of those who have supported me and helped me to become an effective leader". Outside the Council, Cllr Watson has been Chairman of the North East Regional Assembly, Chairman of the English Regions Network and Vice Chairman of the Association of North East Councils.

*Alex Watson OBE*

*Investors in People Award 2007 (l-r) Ian Jones (DDC Head of Organisational Development), Wendy Nichol (DDC Human Resources Officer), Robert Macleod (Managing Director of Assessment North East)*

## Chapter Fifteen
# Derwentside's Enduring Legacy

Throughout its existence Derwentside District Council has been a Labour authority - an authority which is rightly proud of its contribution to the development of the community of North Durham, which it has served in an entrepreneurial and innovative way. As a Council it believes that it has always punched above its weight, contributing, often in partnership but certainly in the lead, to the development of infrastructure which has helped the economy grow and has encouraged housing development to sustain the community. This has involved taking a radical approach to the delivery of services whilst ensuring quality, efficiency and value for money for Council Taxpayers of the District.

Councillor Michael Malone, a driving force behind many of the Council's successes over the last 14 years said; 'One of our most influential initiatives has been the development of Broadband IT infrastructure and services, initially for Derwentside but over recent years also for most of the Councils in the Northern Region, a number of other public sector users - including hospitals, GPs and schools - and, importantly, for many communities throughout North Durham, ensuring that they have been able to benefit through speedy and cheap access to the modern world of technology. Our approach to IT is, however, just but one example of many initiatives and a way of working which has significantly benefited the community of Derwentside'.

The Council's last Chief Executive Mike Clark said: 'Our encouragement of housing development has significantly improved the sustainability of many of our communities whilst helping to replace much of the lost population that departed our area following the closure of Consett Steelworks. In the public sector we created Derwentside Homes in 2006 and transferred the Council's housing stock to it to ensure a sustainable future for tenants in high quality, cost-effective housing. Our approach to regeneration has led to much older housing being demolished and replaced with modern, quality homes, and our approaches to education and training - as well as our employment initiatives - have significantly improved the opportunities for young people and others who live in Derwentside to gain employment either within or outside of the District'.

Although the regeneration of Consett Steelworks Site (Project Genesis) was slow to progress, the Council has left an opportunity for the development of a major new sports complex on the site by Durham County Council, and the project has generated £65 million worth of investment in what could otherwise have been left as a redundant area of open space. Alongside Project Genesis, the Council has also modernised Consett town centre.

However, as Councillor Malone has stated: 'As a Council we are proud of the services we have delivered to the people of the District. Our approach to environmental improvement has received national recognition, with awards being received for our work in the parks at Blackhill and Consett as well as Annfield Plain. We have also invested, sometimes in partnership with the private sector, in our parks, such as Sherburn Park in Consett, and our legacy to the people of South Moor includes a programme for the investment of a half a million pounds in South Moor Park. We have also provided and contributed to activities which have improved community safety within the District. Derwentside was one of the first Districts to fund community safety police officers and as a District we now have over 90 CCTV cameras, funded by the Council but operated from the Project Genesis Control Room. We are proud of the national awards that we have received.

'In addition to the recognition of our work to improve the environment, we have received Beacon Council awards for our work with young people, improving employment opportunities and improving the health of people who live within the District. Our Revenues and Benefits Service has received national recognition, as has the Council's training agency and a number of other services which we provide. At the same time we have reduced the tax burden on residents, having frozen Council Tax levels for the last four years of our existence, "a record second to none!" as far as Alex Watson is concerned.

'Over the last 35 years Derwentside District Council has also raised, and provided directly, a significant amount of funding for initiatives and projects which have benefited the community. As a Council we have provided and renewed leisure facilities in Consett and Stanley. Throughout the District there are many community centres which have been built with assistance from the District Council, and these are providing much valued services for smaller communities. Additionally, the Council has invested heavily in the provision of arts facilities in both Consett and Stanley, with a thriving theatre in Consett, the Empire, and a thriving arts and theatre facility in Stanley at the Lamplight Arts Centre.

'The final acts of the District Council are examples of our approach to investment and initiatives which have benefited people across the District. On 29th January 2009 a private sector funded centre, which will provide care for people well into the future, was officially opened at View Lane Park. This facility has created over £8 million worth of investment from the private sector, and will see over £250,000 of investment by the Council in refreshing and renewing View Lane Park, as well as over £300,000 of investment in a new bowling green at East Stanley. The facility will create over 100 jobs for people in the community of Stanley. This initiative, championed by Councillor Anne Taylor of the Havannah Ward in the face of severe opposition from some interest groups, will create jobs, improve the environment and create new and improved facilities for people of the area for many years to come'.

On the 18th March 2009 Derwentside District Council's final managed business complex was to be completed at Tanfield Lea Industrial Estate, following the investment of Council resources and external grants. This complex is the fifth built and delivered by the District Council over the last 10 years and will be let as managed space for small and medium sized businesses hoping to develop and thrive in Stanley, creating jobs and opportunities for people who live in the area. 'A legacy which will prove its worth to the people and economy of the District for many years to come,' in the opinion of David Llewelyn, the Council's Economy portfolio holder.

Councilor Malone said: 'Members of Derwentside's final Council should be proud of its achievements. Over the last two years alone we provided over £20 million of investment for the District, and we leave capital resources of over £15 million for construction of a new sports complex in Consett, as well as over £65 million worth of assets to the new authority when it takes over on the 1st April 2009.

A message from the Cabinet of Derwentside District Council to the leaders of new Durham County Council is that they hope that the new authority will be as successful in developing and delivering quality services and initiatives for the people of Durham as we in Derwentside have been over recent decades,' said Cllr Malone.

Films shown at Stanley Civic Hall in 1975 included "Battle for the Planet of the Apes","Willie Wonka and the Chocolate factory","Jesus Christ Superstar","Young Winston","Live and let die","The Red Baron" and "The Quiet Man." The Pavilion Cinema, Stanley, known as the "Piv", had a three-manual theatre organ.

*In 1953, the world record for the women's mile was broken in Consett. Anne Oliver clocked 5min 8.0sec on the town's old black shale track, although her time was never ratified because there was only one timekeeper.*

A public house in Shield Row was the setting for a Geordie dialect song by Tommy Armstrong, the pitman's poet, called "The Cat Pie".

*Until the creation of a separate parish in the 19th century, many people from Shotley Bridge were christened, married and buried in Ebchester, including many of the sword-makers and their families. Perhaps the most notable is the monument of Joseph Oley, which reads "The last of the Shotley Bridge swordmakers".*

*River Derwent at Allensford (CFW)*

## Chapter Sixteen
# Last Words

**Mike Clark, Chief Executive Officer**

*"Councils are people-based"*

This book is about the life of a local Council, created in 1974 and coming to an end in 2009. Hopefully, you have found this account of our 35-year history an interesting and readable story of endeavour and success, and one which will have stimulated your thoughts and memories.

*Mike Clark*

Councils are people-based organisations, run by local people for the benefit of the local community. Its policy is decided by councillors, elected by you and drawn from the local community. Their decisions are carried out by Council staff, most of whom live locally and who all have a stake in the area. Staff and councillors alike are all here to serve the interests of the people who live, work and play in Derwentside. It is the people who have worked for the Council and those who have been elected members during our 35-year history, who have made sure that Derwentside District Council has best served the interests of the community. I hope that present and former councillors and staff feel happy that this book has given due recognition to them and their hard work and dedication over the years. This book celebrates their achievements, and rightly so.

As a Council we have achieved many things. Over the last 35 years Derwentside has seen industrial decline and suffered its effects. It is now a place that we can be proud of. Although, sadly for many, Derwentside District Council will become part of history on the 31st March 2009, that should not detract from its success in delivering real improvements throughout the district. Even if I had the space to do so, it would be wrong of me to name individual officers and members in this 'end piece', but I do want to say that during my 19 years here I have enjoyed working with such a close-knit family. We have experienced good and bad times, but always found the time to smile and laugh together.

There are, however, two particular individuals that I would like to mention, who personify the theme of local people and family, but who have sadly died in recent years. They are Mike Bonser, Chief Administrative Officer, and personnel assistant Frankie Bowes, two people for whom I had a particular respect, and for different reasons. Mike was one of those people who glued the organisation together. He died after retirement. Frankie was a real personality, one of those people who smiled his way through work and adversity alike, but who died before he could retire. Both men were loved and respected by staff and members alike. At each of their funerals, the church was filled to overflowing for the occasion, with the Council almost literally coming to a halt each time.

Things will change from the 1st April 2009. We all must embrace that change, hoping that the County Council will build on the success of Derwentside and continue to improve the area for future generations. I am sure that those officers and members who become part of the new Council will continue to work with the same enthusiasm and dedication on behalf of the community. I wish them well, and hope that this book will help remind them of how problems can be overcome and success achieved when people work together for the good of all.

*Mike Clark*

**Alex Watson, Leader of the Council**

*"From Disaster to Success"*

The closure of the Steelworks and the Coal mines dealt a savage blow to the economy of our district. Although at the time we were given every assurance that everything conceivable was being done to address what was considered to be a major catastrophe, the actions taken in the first ten years had little success. Unemployment was still well into double figures, and the population decline and drift away from the area was still continuing at an alarming rate. Clearly we had to do things differently or face the dire consequences of Derwentside becoming tagged as "the District that died".

*Alex Watson*

We needed a radical rethink on the way forward, and so the Council adopted its ambitious Action Plan. From 1993 onwards, changes became apparent. We were starting to move forward, and things were getting better.

In the past we had experienced problems in persuading the private sector to invest in Derwentside, particularly in the major centres and former pit villages. Our new approach began with the Genesis Project, a public/private sector partnership. Genesis clearly sent out the right messages, as Derwentside rapidly gained a reputation – now firmly established - for being a boom area. This new investment in the district has produced real results. Unemployment has dropped from 35% at its peak to our current position of 2.3%. Derwentside's population decline has been arrested from a low of 83,000 to 87,000 and growing, as new housing estates have sprung up all around the district.

Another significant reason for Derwentside's success has been our Council staff. Their commitment has been phenomenal, working tirelessly to turn around the whole economy of the district from doom and gloom to success and prosperity. The demise of Derwentside District Council - which very few people wanted - is certainly a huge disappointment. There was a complete lack of democracy in how the decision was made. In the most recent referendum there was a overwhelming "NO" vote to the abolition of our Council.

I can state with complete confidence that our record in office is second to none. We are in our fourth year when we have not increased Council Tax, we have virtually wiped off £70 million of inherited debt, and Derwentside is one of very few districts in a growth position. Right now, the people of Derwentside enjoy the advantages of a rapidly developing economy in a rural setting. Our quality of life is outstanding, with superb low-cost housing and an ideal mix of first-class state schools. There are many leisure facilities in the area, and almost every type of sport and entertainment is catered for.

What better contrast could there be to the days of the Steelworks and Mining when the area was best known for its pollution and dirt? From the disastrous closures of the 1970s and 1980s, your District Council – elected by you – has brought Derwentside from disaster to a much-improved present and a better future.

"We shall take from the past its fires and not its ashes"

*Alex Watson*

# For the Record

## Chairmen of the Council 1974-2009

1973/74 (shadow year) Wilfred Baker
1974/75 Wilfred Baker
1975/76 John George Parkin
1976/77 William Bell
1977/78 Norman Seymour
1978/79 Sidney George Dixon
1979/80 Kenneth Fredrick Robson
1980/81 James Thompson Stoker Graham
1981/82 Sidney George Dixon
1982/83 Joseph Walker JP
1983/84 James Creegan
1984/85 Brian Charlton
1985/86 Selby Clark Walker
1986/87 James Kenneth Sessford
1987/88 Michael Brough
1988/89 John Keir Pears
1989/90 Mrs Mary Armstrong
1990/91 James Henry Griffiths
1991/92 Keith Murray-Hetherington
1992/93 Benjamen Brenkley
1993/94 Mrs Elizabeth Jane Coulson
1994/95 Eric Turner
1995/96 George Francis Johnson
1996/97 Henry Shaw Guildford
1997/98 Anthony Donaghy
1998/99 Richard McArdle
1999/2000 Mrs Evelyn Wilson
2000/01 Ossie Johnson
2001/02 Leslie Vaux
2002/03 David Gwyn Llewellyn
2003/04 Miss Denise Bennett
2004/05 Mrs Cath Clark
2005/06 Mrs Elizabeth Jane Coulson
2006/07 John Henry Fothergill
2007/08 Mrs Olga Milburn
2008/09 (final year) Eric Turner

## Leaders & Chief Executives

### Leaders of the Council
Norris Oyston 1973-79
Billy Bell 1979-87
Joe Rhind 1987-91
Alex Watson 1991-2009

*In tandem – Alex Watson and Mike Malone have clocked up 14 years as the Council's Leader/Deputy Leader duo (AW)*

### Chief Executives
Joe Quinn 1973 – August 1975
Terry Hodgson December 1975 – October 1987
Neil Johnson January 1988 – August 1997
Mike Clark July 2002 – March 2009

*Mike Clark*

*Joe Quinn*

Cllr Wilf Baker (1974-75)   Cllr John Parkin (1975-76)   Cllr Sid Dixon (1978-79, 1981-82)   Cllr Jimmy Graham (1980-81)

Cllr Joe Walker (1982-83)   Cllr Brian Charlton (1984-85)   Cllr Mary Armstrong (1989-90)   Cllr Harry Guildford (1996-97)

Cllr Tony Donaghy (1997-98)   Cllr Richie McArdle (1998-99)   Cllr Evelyn Wilson (1999-2000)   Cllr Ossie Johnson (2000-01)

Cllr Les Vaux (2001-02)   Cllr David Llewellyn (2002-03)   Cllr Denise Bennett (2003-04)   Cllr Catherine Clark (2004-2005)

Cllr Liz Coulson
(1993-94, 2005-06)
Cllr John Fothergill (2006-07)   Cllr Olga Milburn (2007-08)   Cllr Eric Turner
(1994-95, 2008-09)

*Cllr John Parkin, Hamsterley Colliery Senior Citizens Christmas Party 1975 (JP)*

*Executive 2008 (l-r): Cllr Carl Christer (Community Safety), Cllr Dennis Lavin (Health), Cllr Ossie Johnson (Environment), Cllr Anne Taylor (Strong Communities), Cllr Alex Watson (Leader), Cllr Mike Malone (Deputy Leader), Cllr David Llewellyn (Economic Development) (CFW). Not in picture: Cllr Carl Marshall (Learning)*

*Cllr Carl Marshall*

Christmas Party and a Golden Wedding – all in day's work for a Council Chairman (left)

*Cllr John Parkin, Golden Wedding of Mr & Mrs J Peake 1975 (JP)*

*Careful where you're sticking that pin, Mike!*

*Ashley Rocks-Menon*

*Management Team 2008 (l-r): Dave Watson (Head of Financial Services), John Pearson (Deputy Chief Executive), Alan Hodgson (DurhamNet), Ian Jones Head of Organisational Development), Mike Clark (Chief Executive), Pam Harrison (PA to chief executive), Peter Reynolds (Director of Environmental Services), Gordon Elliott (Director of Corporate Administration & Policy) (CFW). Not in picture: Ashley Rocks-Menon (Legal Officer)*

*African children's choir - highlight for Olga Milburn (2007-08)*

## Elected Members

Derwentside Council has always been Labour-controlled, but the large majorities of past years have gradually been reduced. In the 2007 elections, Labour's overall majority fell to just three, with 29 out of 55 members. The Derwentside Independent group increased to 23, with one other Independent and two Liberal Democrats. A striking feature of the 2007 election was the number of wards where councillors of different parties were elected. A majority of wards, twelve out of 22 wards, were "shared", perhaps indicating that people were casting their votes more for candidates as individuals rather than the straight "party ticket". No fewer than 23 councillors – over 40% of the council – were elected for the first time in 2007, and thirteen were first-timers in 2003.

By the time the Council came to its end in 2009, there were only four councillors with more than twenty years' service. Council Leader Alex Watson was the longest-serving member. He was first elected in 1979 and now completes 30 years on the council. Independent Marion Wotherspoon, elected for the Castleside ward in a by-election in July 2008, was the shortest-serving member, her term of office due to end after only eight and a half months. From 2009, the people of Derwentside will have two-thirds fewer councillors to represent them. For the previous 35 years, the area was represented by 55 district and eleven county members. These 66 councillors were to be replaced by 22 members of the new Durham County (Unitary) Council, elected on 1st May 2008. If the Boundary Commission has its way, these 22 will be reduced still further at the next county election, which could come as early as 2010. The results in Derwentside reflected the 2007 district elections, the numbers gained by each party being Labour eleven, Derwentside Indendents ten and LibDems one. Fourteen of the 22 new county councillors are current members of the District Council.

## 1973
### Labour takes control

This first election – the new Council had a "shadow year" before taking over in 1974 – saw a big majority for Labour with 44 members elected. The eleven non-Labour councillors were a mixed bunch: three Liberals, one Conservative, one Independent; four councillors who described themselves as "Retired", plus Benfieldside members, the redoubtable Rena Mohon JP (Progressive) and the well-known local businessman and choir leader Willie Westgarth who stood as "Estate Agent." There were only seven women councillors. Labour leader Norris Oyston became the first Council Leader, with Selby Walker as Group Secretary. Mrs Mohon was leader of the opposition. Cllr Wilf Baker was Chairman of the shadow Council 1973/74, and Derwentside's first Chairman 1974/75. Members: **Annfield Plain:** James Joseph Elliott, Edwin Urwin (Ted) Lightfoot; **Benfieldside:** Mrs Rena Mohon JP (Progressive), Sydney Unsworth (Retired), William Edwin (Willie) Westgarth MBE (Estate Agent); **Blackhill:** Mrs Sarah Donnelly, Vincent Kelly, Kenneth Frederick (Ken) Robson;

**Burnopfield:** Walter Armstrong, Wilfred Baker, Brian Charlton; **Catchgate:** William Bell, John Evans; **Collierley:** Cecil Johnson, Norris William Oyston; **Consett North:** Norman Heaviside (Retired), Lawrence Arthur (Larry) Thomas (Con); **Consett South:** Stanley Armstrong Breen, Derek McVickers (Ind), Joseph Redshaw; **Cornsay & Hedleyhope:** Charles Wade Hunwick (Retired); **Craghead:** Harry Feenan, Thomas Wilkinson; **Delves Lane & Crookhall:** Robert Bell, Edward Humphreys, Ronald George (Ronnie) Knowles, James Kenneth (Ken) Sessford; **Ebchester:** Robert Telford (Bob) Gardner JP; **Esh:** John Kevin Elliott (Lib), Vincent Taylor (Lib), Brain Anthony Tulip (Lib); **Greencroft, Lanchester & Langley:** David Arthur Cairns, William Coates, Sydney George Dixon, Ralph Kell; **Havannah:** Edward (Ted) Defty, Norman Seymour, Albert Wilson, Mrs Ann (Annie) Wilson JP; **Healeyfield, Mugglewick & Satley:** David Young (Retired); **Leadgate:** Lawrence Allen (Larry) Brown, William Thomas (Bill) Thompson, William Walton BEM JP; **Medomsley:** John George Parkin, Mrs Isabella (Bella) Williamson JP; **South Moor:** Mrs Margaret Ellen Errington, Mrs Catriona Janet (Cathy) Smith, Lawrence (Larry) Welsh; **Tanfield:** Ronald Dodd, Selby Clark Walker; **Towneley:** Sydney Davies, James Thompson Stoker (Jimmy) Graham, Oswald (Ossie) Johnson, Mrs Nora Ann Kelly, George William Ward. (all Labour except where shown; Con = Conservative, Ind = Independent, Lib = Liberal).

## 1976
### Labour maintains grip

Despite gaining 22 uncontested seats, Labour lost five seats to finish up on 39. There were eight Independents with various labels, five Liberals and three Conservatives, giving Labour an overall majority of 23. There were six women councillors, increased to seven in a by-election. Members: **Annfield Plain:** James Joseph Elliott, Edward Urwin Lightfoot [17.3.77 Albert James Spurr]; **Benfieldside:** Mrs. Rena Mohon JP (Progressive), Sydney Unsworth (Retired), William Edwin Westgarth MBE (Estate Agent); **Blackhill:** John Nicholas Gillinder (Lib), Vincent Kelly, Kenneth Frederick Robson; **Burnopfield:** Brian Charlton, Thomas Norman Hall (Ind), Alan Neil Cole Holmes (Ind); **Catchgate:** William Bell, John Evans; **Collierley:** Norris William Oyston, Joseph Walker; **Consett North:** Norman Heaviside (Retired), Lawrence Arthur Thomas (Con); **Consett South:** James Creegan, Derek McVickers (Ind), Joseph Redshaw; **Cornsay & Hedleyhope:** Thomas Johnson; **Craghead:** Harry Feenan, Martin Quinn; **Delves Lane & Crookhall:** Wilfred Craggs, Ala Laybourn (Lib), James Kenneth Sessford, John Whitfield; **Dipton:** Norris William Oyston, Joseph Walker; **Ebchester:** Robert Telford Gardner JP; **Esh:** John Kevin Elliott (Lib), Joseph Hennessy (Lib), Vincent Taylor (Lib) [1.9.77 Jean Taylor (Lib)]; **Greencroft, Lanchester & Langley:** David Arthur Cairns, William Coates, Stanley George Dixon, Andrew Linden Laing (Con); **Havannah:** Edward Defty, Norman Seymour, Albert Wilson, Mrs. Ann Wilson JP; **Healeyfield, Mugglesswick & Satley:** Dorothy Audrey Graham (Con); **Leadgate:** Lawrence Allen Brown, William Thomas

Thompson, William Walton BEM, JP; **Medomsley:** John George Parkin, Mrs. Isabella Williamson JP; **Tanfield:** Ronald Dodd, Selby Clark Walker; **Towneley:** James Thompson Stoker Graham, Alan Huggins, Oswald Johnson, Mrs. Norah Ann Kelly, George William Ward. (all Labour except where shown; Con = Conservative, Ind = Independent, Lib = Liberal) [by-election].

## 1979
## Oyston voted out

Labour suffered a further loss of seats, including leader Norris Oyston who lost by 20 votes to Independent James Downs in Dipton, reducing from 39 to 30. Increasing the number of wards from 21 to 23 could have been a factor. There were 16 Independents, six Conservatives and three Liberals, for an overall majority of just five. There were six women councillors, and 21 Labour members had been returned unopposed. Labour regained three seats from the Independents in by-elections to increase their majority to eleven. Members: **Annfield Plain:** Frederick Armstrong Daglish (Ind), John Henderson (Ind); **Benfieldside:** Alice Muriel Howe (Con), Mrs. Rena Mohon JP (Progressive), William Edwin Westgarth MBE (Estate Agent); **Blackhill:** Robert Atkinson (Steelworks Manager), Vincent Kelly, Kenneth Frederick Robson; **Burnhope:** William Coates; **Burnopfield:** Brian Charlton, Thomas Norman Hall (Ind), Alan Neil Cole Holmes (Ind) 11.9.80 Walter Armstrong, William Walker Dobson]; **Castleside:** Dorothy Audrey Graham (Con); **Catchgate:** William Bell, Keith Elliott (Ind) [26.3.81 John Evans]; **Consett North:** Lawrence Arthur Thomas (Con), Alexander Watson; **Consett South:** James Creegan, Joseph Redshaw, Philip Reilly; **Cornsay:** Thomas Johnson; **Craghead:** Harry Feenan, Martin Quinn; **Crookhall:** George Nicholson Brown; **Delves Lane:** Wilfred Craggs, James Kenneth Sessford, John Whitfield [16.7.81 Eric John Shaw Edwards]; **Dipton:** James Downs, Joseph Walker; **Ebchester & Medomsley:** Robert Telford Gardner JP, Robert Russell (Con), Mrs. Isabella Williamson JP; **Esh:** Joseph Hennessy (Lib), Jean Taylor (Lib), Vincent Taylor (Lib); **Havannah:** Walter Scott Peacock (Ind), Ean Thomas Reed (Ind), Ernest Tuckerman (Ind); **Lanchester:** Denise Bullivant (Con), Sydney George Dixon, Edwin Tallentire (Con); **Leadgate:** John Keir Pears, William Coulthard Stockdale (Ind), William Walton BEM, JP; **South Moor:** James Findlay Graham (Ind), David Ledger Robson (Ind), Alan Crawford Westwater (Ind) [20.3.80 George Davis Hole (Ind)]; **South Stanley:** James Thompson Stoker Graham, Oswald Johnson, George William Ward; **Stanley Hall:** Michael Brough, Alan Huggins, Greta Taylor; **Tanfield:** Ronald Dodd, Selby Clark Walker. (all Labour except where shown: Con = Conservative, Ind = Independent, Lib = Liberal) [by-election].

## 1983
## Increased Labour majority

Five unopposed seats helped Labour win 36 in all, an increase of six. With 12 Independents, four Conservatives and three Liberals, Labour had a 17-seat majority. Oyston again lost to Down, this time by 75 votes. There were ten women councillors. Labour gained a further

four seats in by-elections, one by the "drawing of lots" in Benfieldside when Labour's Joe Toner was declared the winner after having equal votes with Independent Barry Hoggarth. Another Labour win came in Dipton with future leader Joe Rhind elected. Members: **Annfield Plain:** Joseph Kenneth Gilbert, Bart Kelly; **Benfieldside:** Derek Hume (Ind), John Jeffrey (Con), Owen Leighton Temple (SDP/Lib) [20.11.86 Joseph Toner]; **Blackhill:** Robert Atkinson (Ind), Vincent Kelly, Kenneth Frederick Robson; **Burnhope:** William Coates; **Burnopfield:** Walter Armstrong, Brian Charlton, William Walker Dobson; **Castleside:** Dorothy Audrey Graham (Con); **Catchgate:** William Bell, John Evans; **Consett North:** Patricia Holmes (Ind), Alexander Watson; **Consett South:** James Creegan, Derek McVickers (Ind), Philip Reilly; **Cornsay:** Thomas Johnson; **Craghead:** Harry Feenan, Martin Quinn; **Crookhall:** David Hodgson; **Delves Lane:** Eric John Shaw Edwards, James Kenneth Sessford, John Whitfield; **Dipton:** James Down (Ind), Joseph Walker [4.7.85 Joseph Rhind]; **Ebchester & Medomsley:** William Brown, Joanne Carr, Robert Telford Gardner JP [4.7.85 Kenneth Walker]; **Esh:** William Patrick Beavis, Joseph Hennessy (SDP/Lib), Jean Taylor (SDP/Lib) [5.7.84 Neil Gregory]; **Havannah:** Walter Scott Peacock (Ind), Evan Thomas Reed (Ind), Ernest Tuckerman (Ind); **Lanchester:** Sydney George Dixon, Christine Hewitt (Con), Edwin Tallentire (Con) [24.1.86 Margaret Denise Bulivant (Con), Derek Iceton (Con)]; **Leadgate:** John Keir Pears, William Coulthard Stockdale (Ind), William Walton BEM, JP; **South Moor:** George David Hole (Ind), David Ledger Robson (Ind), Alan Crawford Westwater (Ind) [17.10.85 Elizabeth Jane Coulson]; **South Stanley:** Mary Armstrong, James Thompson Stoker Graham, James Henry Griffiths; **Stanley Hall:** Michael Brough, Alan Huggins, Anne Eve Sirkett [17.10.85 Janet Temperley Greener]; **Tanfield:** Ronald Dodd, Selby Clark Walker. (all Labour except where shown: Con = Conservative, Ind = Independent, SDPLib = SDP/Liberal Alliance) [by-election].

## 1987
## Billy Bell out

Labour Leader Billy Bell, who had taken over from Norris Oyston as Council Leader in 1979 when Oyston lost his seat, likewise lost his seat in 1987. Joe Rhind became Leader, only for him to lose his seat four years later. Eight seats were uncontested in 1987, and twelve women members were elected. There were nine Independents, three Conservatives, no Liberals and 43 Labour members with an overall majority of 31. Alex Watson, voted in as deputy leader in 1987, lost out to Dave Hodgson the following year. Hodgson held the post for two years, only for Watson to return as deputy in 1990. In 1988 there were no opposition members on the 17-strong Policy Committee. Members: **Annfield Plain:** Joseph Kenneth Gilbert, Bart Kelly; **Benfieldside:** Barry Hoggarth (Ind), Derek Hume (Ind), Joe Toner; **Blackhill:** Robert Atkinson (Ind), Kevin Earley, David Gwynn Llewellyn; **Burnhope:** Janice Taylor; **Burnopfield:** Walter Armstrong, Brian Charlton, Thomas Edward Charlton (Ind); **Castleside:** Derek McVickers (Ind); **Catchgate:** John Evans, Anthony William Grainger; **Consett North:** Patricia Holmes (Ind), Alex Watson; **Consett South:** Colin

Anderson, James Creegan JP, Derek Hicks (Ind); **Cornsay:** John Allinson Scanlan; **Craghead:** Harry Feenan, Martin Quinn; **Crookhall:** David Hodgson; Delves Lane: Allan Atkinson, Eric Edwards, John Whitfield; **Dipton:** Richard Michael Christon, Joseph Rhind; **Ebchester & Medomsley:** William Brown, Joanne Carr, Kenneth Walker [Eric Turner 26.1.89]; **Esh:** Walter Patrick Beavis, Ben Brenkley, Neil Gregory; **Havannah:** Lyn Boyd, George Derrick Little, Aidan Patrick Thomas Murphy; **Lanchester:** Margaret Denise Bullivant (Con), Derek Iceton (Con), Edwin Tallentire (Con); **Leadgate:** Jean Huntley, John Keir Pears, William Coulthard Stockdale (Ind); **South Moor:** Elizabeth Jane Coulson, Joyce Elizabeth James, Dorothea Jamila Khamis; **South Stanley:** Mary Armstrong, James Thompson Stoker Graham, James Henry Griffiths; **Stanley Hall:** Michael Brough, Janet Temperley Greener, Alan Huggins; **Tanfield:** Victoria Ena Binney, Barry Douglas Coulthard. (all Labour except where shown: Con = Conservative, Ind = Independent).

*Civic Centre, Consett (CFW)*

## 1991
### Watson becomes Leader

Although 18 new councillors were elected, the political balance of the Council was little changed at Labour 39, Independents 14, Conservatives 2. Despite taking twelve seats unopposed, Labour's numbers dropped from 43 to 39 for a 23-seat overall majority. Peter Murphy, candidate for the "Catchgate People's Party" failed to get elected. Fifteen women members were elected, the most there had ever been up to that point. This increased to 16 through a by-election. Alex Watson was elected Leader, and Kevin Earley as Deputy. Bill Stockdale again led the Independent group, Margaret Bullivant the Conservatives. Members: **Annfield Plain:** Joseph Kenneth Gilbert, George Francis Johnson [17.6.93 Alan Atkinson]; **Benfieldside:** Barry Hoggarth (Ind), Derek Hume (Ind), Joe Toner; **Blackhill:** Kevin Earley, David Gwynn Llewellyn, Michael John Malone; **Burnhope:** Janice Taylor; **Burnopfield:** Robert Alderson (Ind), Walter Armstrong, Thomas Edward Charlton (Ind); **Castleside:** Derek McVickers (Ind); **Catchgate:** Anthony William Grainger, George Harrison (Ind) [11.3.93 Eileen Wiliamson]; **Consett North:** Patricia Holmes (Ind), Alex Watson; **Consett South:** Colin Anderson, James Creegan

JP, Derek Hicks (Ind) [12.7.91 Derek Drafan (Ind); 17.6.93 Anthony Donaghy]; **Cornsay:** Francis Sydney Duggan (Ind); **Craghead:** Patricia Paule Hall, Martin Quinn; **Crookhall:** David Hodgson [23.11.93 Alan William Stephens]; **Delves Lane:** Allan Atkinson, Eric John Shaw Edwards, Kathleen Harrison; **Dipton:** Richard Michael Christon, Thomas Senior Foggett (Ind); **Ebchester & Medomsley:** Joanne Carr, Eric Turner, Kenneth Walker; **Esh:** Benjamin Brenkley, Harry Shaw Guildford, Ruth Hughes; **Havannah:** Lyn Boyd, John Pallas, Anne Taylor; **Lanchester:** Margaret Denise Bullivant (Con), Joyce Lawson (Con), John Frederick Wilson [12.9.91 John Redvers Sudder]; **Leadgate:** Terence Richardson, George Siddaway (Ind), William Coulthard Stockdale (Ind); **South Moor:** Elizabeth Jane Coulson, Joyce Elizabeth James, Dorothea Jamila Khamis; **South Stanley:** Mary Armstrong, James Thompson Stoker Graham, James Henry Griffiths; **Stanley Hall:** Michael Brough, Janet Temperley Greener, Keith Murray-Hetherington JP; **Tanfield:** Arthur Norman Carr (Ind), Paul Lee Devlin (Ind). (all Labour except where shown: Con = Conservative, Ind = Independent) [by-election].

## 1995
### Biggest ever Labour win

Labour swept to their biggest ever victory on the Council, winning 50 of the 55 seats with just one place unopposed. With only five opposition members, all Independents, Labour had a majority of 45. There were 18 women councillors, later increased to a record 20 thanks to by-elections. Alex Watson continued as Leader, with Mike Malone taking over from Kevin Earley as Deputy Leader. In 1997/98 the Local Government Commission carried out a review of the District. The council remained at 55 members, but the 23 wards were reduced to 22, with boundary changes to 18 wards. Members: **Annfield Plain:** Alan Atkinson, George Francis Johnson [20.2.97 Maureen Elizabeth Baggett; 7.5.98 Michele Hodgson]; **Benfieldside:** John Davies, Derek Hume (Ind), Joe Toner; **Blackhill:** Kevin Earley, David Gwynn Llewellyn, Michael John Malone; **Burnhope:** Denise Bennett; **Burnopfield:** Robert Anderson (Ind), June Pamela Armstrong, Walter Armstrong **Castleside:** William Rochester Golightly; **Catchgate:** Anthony William Grainger, Eileen Williamson; **Consett North:** Anthony Donaghy, Alexander Watson; **Consett South:** John Ian Agnew, Doreen Atherton, Andrew McDonald; **Cornsay:** Francis Sydney Duggan (Ind); **Craghead:** Janice Docherty, Elizabeth James; **Crookhall:** Alan William Stephens; **Delves Lane:** Allan Atkinson, Eric John Shaw Edwards, Kathleen Harrison [22.2.96 Richard McArdle]; **Dipton:** Joanne Carr, Thomas Senior Foggett (Ind); **Ebchester & Medomsley:** Colin Bell, Eric Turner, Kenneth Walker; **Esh:** Neil Gregory, Harry Shaw Guildford, Alison Mary Hiles; **Havannah:** Lyn Boyd, John Pallas, Anne Taylor; **Lanchester:** Colin Burton, John Redvers Sudder, Evelyn Wilson [22.2.96 Oswald Johnson]; **Leadgate:** Jean Huntley, Terence Richardson, William Coulthard Stockdale (Ind); **South Moor:** Elizabeth Jane Coulson, Dorothea Jamila Khamis, Leslie (Les) Vaux; **South Stanley:** Mary Armstrong, James

*Full Council meeting, 21st October 2008. Names are listed along each bench from front (nearest to camera) to back of picture, (left rear): John Williams, Ray Ellis, Bob Cook, Owen Temple, Keith English, Denise Bennett, Tom Pattinson, David Walton, Richard Young, Malcolm Campbell, Tony Westgarth; (left front): Bob Alderson, Derek Hume, Duncan Barnett, Roland Hemlsely, Wallace Tyrie, Ian McElhone, Michael Malone, Alex Watson, Tom Clark; (centre): Eric Turner (Chairman)*

Thompson Stoker Graham, James Henry Griffiths; **Stanley Hall:** Michael Brough, Janet Temperley Greener, Keith Murray-Hetherington JP [25.9.97 Peter Mingins]; **Tanfield:** George Derrick Little, Olga Milburn. (all Labour except where shown: Ind = Independent) [by-election].

## 1999
### Eleven unopposed seats
The Independents increased their numbers from five to eight, but again there were no other opposition members. Labour's majority fell to 39 with eleven returned unopposed. There were 15 women members, two more coming in via by-elections. Members:
**Annfield Plain:** Alan Atkinson, Michelle Hodgson [3.8.01 Carl David Christer]; **Benfieldside:** John Davies, Derek Hume (Ind), Joe Toner [2.5.02 Thomas Clark]; **Blackhill:** Kevin Earley, David Gwynn Llewellyn, Mike Malone; **Burnhope:** Denise Bennett; Burnopfield: Robert Alderson (Ind), Walter Armstrong, Thomas Edward Charlton (Ind); **Castleside:** Gordon Campbell Glass (Ind); **Catchgate:** Anthony William Grainger, Eileen Williamson; **Consett North:** Anthony Donaghy, Alex Watson; **Consett South:** John Ian Agnew, Doreen Atherton, Andrew McDonald [15.3.01 William Golightly; 17.1.02 Catherine Clarke]; **Cornsay:** George Ian Forsyth Blacklock; **Craghead:** Janice Docherty, Garry Edward Reed [15.11.01 John Henry Fothergill]; **Crookhall:** Barry Thomas Breeze; **Delves Lane:** Carolyn Carrick McArdle, Richard McArdle, Eric John Shaw Edwards; **Dipton:** Joanne Carr, Thomas Senior Foggett (Ind); **Ebchester & Medomsley:** Colin Bell, Watts Stelling (Ind), Eric Turner; **Esh:** Neil Gregory, Henry Shaw Guildford, Alison Mary Hiles; **Havannah:** Lyn Boyd, John Pallas, Anne Taylor; **Lanchester:** Colin Burton, Ossie Johnson, Evelyn Wilson; **Leadgate:** Jean Huntley, Terry Richardson, William Coulthard Stockdale (Ind); **South Moor:** Elizabeth Jane Coulson, Dennis Lavin, Leslie (Les) Vaux; **South Stanley:** James Thompson Stoker Graham, James Henry Griffiths, Sheila Veronica Kelly; **Stanley Hall:** Michael Brough, Janet Temperley Greener, Peter Mingins; **Tanfield:** Olga

Milburn, Janice Wilson (Ind) [22.6.00 Elizabeth Minto (Ind)]. (all Labour except Ind = Independent) [by-election].

## 2003
### Independents double numbers
Now officially registered as the Derwentside Independents, the group doubled its numbers by taking 16 seats, Watts Stelling taking over from Bill Stockdale as leader. With one Liberal Democrat and one "Independent Independent" elected, Labour's numbers were down to 37 and their majority to 19. Four seats were unopposed, and 12 women elected. This became 13 when Barbara Armstrong won a by-election which saw Labour gain a seat from the DIs. The 23 wards had been reduced to 22, and a new Consett East ward created. Members 2003: **Annfield Plain:** Alan Atkinson, Carl Christer, Dennis Lavin; **Benfieldside:** Duncan Ian Barnett (DerwInd), Keith English (LibDem), Derek Hume (DerwInd); **Blackhill:** Thomas Clark, David Gwyn Llewellyn, Michael John Malone; **Burnhope:** Denise Bennett; **Burnopfield:** Robert Alderson (DerwInd), Walter Armstrong, Thomas Edward Charlton (DerwInd); **Castleside:** Gordon Campbell Glass (Ind); **Catchgate:** Hilary Christer, William Proud; **Consett East:** Frederick Todd (DerwInd); **Consett North:** Catherine Clark, Tony Donaghy, Alex Watson; **Consett South:** John Ian Agnew, Derek Hicks (DerwInd); **Cornsay:** John Pickersgill (DerwInd) [16.2.06 Barbara Armstrong]; **Craghead & South Stanley:** Janice Docherty, Tracy Davinson, John Henry Fothergill; **Delves Lane:** Barry Thomas Breeze, Eric John Shaw Edwards, Atherley Edward Hodgson; **Dipton:** Tom Foggett (DerwInd), Reg Ord (DerwInd); **Ebchester & Medomsley:** Colin Bell, Eric Turner, Carol Tracy Watson (DerwInd); **Esh:** Gordon Coulson, Harry Shaw Guildford, Wallace Joseph Tyrie (DerwInd); **Havannah:** Kevin Howe, George Derrick Little, Anne Taylor; **Lanchester:** John Gordon Ingham (DerwInd), Ossie Johnson, Richard Young (DerwInd); **Leadgate:** Jean Huntley, Margaret Jopling (DerwInd), Watts Stelling

(centre): Sue Rothwell (Vice Chairman); (right front): Watts Stelling, Fred Todd, Marion Wotherspoon, Derek Hicks, Gina Reid, Ossie Johnson, David Llewellyn, Ian Agnew, Gordon Coulson; (right rear): John Hunter, Joan Nicholson, Dennis Lavin, Alan Atkinson, Carl Christer, Anne Taylor, Hilary Christer, Olga Milburn, Bill Gray, Joe Wilson, Eric Edwards.
Panorama photograph by Mark Wilkinson (MW)

(DerwInd); **South Moor:** Elizabeth Jane Coulson, James Thompson Stoker Graham, Darren Vincent McMahon; **Stanley Hall:** David Broadley, Janet Temperley Greener, Claire Louise Vasey [29.9.05 Carl Marshall]; **Tanfield:** Thomas Alan Henderson, Olga Milburn, Joe Wilson. (all Labour except Ind = Independent, LibDem = Liberal Democrat) [by-election].

## 2007
## Labour majority only three
Labour's overall majority was reduced to three, its lowest ever. There were 29 Labour councillors, 23 Derwentside Independents, two Liberal Democrats and one Independent. Even then, there were still only thirteen women councillors out of 55. A by-election in 2008 brought it up to fourteen. The DI group lost two members: Burnopfield councillor Bob Cook switched to the LibDems, and Iain McElhone (Delves Lane) became an Independent Independent. Members: **Annfield Plain:** Alan Atkinson, Carl Christer, Dennis Lavin; **Benfieldside:** Duncan Ian Barnett (DerwInd), Keith English (LibDem), Derek Hume (DerwInd); **Blackhill:** Tom Clark, David Gwyn Llewellyn, Michael John Malone; **Burnhope:** Denise Bennett; **Burnopfield:** Robert Alderson (DerwInd), Bob Cook (DerwInd), Roland Hemsley (DerwInd); **Castleside:** Gordon Campbell Glass (Ind) [17.7.08 Marion Wotherspoon]; **Catchgate:** Hilary Christer, Joan Nicholson (DerwInd); **Consett East:** Frederick Todd (DerwInd); **Consett North:** Owen Leighton Temple (LibDem), Alex Watson (Lab), Mary Westgarth (DerwInd); **Consett South:** John Ian Agnew, Derek Hicks (DerwInd); **Cornsay:** Malcolm Campbell (DerwInd); **Craghead & South Stanley:** Janice Docherty, Linda Marshall, Tina Marie Parry; **Delves Lane:** Eric John Shaw Edwards, Iain McElhone (DerwInd), Tony Westgarth (DerwInd); **Dipton:** Reg Ord (DerwInd), Gina Reid (DerwInd); **Ebchester & Medomsley:** Ray Ellis (DerwInd), Alan Shield (DerwInd), Eric Turner; **Esh:** Gordon Coulson, Susan Jane Rothwell, Wallace Joseph Tyrie (DerwInd); **Havannah:** Tom Pattinson (DerwInd),

Anne Taylor, David Walton (DerwInd); **Lanchester:** Bill Gray, Ossie Johnson, Richard Young (DerwInd); **Leadgate:** Peter Damian Hughes, Watts Stelling (DerwInd), John Williams DerwInd); **South Moor:** Gary Beckwith, Darren Vincent McMahon [resigned November 2008], Paula Murray; **Stanley Hall:** David Broadley, Carl Marshal, Susan Ellen Mellor; **Tanfield:** John Charles Hunter (DerwInd), Olga Milburn, Joe Wilson. (all Labour except: DerwInd = Derwentside Independent, Ind = Independent, LibDem = Liberal Democrat) [by-election].

## Key to members

01 John Ian Agnew
02 Robert Alderson
03 Alan Atkinson
04 Duncan Ian Barnett
05 Gary Beckwith
06 Denise Bennett
07 David Broadley
08 Malcolm Campbell
09 Carl Christer
10 Hilary Christer
11 Thomas Clark
12 Bob Cook
13 Gordon Coulson
14 Janice Docherty
15 Eric John Shaw Edwards
17 Keith English
18 Bill Gray
19 Roland Hemsley
20 Derek Hicks
21 Peter Damian Hughes
22 Derek Hume
23 John Charles Hunter
24 Ossie Johnson
25 Dennis Lavin
26 David Gwyn Llewellyn
27 Iain McElhone
28 Darren Vincent McMahon
29 Michael John Malone
30 Carl Marshal
31 Linda Marshall
32 Susan Ellen Mellor
33 Olga Milburn
34 Paula Murray
35 Joan Nicholson
36 Reg Ord
37 Tina Marie Parry
38 Tom Pattinson
39 Gina Reid
40 Susan Jane Rothwell
41 Alan Shield
42 Watts Stelling
43 Anne Taylor
44 Owen Leighton Temple
45 Frederick Todd
46 Eric Turner
47 Wallace Joseph Tyrie
48 David Walton
49 Alex Watson
50 Anthony Westgarth
51 Mary Westgarth
52 John Williams
53 Joe Wilson
54 Marion Wotherspoon
55 Richard Young

# Final Roll Call

Members 2009 (54 members, one vacancy) showing year first elected. (*) member of new unitary Durham County Council

**1. John Ian Agnew** (Lab) 1995 Consett South. Has seen many improvements in The Grove and Moorside. "Now we have a real community which wasn't there before".

**2. Robert (Bob) Alderson** (Derwlnd) 1991 (*) Burnopfield. Born South Moor, has lived in Burnopfield since 1956, quality controller/inspector at Ever Ready until redundancy in 1988. With fellow councillor, the late Tom Charlton, helped action group's successful campaign to stop opencasting near village.

**3. Alan Atkinson** (Lab) 1993 Annfield Plain. Sixty-three when first elected, "retires" as a councillor at 79 after 16 years' service. Committee chairman, governor of two local schools, supported football and kick-boxing clubs and other community organisations. "made many new friends" and always followed up constituent's problems, ensuring every one got a reply.

**4. Duncan Ian Barnett** (Derwlnd) 2003 (*) Benfieldside. An unusual occupation – criminologist. Born in Blackhill. Helped get improved disabled access to community facilities, restoration of community garden, improved bus shelters. "An independent voice."

**5. Gary Beckwith** (Lab) 2007 South Moor.

**6. Denise Bennett** (Lab) 1995 Burnhope. Council Chairman 2003/04.

**7. David Broadley** (Lab) 2003 Stanley Hall. Born in Hexham, retired.

**8. Malcolm Campbell** (Derwlnd) 2007 (*) Cornsay. Retired Police Inspector with the Northumbria force. Born Consett, went to Blackfyne Secondary School, brother of Alan Campbell, Labour MP for Tynemouth. "Closely involved with many local people and real, local issues, making my role a pleasure. The parishes of Satley, Hedleyhope & Cornsay are great old communities with mining and farming histories".

**9. Carl Christer** (Lab) 2001 Annfield Plain born Wallsend, healthcare specialist advisor. Executive member, Community Safety Portfolio holder. Board Chairman, Derwentside Homes Ltd. Much involved in community, trades union & Labour Party organisations.

**10. Hilary Christer** (Lab) 2003 Catchgate Chair of Licensing Committee, Chair of Council Labour Group; Ward Secretary, Annfield Plain & Catchgate Branch; Governor of Catchgate Primary school; Board Member, Surestart. Took the lead on the regeneration of Catchgate, 2003 to the present, working with Catchgate Residents & Partnership Groups.

**11. Thomas Clark** (Lab) 1999 Blackhill. Vice Chair, Development Control.

**12. Bob Cook** (LibDem) 2007 Burnopfield. Elected as Derwlnd.

**13. Gordon Coulson** (Lab) 2003 Esh retired joiner, union convenor. Started work with Lanchester Council in 1946, aged 16, under architect Mr Simkins. One benefit of the new council being set up in 1974 was that Lanchester council workmen got into a bonus scheme for the first time.

**14. Janice Docherty** (Lab) 1995 (*) Craghead & South Stanley. Born in Craghead and has lived there most of her life. Works as chief officer of Derwentside Community for Voluntary Service. Janice was a school governor and playgroup organizer when first elected in 1995. Since then she has been a portfolio holder and had held other positions, including chair of Derwentside Rural Challenge.

**15. Eric John Shaw Edward**s (Lab) 1981 Delves Lane first elected to represent the Delves Lane & Crookhall ward in a by-election in August 1981. Has worked as a railway guard, a factory supervisor with Amoco, and as a care worker with the county council. In 2007 Eric, who "likes to help the people", received recognition for his first 25 years on the council, albeit a year late.

**16. Ray Ellis** (Derwlnd) 2007 Ebchester & Medomsley. Born Dunston, 40 years an electrical distribution design engineer. Produced a monthly Community Newsletter since 1998. "Ongoing sense of satisfaction in being able to help and serve my local community, which is really what it's all about".

**17. Keith English** (LibDem) 2003 Benfieldside.

**18. Bill Gray** (Lab) 2007 Lanchester born Success Road, Philadelphia, Houghton-le-Spring, first ever honours music graduate from Newcastle University, 43 years teaching music in NW Durham schools & colleges, still teaching part-time. Accompanist/organist in churches, clubs, operatic societies, schools and at music festivals. Vice Chair, Licensing Committee. Lanchester Parish Councillor.

**19. Roland Hemsley** (Derwlnd) 2007 Burnopfield. "It has been a great joy and pleasure to serve the people in the ward".

**20. Derek Hicks** (Derwlnd) 2003 Consett South.

**21. Peter Damian Hughes** (Lab) 2007 Leadgate. Vice Chair, Economy & Learning Scrutiny Panel.

**22. Derek Hume** (DerwInd) 1983 Benfieldside.

**23. John Charles Hunter** (DerwInd) 2007 (*) Tanfield. Auto electrical engineer from Shield Row. Found the experience of working for and with local people enjoyable. "People value the work done in their community and have a strong pride in their community and the area they live in."

**24. Ossie Johnson** (Lab) 1996 (*) Lanchester. School teacher. E xecutive member, Environment Portfolio holder. Proud to be "Centenary Chairman" of the Council, 2000/01. Passionate about the environment.

**25. Dennis Lavin** (Lab) 1999 Annfield Plain. Lived in Annfield Plain since 1946, mainly in New Kyo. First elected for South Moor, then for Annfield Plain after boundary changes. Executive member, Portfolio holder for Health.

**26. David Gwyn Llewellyn** (Lab) 1987 Blackhill. Executive member, Portfolio holder for Economy, particularly pleased: to officiate at the reopening of Blackhill & Consett Park as Council Chairman 2002/03; role as Exec member for economic development; being part of team gaining Beacon Status for business start-ups.

**27. Iain McElhone** (IndInd) 2007 Delves Lane. Elected as DerwInd. Born and brought up in Blackhill, Iain had three years' Army service, was then a civilian with the Army Fire Service, joined the Durham Fire Service in 1994, still full-time & based at Villa Real FS in Consett. Iain helped bring about three main improvements in his ward: restoring a local bus service, the installation of a pedestrian crossing, and improved recreation facilities.

**28. Darren Vincent McMahon** (Lab) 2003 South Moor. [resigned November 2008]. Member of Stanley Town Council.

**29. Michael John Malone** (Lab) 1991 Blackhill. Born near Durham. Merchant Navy/steelworker/teacher. Deputy Council Leader 1995-2009. Studies every report in detail. Personal highlights include facilitating the visit from the people of Omagh with Mo Mowlam in attendance, and recognising the award of the Military Cross to a soldier from Bridgehill with a Civic Reception.

**30. Carl Marshall** (Lab) 2005 (*) Stanley Hall. At 24, was youngest ever DDC councillor and later one of youngest cabinet members in UK. Community development officer/regeneration manager. Executive member, Portfolio holder for Learning.

**31. Linda Marshall** (Lab) 2007 Craghead & South Stanley. Chair, Community Safety & Strong Communities Scrutiny Panel.

**32. Susan Ellen Mellor** (Lab) 2007 Stanley Hall. Born Buxton, Derbyshire. Ex-social worker specialising in residential care. "The best thing about being a councillor is the satisfaction when a problem that a constituent has brought to you has been solved".Vice Chair, Executive & Leader/Deputy Leader Scrutiny Panel.

**33. Olga Milburn** (Lab) 1995 Tanfield. Born Dipton. Tenant support worker with Stonham. School governor since 1989. Chair, Derwentside Domestic Abuse management committee. Council Chairman 2007/08.

**34. Paula Murray** (Lab) 2007 South Moor. Vice Chair, Environment & Health Scrutiny Panel. Member of Stanley Town Council.

**35. Joan Nicholson** (DerwInd) 2007 Catchgate. Florist, married with two children. Enjoyed her short time on the District Council. Member of Stanley Town Council.

**36. Reg Ord** (DerwInd) 2003 Dipton.

**37. Tina Marie Parry** (Lab) 2007 Craghead & South Stanley. Vice Chair, Community Safety & Strong Communities Scrutiny Panel. Member of Stanley Town Council.

**38. Tom Pattinson** (DerwInd) 2007 Havannah. Born Kip Hill, Stanley, retired project engineer in the electricity supply industry. In his short time on the Council, found committee work "interesting & rewarding", the best aspect being the ability to help residents with their problems. Chairman of Stanley Town Council.

**39. Gina Reid** (DerwInd) 2007 Dipton. Born in Sunderland, now retired. Described herself as "single with ten grown-up children." Chair of Dipton Residents Association, trustee of Derwentside Rural Crime Initiative. Worked with young people and started a Faith group in Dipton which for some was the only social event of the week.

**40. Susan Jane Rothwell** (Lab) 2007 Esh. Vice Chairman of Council 2008/09 – last to hold this office.

**41. Alan Shield** (DerwInd) 2007 (*) Ebchester & Medomsley. Born Consett, industrial chemist/quality technician/manufacturing manager/advice worker. Chair, Economy & Learning Scrutiny Panel. "You don't need to be a politician to be in politics, you need to be a representative of the people".

**42. Watts Stelling** (DerwInd) 1999 (*) Leadgate. "A Leadgate lad", industrial chemist/lab manager. Leader of Derwentside Independent Group. "We are a regular political party but we are not involved in national politics".

**43. Anne Taylor** (Lab) 1991 Havannah. Born Stanley, early years practitioner. In her fifth term of office, Executive member, Portfolio holder for Strong Communities. Has held a number of other posts including Chair of Equal Opportunities and Chair of Standards. Highlights include: awarding of Beacon Status for Youth Inclusion; establishing mobile youth facility, the "Ellie Bus".

**44. Owen Leighton Temple** (LibDem) 2007 (*) Consett North. London-born, teacher/ financial advisor. Leader of Liberal Democrat Group. Previously on the Council 1985/87.

**45. Frederick Todd** (DerwInd) 2003 Consett East. Engineer, born in Crookhall.

**46. Eric Turner** (Lab) 1989 Ebchester & Medomsley. Joiner by trade. Twice Council Chairman 1994/95, 2008/09 – last ever to hold the office. Chairman of the planning committee for ten years, a record stint.

**47. Wallace Joseph Tyrie** (DerwInd) 2003 Esh. David Stanley Walton (DerwInd) 2007 Havannah. Member of Stanley Town Council.

**48. David Stanley Walton** (DerwInd) 2007 Havannah. Member of Stanley Town Council.

**49. Alexander Watson** (Lab) 1979 Consett North. Born Consett. 29 years auto-setter operator with RB Bolton, & AEU works convener. Council Leader 1991-2009, proud of what has been achieved under his leadership.

**50. Anthony Westgarth** (DerwInd) 2007 Delves Lane. Born in Leadgate. Retired supervisor. "My greatest achievement as councillor is to have gained the respect of the people of the ward by listening to their concerns and addressing their issues wherever I could".

**51. Mary Westgarth** (DerwInd) 2007 Consett North. Unit residential manager in an elderly care home. All three councillors for the ward from different parties have worked together in partnership. Will continue to work within the community to make Consett a "great" place to live in. Chair, Executive & Leader/Deputy Leader Scrutiny Panel.

**52. John Williams** (DerwInd) 2007 Leadgate. Born in Chipping Norton, was a Merchant Navy Officer for 15 years before becoming a senior lecturer. "The Independents are a force to be reckoned with – oh for a little more time…."

**53. Joe Wilson** (Lab) 2003 (*) Tanfield. Born at Richard Murray Hospital, Shotley Bridge, has the unusual job of funeral director. Member of the working group that got a children's play area in every ward; new office complex on Tanfield Lea industrial estate. Member of the Tanfield Lea Partnership which helped win the County Durham Village of the Year 2008. Chair, Environment & Health Scrutiny Panel.

**54. Marion Wotherspoon** (Ind) 2008 Castleside. Last person to be elected to the Council (by-election 17th July 2008). Occupational therapist, lived in Castleside for 20+ years, Parish Councillor, involved with Castleside & Muggleswick Partnership, "completely independent".

**55. Richard Young** (DerwInd) 2003 (*) Lanchester.

(DerwInd = Derwentside Independent, Ind = Independent, Lab = Labour, LibDem = Liberal Democrat. There was a vacancy in the South Moor ward. Labour Councillor Darren McMahon had resigned in November 2008, and election rules did not allow a by-election in the last six months of the Council.

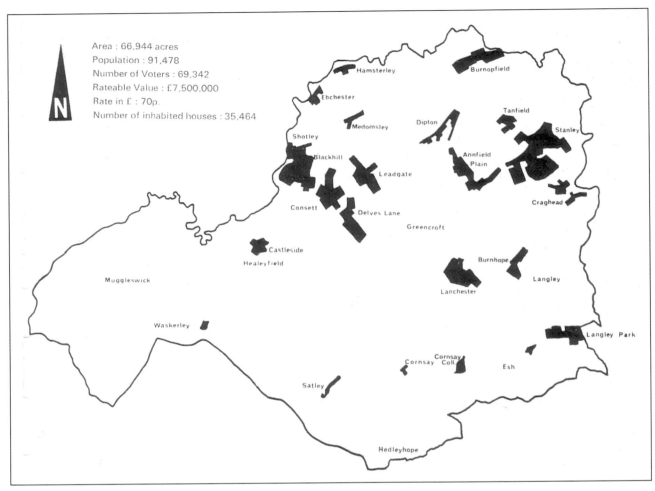

Area : 66,944 acres
Population : 91,478
Number of Voters : 69,342
Rateable Value : £7,500,000
Rate in £ : 70p.
Number of inhabited houses : 35,464

*Derwentside District 1974*

*North East England*

Derwentside is the North West corner of County Durham. Its northern boundary is shaped by the River Derwent, which is also the boundary between Durham and Northumberland. The River Browney, which flows into the Wear, is in the south of the District. Derwentside's two largest towns, Consett and Stanley, are respectively twelve and eight miles from the City of Newcastle upon Tyne. Lanchester, by the Browney, is seven miles from the City of Durham.

Allendale Cottages….

….are no more

Allensford Park

Annfield Plain

Benfieldside

Berry Edge

Blackhill

Bradley Cottages, nr Leadgate

Bridgehill

Bryan's Leap, Burnopfield

Burnhope Memorial

Burnhope Mast

Castleside

Catchgate Library

Clough Dene, Tantobie

Consett, Middle Street

Cornsay

Cornsay Colliery

## Gazetteer

**Allendale Cottages** small mining village North of Medomsley.

**Allensford** formerly Allansford, where the A68 crosses the River Derwent, to the West of Consett. Named from Alan de Chilton, ancient Lord of Healeyfield.

**Annfield Plain** large village between Stanley and Consett, originally Annfield Plane, in 1820 a small hamlet consisting of a single street.

**Bantling Castle** see East Castle.

**Benfieldside** nr Shotley Bridge north of Consett. Benfieldside probably comes from the Celtic ben, an elevated place, and the Anglo-Saxon feld, a forest clearing.

**Berry Edge, Consett** site of former steelworks, close to town centre.

**Blackhill** district of Consett, not named because of industrial grime, but because the rising sun casts a shadow over its west-facing slope.

**Bloemfontein** see The Middles.

**Bradley Cottages** ex-mining community next to Pont Bungalows, Leadgate.

**Bridgehill** district west of Consett.

**Browney** River south of District.

**Burnhope** nr Lanchester the only place that the Durham Miners' Gala has been held apart from Durham. This was in 1926, the year of the General Strike. The Burnhope transmitter mast, opened in 1959 for the ITV Tyne Tees television service, now the home of Channel 5 and some local radio services.

**Burnopfield** large village, NW corner of District.

**Butsfield** nr Satley twin villages East and West, south of Consett. Originally the stone from Butsfield's quarries was transported by horse & cart, but later an aerial ropeway was built to take it direct to the Consett Iron Co works.

**Castleside** SW of Consett, adjoins the A68. The name Castleside comes from Castle Hill where a farmer called Castle settled in the late 18th century. Castleside Parish was formed in 1873. In 1974 Castleside won the award for the tidiest industrial village in County Durham.

**Catchgate** nr Annfield Plain once had a toll gate;

**Clough Dene** nr Tantobie.

**Consett** Derwentside's largest town, high on the edge of the Pennines in NW Durham. In ancient times variously named Conekesheved, Conside, Conshead. First called Consett in reign of Henry VIII. Population in 1841 was just 145. Coking coal, iron ore and limestone, the three ingredients needed to produce iron and steel, were readily obtainable locally. With cutlery and sword-making already established at nearby Shotley Bridge, Consett expanded rapidly to become one of the UK's main producers of iron and steel.

**Co-operative Villas** nr Stanley - see No Place.

**Cornsay village** SSW of Lanchester.

**Cornsay Colliery** south of Lanchester, some distance from Cornsay village;

**Craghead** ex-mining village SW of Stanley.

**Crookgate** nr Burnopfield.

**Crookhall** East of Consett has a strong & distinct identity.

**Delves Lane** SE of Consett name derived from the delf holes dug by the German swordmakers seeking iron-ore deposits.

**Derwent Cottages** small mining village West of Medomsley.

*Craghead, St Thomas Church*

*Crookgate, Grove Terrace*

*Crookhall, Sixth Street*

*Delves Lane*

*Derwent Cottages, once here*

*Dipton, St John the Evangelist Church*

*East Butsfield*

*East Castle*

*East Hedleyhope*

*East Law nr Ebchester*

*Ebchester Bridge*

*Esh, St Michaels RC Church*

**Derwent** River northern boundary of Derwentside. Gave the District its name, from the Celtic word for "clear, bright water", also "laughing or smiling waters". Also could mean "valley of the wooded oaks".

**Dipton** large village ENE of Consett name derived from "deep dene". Dipton and Collierley were mentioned by Bishop Pudsey in 1166. Drift mining dates at least from 1333, and a coal mine was sunk in 1731.

**East Butsfield** – see Butsfield.

**East Castle** small mining village between Leadgate and Annfield Plain.

**East Hedleyhope** south side of the district, nr Tow Law.

**East Kyo** West of Stanley.

**East Law** Ebchester.

**Ebchester** north of Consett was Upchester (= "the camp on the height"). Much of the stone in the walls and doorway of the parish church of St. Ebba was taken from the nearby Roman fort of Vindomora (= "on the edge of the black moor"). Ebchester was once owned by Sherburn Hospital.

**Elm Park** on the outskirts of Shotley Bridge, had a zoo in the early 1900s, also a coal drift mine, 1961-72.

**Esh** hilltop village nr Langley Park. Esh is a Saxon term for Ash.

**Flint Hill** nr Tantobie.

**Greencroft** village nr Annfield Plain. Greencroft Hall was built by the Clavering family in 1670.

**Hamsteels** south of Lanchester.

**Hamsterley Colliery** nr Ebchester, ex-mining village.

**Harelaw** nr Annfield Plain.

**Harperley** nr Stanley. The Harperley Hotel was originally a corn mill driven by water from the Kyo Burn. It later became Tanfield Lea workingmens club.

**Havannah** central Stanley.

**Healeyfield** nr Castleside. In 1170 Bishop Hugh Pudsey granted Healeyfield to Alan de Chilton. The Healeyfield Mining Company at Castleside produced large amounts of good quality lead with a high silver content until 1891.

**Hedley Hill** nr Cornsay.

**Hedleyhope** see East Hedleyhope.

**High Westwood** nr Ebchester, small ex-mining community.

**Hill Top** nr Langley Park.

**Hill Top** nr Tantobie.

**Hisehope** reservoir nr Waskerley.

**Hobson** NW of Consett.

**Hollinside** nr Lanchester, former mining village.

**Holmside** nr Craghead.

**Honey Hill** nr Waskerley, site of water treatment works, and also a pub;

**Hownsgill**, formerly Howen's Gill, deep ravine near Consett.

**Hurbuck Cottages** between Consett and Lanchester. A Viking sword, axe heads and scythes were found in a nearby stream.

**Iveston** pleasant village east of Consett. Mentioned in the Boldon Book of 1183. A coal pit was sunk here in 1621. Much sought-after location.

**Kip Hill** village north of Stanley, near Shield Row. Has two pubs, the Blue Bell Inn and the Ball Alley (its original name, for some years it was the Shield Row Hotel).

**Knitsley** small village south of Consett. Once owned by the Surtees family. Had its own railway station until 1964.

Flint Hill nr Dipton, East Terrace

Greencroft

Hamsteels Hall

Hamsterley Mill (DDC)

Hamsterley, Christ Church

Harelaw nr Annfield Plain

Harperley nr Stanley

Hedleyhope Fell

High Westwood nr Ebchester

Hill Top, nr Langley Park

Hobson, Wigham Terrace

Hollinside nr Lanchester

Holmside nr Burnhope

Honey Hill, Moorcock Inn

Hownsgill Park

Hurbuck Cottages

Iveston

Kip Hill, Ball Alley pub

Knitsley, Station House

Lanchester, village entrance

Langley Park, Front Street

Leadgate

Leazes nr Burnopfield, Syke Road

Lintz Cricket Club

Lintzford Mill

Low Westwood nr Ebchester

Maiden Law

Malton nr Lanchester

Medomsley, St Mary Magdalen Church

Moorside, new housing

Muggleswick

New Kyo, Jubilee Terrace

Newbiggin nr Lanchester

No Place nr Stanley

Oxhill, Eden Terrace

Pont Bungalows, Leadgate

**Lanchester** large village by the River Browney, on the main road between Durham and Consett. Its name comes from the Roman fort of Longovicium, half a mile SW of the village. Before the Romans, the valley was inhabited by the Brigante tribe. The disused railway line is now the Lanchester Valley Walk. The centre of Lanchester was designated as a conservation area in 1972. In 1974 Lanchester came third in the main section of the County Durham tidy village competition.

**Langley Park** on the east side of the district, four miles from Durham. Most likely named after Bishop Langley of Durham. Childhood home of former England soccer manager Sir Bobby Robson. Langley Park Colliery, where Bobby and his father both worked, was opened in 1873 by the Consett Iron Co. It closed on 31st October 1975.

**Leadgate** just outside Consett, was on the turnpike road between Consett and Dipton. Parish formed in 1863. Local Board was formed in 1866. Population in 1894 was 4,900. Eden Colliery, Leadgate, closed 18th July 1980, the last pit in the area to close. There are Leadgate villages in Northumberland and Cumbria, and in Gateshead.

**Leazes** nr Burnopfield.

**Lintz** small village SW of Burnopfield.

**Lintzford** named after the DeLintz family, Austrian refugees who settled in Lintz Hall in the 12th century.

**Low Westwood** mining community nr Hamsterley.

**Maiden Law** between Lanchester and Annfield Plain.

**Malton** between Lanchester and Langley Park.

**Medomsley** village NE of Consett. Mentioned in the Boldon Book of 1183. Until the creation of Shotley Bridge parish in the 19th century, Medomsley's church of St. Mary Magdalene was used by sword-makers from there for christenings, marriages and funerals. In 1811 had a population of 391, in 1891, 5,306. Had two collieries which employed 2,000 men and boys.

**Moorside** residential area West of Consett, near to the former steelworks. There are at least nine other Moorsides around the country.

**Muggleswick** scattered rural village close to the River Derwent between Castleside and Edmundbyers.

**New Kyo** nr Stanley.

**Newbiggin** nr Lanchester.

**No.1** district NE side of Consett, named after the No.1 ironstone mine situated there.

**No Place** really does exist! Small village nr Stanley, also known as Co-operative Villas.

**Oxhill** nr Stanley. There is an Oxhill village in Warwickshire.

**Pont Bungalows** Leadgate, ex-mining community.

**Pontop Pike** nr Annfield Plain. Television transmitter mast put up in 1953, originally 300ft high, later extended to 500ft.

**Quaking Houses** village near Stanley originally settled by Quakers. Supposedly once known as "Quakies" or "Nanny Goat Island".

**Quebec** village south of Lanchester. The Roman road Dere Street passed through Quebec on its way from Yorkshire to Hadrian's Wall via the fort at Lanchester. The Canadian province of Quebec occupies a vast territory nearly three times the size of France or Texas.

**Rowley** tiny village on the A68 near Castleside. Its former railway station was taken down and rebuilt at Beamish Museum. There are Rowley towns in Massachusetts and

*Pontop Pike*

*Quaking Houses*

*Quebec*

*Rowley*

*Satley Church*

*Shield Row, Stanley*

Sleepy Valley nr Tantobie

Snows Green, Shotley Bridge

South Moor

South Stanley, Engels Terrace

Stanley, Front Street (DDC)

Stobbilee nr Lanchester

Stony Heap, Hanging Stone

Tanfield Lea

Tanfield, St Margaret of Antioch Church

Tantobie, South View Terrace

Templetown, Temple Gardens

The Dene

The Grove

The Middles, Craghead

Ushaw College (YG)

Shotley Bridge (YG)

Shotley Spa

Waskerley Station

Iowa in the USA, Alberta in Canada; Rowley villages in Yorkshire and Shropshire; and a former Rowley parish in Barnet, north London.

**Satley** rural village SW of Lanchester.

**Shield Row** north side of Stanley, from "shiel" meaning a shepherd's hut. Shield Row station, opened in 1894, was the busiest on the Annfield Plain branch line, often taking £100 before noon on a Saturday.

**Shotley Bridge** West of Consett, mentioned in 1356. Shotley is believed to be a corruption of Scotley, meaning the ley, or woodland clearing of a Scotsman or a clearing where pigeons are to be found. Shotley Bridge was once the heart of Britain's swordmaking industry. In 1685, Lutheran swordmakers from Solingen in Germany came to Britain, and by 1690 were settled at Shotley Bridge. Other industries such as paper-making followed. Shotley Spa flourished in the 19th century.

**Sleepy Valley** nr Tantobie. Showpiece housing estate built by Durham County Council in the 1930s to provide the best possible housing for working people.

**Smiddy Shaw** reservoir nr Waskerley.

**Snows Green** Shotley Bridge.

**South Moor** separate district of Stanley, originally the South Moor of Beamish. CHIP – Craghead Housing Intervention Project – won £700,000 funding in 2008/09 for the revitalisation of South Moor Park.

**South Stanley** district of Stanley with its own distinct community.

**Stanley** second largest town in Derwentside (also see West Stanley). The known history of Stanley goes back to AD 120-240 when there was a Roman camp with turf walls and surrounded by a ditch, to protect cattle and sheep from the maurauding Scots. Stanley was first mentioned in 1211 when Philip de la Leigh granted land named Stanleigh, the name derived from the Old English for "stoney field". Former world cruiserweight boxing champion Glenn McCrory is from Stanley, as is ex-Sunderland FC star Barry Venison. Kevin Keegan's grandfather and Hilary Clinton's grandfather both came from Stanley. See also West Stanley.

**Stobbillee** nr Lanchester.

**Stony Heap** also Stoney Heap, between Lanchester and Consett. Stony Heap pit was the last NCB mine in the area. Very little remains of this former mining community.

**Tanfield & Tanfield Lea** former mining village north of Stanley, takes its name from the river Thame or Tame that runs through the village. Monks from Chester le Street built a church here around 900. At the time of William the Conquerer, Tanfield was listed as a manor. Location of the Tanfield Railway and Causey Arch. Tanfield was the home of Tommy Armstrong (1848-1919), the "Pitman Poet", whose grave is in the village cemetery.

**Tantobie** former colliery village NW of Stanley.

**Templetown** district south of Consett.

**The Dene** housing estate nr Medomsley.

**The Grove** residential area West of Consett, close to the former steelworks.

**The Middles** Craghead, nr Stanley, also known as Bloemfontein.

**Ushaw College** nr Langley Park. Roman Catholic seminary, founded at Douai in France in 1568, which moved to Ushaw Moor in 1808. The main college buildings are grade II listed, the College Chapel is grade II* and the Chapel of St Michael

*Watling Bungalows, Leadgate*

*West Butsfield*

*West Kyo nr Annfield Plain*

*White Hall nr Castleside*

*White-le-Head, Tantobie*

*Wilk's Hill, Quebec*

is grade I. The College Chapel and Refectory were designed and built by Pugin. The original college buildings were designed by James Taylor.

**Villa Real Bungalows** nr Consett, once had a hosiery factory.

**Waskerley** former railway town. Nearby are three reservoirs (Waskerley, Hisehope & Smiddy Shaw) and a water treatment works (Honey Hill).

**Watling Bungalows** ex-mining community nr Leadgate.

**West Butsfield** see Butsfield.

**West Kyo** nr Annfield Plain.

**West Stanley** previous name of the town of Stanley: hence West Stanley Co-op, Building Society, Football Club etc. One of the worst mining disasters of the 20th Century occurred at the West Stanley Colliery, Durham, on 16th February 1909 when 168 men & boys lost their lives. See also Stanley.

**Wheatley** nr Burnhope.

**Whitehall** nr Castleside.

**White-le-Head** tiny village nr Tantobie, once had a football team famous for its giant-killing exploits.

**Wilk's Hill** hamlet nr Quebec.

*Except where shown, all Gazetteer photographs by Chris Foote Wood.*

*Welcome to Delves Lane*

*Satley Church*

*Lintzford Bridge*

## References

Most of the information in this book has come from Council minutes, reports, surveys, magazines, newspapers, newsletters and other material supplied by Derwentside District Council, plus a wealth of old programmes, booklets and memorabilia loaned to me by helpful individuals. In addition, I have conducted upwards of eighty face-to-face interviews and at least as many again by letter, telephone and email. I have consulted numerous websites including Wikipedia and the Lanchester Parish Council website. There's almost always an argument about the origin of place names. Most references as to how the River Derwent got its name quote the Celtic for oak, daru or derw, giving Derwent as "a valley thick with oaks". I prefer an alternative derivation from the Celtic deifr, meaning "waters", or dwr gwin, the bright clear water. As far as I can make out, the Latin Derventio simply means "the people of the Derwent". No doubt people far more learned that I will tell me that I'm wrong, but as the derivation of the name Derwent is uncertain, I have picked the one I like best – "land of the bright clear water". CFW

## Publications

*1725 onwards, a guide to the Tanfield Railway, Tyneside* Locomotive Museum Trust 1998

*A Day to Remember,* Friends of Consett Park 2002

*Annfield Plain & District* by Jack Hair, The People's History 2002

*Around Stanley* by Jack Hair & Alan Harrison, Chalford Publishing Co 1997

*Canny Crack,* Craghead Village newsletter 2000

*Consett a town in the making* by Tommy Moore, County Durham Books 1992

*Consett in old picture postcards* by Bob Gibbon, European Library 1993

*Derwentside in old picture postcards* by Bob Gibbon, European Library 1994

*Durham Advertiser Series*

*Ebchester the story of a North Durham Village,* Ebchester Village Trust 1984

*Evening Chronicle*

*Longovicium, Lanchester's Roman Fort,* Friends of Longovicium 2008

*Looking back at Stanley* by Jack Hair, People's Press 2000

*Newcastle Journal*

*Northen Echo*

*Shotley Bridge, Village Survey & brief history,* Shotley Bridge Village Community Trust 1989

*Stanley & District Then & Now* by Ron Hindhaugh, County Durham Books 2006

*Stanley in old picture postcards vol 1* by Ronald Hindhaugh, European Library 1988

*Stanley in old picture postcards vol 2,* Stanley Past & Present History Group, European Library 1993

*Stanley Remembered* by Alan Harrison & Jack Hair, The People's History 1999

*The Banner* (Iron & Steel Trades Confederation) 1980

*The Coal Miners of Durham* by Norman Emery, Alan Sutton Publishing 1992

*The Consett Story,* Consett Lions' Club 1963

**Chris Foote Wood** has spent most of his working life as a freelance journalist, writer and broadcaster. After completing an honours degree course in civil engineering at King's College, Newcastle in 1962 (no degree awarded), Chris worked as an engineer & surveyor for two local authorities in the North East before setting up and running a group of six local free newspapers with his first publishing venture "Durham Free Press", 1968-71. In 1974 Chris started his own regional press agency "North Press News & Sport" and ran it for 30 years. He gave up the agency in 2004 to concentrate on writing books, publishing his own and other authors' work with his latest venture "Northern Writers". Chris is an accomplished biographer and "ghost writer", and has edited a number of newspapers, magazines and books. Chris's late father Stanley was a successful author, stage & radio playwright and "Coronation Street" scriptwriter, and his sister Victoria is the hugely talented and much-loved comedienne, singer-songwriter, actress and producer Victoria Wood. Chris has been married to Frances Foote OBE for 32 years, and has three children from his first marriage and two grandchildren. Chris was a district councillor in Bishop Auckland for 40 years, including six years as Council Leader, and was also a County and Parish councillor. He stood down in 2007 and is now an Honorary Alderman of both Wear Valley and Durham County. Chris has run 25 Great North Runs, and still competes as a veteran in athletics, cycling and the triathlon.

*Chris Foote Wood*

Other books by Chris Foote Wood: *"Nellie's Book – the early life of Victoria Wood's Mother"* (Sutton Publishing, now with History Press), foreword by Victoria Wood, how as a young girl their mother struggled to overcome poverty and prejudice in industrial Manchester in the 1920s and 30s; *"Tindale Towers - New Art Deco Mansion, how Mike Keen's dream home was planned, designed & built 2005-2007"* (Northern Writers); *"Baghdad Trucker – Adventures of a Truck Driver"* (Northern Writers), as co-author, with Kevin Noble; *"Proud to be a Geordie – the life & legacy of Jack Fawcett"* (Dysart Associates), authorised biography, private publication, not for sale; *"When I'm Sixty-Four – 1001 things to do at 60+"* (Capall Bann), inspirational lifestyle book; *"Walking Over the Waves – Quintessential British Seaside Piers"* (Whittles Publishing), details & photos old & new of all 56 remaining UK seaside pleasure piers; *"My Great British Pier Trip – 66 seaside piers in 21 days"* (Northern Writers); *"Land of the 100 Quangos"* (North Press), the largely unknown and unaccountable organizations that run the North East; *"Bishop Auckland in Old Picture Postcards"* (European Library), local history in words & pictures; *"Kings of Amateur Soccer"* (North Press), official centenary history of Bishop Auckland FC; *"Life of Brian in Black & White – Fifty years following Newcastle United"* by lifelong NUFC fan Brian Hall, cartoons by Paul Burke, edited by Chris Foote Wood (Northern Writers). In production: *"Tales from the Council Chamber"* as co-author, with Hon Alderman Olive Brown; a biography of a major North East politician; the definitive story of the "Category D" Villages of County Durham.

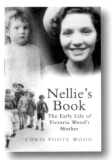

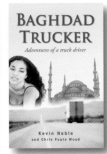

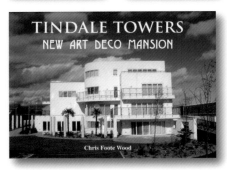

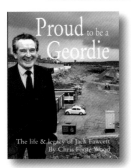

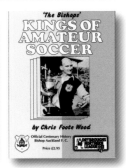

## Acknowledgements

This book, the official history of Derwentside District Council, was researched and written from scratch in just six months. This huge task was achieved only thanks to the ready co-operation and help of many individuals, mainly of course the Members and Officers of the Council who were already having to cope with the impending Local Government Reorganisation as well as their normal work. In particular I must thank Alex Watson, Leader of the Council, and Chief Executive Mike Clark and their respective PAs, Susan Gettings and Pam Harrison, and their deputies Mike Malone and John Pearson, for their patience and kindness in dealing with my all-too-numerous requests for information and advice. The sterling work done by my assistant Yvonne Golightly has been invaluable. Darren Knowd readily agreed to vacate his Civic Centre office for my use, and his colleagues Ian Williams and Kelly Stewart were always on hand to assist when needed. Many other members of staff dealt with my requests without complaint.

Print Manager Charlie Stephenson ensured the smooth production of the book in a very tight timeframe, as he and I renewed our professional acquaintance of forty years ago when he was a fresh-faced apprentice working on the Consett Post, one of my "Durham Free Press" series of six local newspapers I edited and published, at Ramsden Williams printers in Consett, 1968-71. Senior graphic designer Darin Smith has done a superb job with the cover design, as has he and graphic designer Tracy Wilkinson with the page layouts, turning my basic ideas into sparkling reality. All the staff at InPrint involved in this production are to be congratulated on their professionalism and application. When I started this process, the Council's PRO John Davis became my guide and mentor – my special thanks to him. The great majority of the Council's 55 members helped me with the information I requested, and often with much more. They will understand if I do not single out any one of them, but thank them all.

Many people outside the Council have also helped bring this book to life. They include former Officers and Members of the Council, current and former MPs, senior staff of other organisations, business people, members of local history societies, and quite a number of others who have been involved with the Council in all sorts of ways. Sir Bobby Robson graciously agreed to my request for him to write the Foreword. I have tried to list all those who have been particularly helpful, but if your name is absent, please forgive me. For all of you, I hope this unique publication will have made it all worthwhile. Finally, I must commend the Council as a body for envisioning this book and for giving me the opportunity to write and edit it – for me, as a professional writer for over thirty years, and former local councillor for forty years, truly the opportunity of a lifetime. Thank you everyone.

**Chris Foote Wood**
*Bishop Auckland*
*March 2009*

## Photographs

Photographs are of equal importance to the text in this book, so equal thanks must go to those who supplied them. The photographer/supplier/copyright holder is identified by the initials in brackets at the end of each photo caption eg (CFW) = Chris Foote Wood. All photographs in this book have been accepted on the basis that permission has been given for publication: any claims of alternative or prior copyright should be addressed to Northern Writers. Photographer Key:

**AP** Arnold Parkin 01207505321
**AT** Anne Taylor
**AW** Alex Watson 01207501321
**BGP** Book Guild Publishing info@bookguild.co.uk
**BT** Bessie Thomas
**CB** Colin Bell
**CFW** Chris Foote Wood footewood@btconnect.com
**CHS** Castleside Local History Society
**CO** Craig Oliphant railprint@googlemail.com
**DH** Derwentside Homes g.wilcox@derwentsidehomes.co.uk
**DK** Darren Knowd
**DL** Dennis Lavin
**DS** Darin Smith
**EPC** Esh Parish Council
**FF** Frances Foote footewood@btconnect.com
**GD** George Devanney 01207506004
**GS** Gerard Smith smithged1963@aol.com
**IP** InPrint 01207218345
**JH** Jack Hair jackhair@tiscali.co.uk
**JP** John Parkin
**LHA** Leadgate Historical Association
**LW** Leisureworks
**MC** Michael Curran
**MJM** Michael J Malone
**MW** Mark Wilkinson 01207502387
**NO** Norris Oyston
**OJ** Ossie Johnson
**PR** Peter Reynolds
**RG** Robert Gardner
**RH** Ruth Harrison
**RM** Richie McArdle richymcardle@talk21.com
**SW** Sadie Walton 01207503992
**UB** United Biscuits
**WS** Bill Stockdale
**YG** Yvonne Golightly
*Other photographs supplied by Derwentside District Council.*

As well as members and officers of Derwentside District Council, the contributions of the following individuals are gratefully acknowledged: Emma Andrews, Rt Hon Hilary Armstrong MP, Walter Armstrong, Sadie Ayton, Dave Barrett, Colin Bell, Sandra Clennell, Tony Cooke, Michael Curran, George Devanney, Bob Gardner, John Grant, Gilbert Green, Stan Green, Harry Guildford, Jack Hair, John Hall, Ruth Harrison, Joe Hennessy, Alan Hodgson, Terry Hodgson, Pat Holmes, Judith Horey, Helen Jobling, Neil Johnson, Kevan Jones MP, Arthur Lambert, Richie McArdle, Owen McFarlane, Dave McNulty, Brian Page, Arnold Parkin, John Parkin, Rt Hon Lord (Giles) Radice, Joe Rhind, Sir Bobby Robson, Don Robson, Mandy Scott, Gerard Smith, Lee Spraggon, Bill Stockdale, Bessie Thomas, Ray Thompson, Sadie Walton, David Watkins, Martin Weston, Geraldine Wilcox, Tony Wilson. CFW.